Interpreting Human Rights

In recent decades, human rights have come to occupy an apparently unshakable position as a key and pervasive feature of contemporary global public culture. At the same time, human rights have become a central focus of research in the social sciences, embracing distinctive analytical and empirical agendas for the study of rights. This volume gathers together original social-scientific research on human rights, and in doing so situates them in an open intellectual terrain, thereby responding to the complexity and scope of meanings, practices, and institutions associated with such rights. Chapters in the book examine diverse theoretical perspectives and explore such issues as health, indigenous peoples' rights, cultural politics, the United Nations, women and violence, the role of corporations and labour law. Written by leading scholars in the field and from a range of disciplines across the social sciences, this volume combines new empirical research with both established and innovative social theory.

Rhiannon Morgan is Lecturer in Political Sociology at Oxford Brookes University. From 2004 to 2007 she was an ESRC Postdoctoral Fellow in the Department of Sociology at the University of Cambridge. Her publications include (2004) 'Advancing Indigenous Rights at the United Nations: Strategic Framing and its Impact on the Normative Development of International Law', *Social and Legal Studies* 13(4): 481–501 and (2007) 'On Political Institutions and Social Movement Dynamics: The Case of the United Nations and the Global Indigenous Movement', *International Political Science Review* 28(3): 273–92. She is also author of *Transforming Law and Institution: Indigenous Peoples, the United Nations, and Human Rights* (Ashgate, forthcoming, 2009).

Professor Bryan S. Turner is currently Alona Evans Distinguished Visiting Professor of Sociology at Wellesley College, USA. He is the research leader of the cluster on religion and globalisation in ARI, and is currently writing a study of the sociology of religion for Cambridge University Press. He edited the *Cambridge Dictionary of Sociology* (2006) and *Vulnerability and Human Rights* (Penn State University Press, 2006). Professor Turner is a research associate of GEMAS (Centre National de la Recherche Scientifique, Paris), an honorary professor of Deakin University, and an adjunct professor of Murdoch University Australia. He is the founding editor of the journal *Citizenship Studies* and, with John O'Neill, co-founder of the *Journal of Classical Sociology*.

Routledge Advances in Sociology

Interpreting Human Rights

Social science perspectives

**Edited by Rhiannon Morgan and
Bryan S. Turner**

Routledge
Taylor & Francis Group

LONDON AND NEW YORK

First published 2009
by Routledge
2 Park Square, Milton Park, Abingdon, Oxon, OX14 4RN

Simultaneously published in the USA and Canada
by Routledge
711 Third Avenue, New York, NY 10017

Routledge is an imprint of the Taylor & Francis Group, an informa business

First issued in paperback 2012

© 2009 Rhiannon Morgan and Bryan S. Turner, selection and editorial
matter; individual contributors, their contributions

Typeset in Times New Roman by Pindar NZ, Auckland, New Zealand

British Library Cataloguing in Publication Data
A catalogue record for this book is available from the British Library

Library of Congress Cataloging-in-Publication Data
A catalog record for this book has been requested

ISBN 13: 978-0-415-48615-6 (hbk)
ISBN 13: 978-0-415-53419-2 (pbk)
ISBN 13: 978-0-203-88053-1 (ebk)

Contents

List of contributors

Judith Blau is Professor of Sociology at the University of North Carolina, Chapel Hill, US, and president of the US chapter of Sociologists without Borders. She has published books on the sociology of architecture, arts in America, urban planning, economy and society, race in American public schools, and is editor of *The Blackwell Companion to Sociology* (2004). During the past five years she has been working in the area of human rights, and is co-author with Alberto Moncada of *Human Rights: Beyond the Liberal Vision* (2005), *Justice in the United States: Human Rights and the U.S. Constitution* (2006), and *Freedom and Solidarities* (2007), published by Rowman & Littlefield.

Michael Freeman is a Research Professor in the Department of Government, University of Essex, where he teaches political theory. He is author of *Human Rights: An Interdisciplinary Approach* (Polity 2002), and many journal articles on human rights, political theory and the philosophy of the social sciences. In 2006 he was Torgny Segerstedt Visiting Professor at the Institute for the Study of Human Rights, Gothenburg University, Sweden. He is also a member of the Board of Overseers, Human Rights Institute, University of Connecticut, US. He has lectured on human rights in more than 20 countries, from China to Brazil.

Todd Landman was Co-Director of the Human Rights Centre at the University of Essex between August 2003 and June 2005. He is Reader in the Department of Government at the University of Essex and Director of the Centre's State of Democracy Project run jointly with the International Institute for Democracy and Electoral Assistance (International IDEA). His research and teaching interests lie in the areas of democracy, development and human rights, and quantitative and qualitative political methodology. He is the author of *Studying Human Rights* (2006), *Protecting Human Rights: A Global Comparative Analysis* (2005), *Issues and Methods in Comparative Politics* (2000, 2003); (with Joe Foweraker) *Citizenship Rights and Social Movements: A Comparative and Statistical Analysis* (1997, 2000); (with Joe Foweraker and Neil Harvey) *Governing Latin America* (2003). His current research involves the application of systematic comparative analysis to human rights protection and the methodological concerns involved in human rights measurement and impact assessment. He is an international expert working with the Office of the High Commissioner for Human Rights on indicators for monitoring state compliance with treaty obligations, and he has authored the user guide on indicators for human rights-based approaches to development for the United Nations Development Programme (UNDP).

Alberto Moncada is a sociologist who has taught at the University of Madrid, Stanford University, the International University of Florida and Alcalá. He has been a consultant for UNESCO, the Organization of American States (OAS), and the Council of Europe, especially in the areas of education and development. He has published numerous books on a wide range of topics including Opus Dei, globalisation, religion, and education, and is co-author with Judith Blau of a trilogy on human rights, published by Rowman & Littlefield. Currently he is president of Sociologists without Borders.

Rhiannon Morgan is Lecturer in Political Sociology at Oxford Brookes University, UK. She received her PhD from the University of Essex in 2004, and from 2004 to 2007 she was an ESRC Postdoctoral Fellow at the Faculty of Social and Political Sciences at the University of Cambridge. She has published articles on indigenous peoples, human rights and social movements, and is currently working on *Transforming Law and Institution: Indigenous Peoples, the United Nations, and Human Rights* (Ashgate 2009).

Kate Nash is Reader in the Department of Sociology at Goldsmiths College, University of London, and Faculty Fellow at the Center for Cultural Sociology, Yale University. She has published widely on human rights, including *The Cultural Politics of Human Rights: Comparing the US and UK*, (Cambridge University Press 2009). She is also the author of *Contemporary Political Sociology* (Blackwell 2000), and *Universal Difference* (Macmillan 1998), and co-editor (with Alan Scott) of *The Blackwell Companion to Political Sociology* (2001) and (with Alan Scott and Anna Marie Smith) of *New Critical Writings in Political Sociology* (Ashgate 2009).

Colin Samson is a sociologist and director of the Humanities Program at the University of Essex, England. He has been working with the Innu peoples of the Labrador-Quebec peninsula since 1994. Much of his research has sought to understand the health impacts and human rights implications of forced changes to the Innu way of life. His book *A Way of Life that does not Exist: Canada and the extinguishment of the Innu* (Verso Press, 2003) won the International Council for Canadian Studies' Pierre Savard Award in 2006. He is currently writing a book on the social and environmental benefits of cultural continuity for indigenous peoples globally. Recently he has published articles on the impact of international human rights for indigenous peoples and globalization and indigenous rights. In 2009 he will embark upon a British Academy sponsored collaborative film project with the Innu community of Natuashish and the photographer Sarah Sandring.

Gideon Sjoberg is Professor of Sociology at the University of Texas at Austin. He is author of, among other works, *The Preindustrial City* (1960) and (with Roger Nett) *A Methodology for Social Research: With a New Introductory Essay* (1996). In recent years he has sought to formulate an alternative theory of organisations (one founded on integrating the Dewey-Mead heritage with that of Weber) and to advance the view that human rights in the modern world are the basic moral counterforce to the social degradation wrought by powerful organisational relations.

Bryan S. Turner was Professor of Sociology at the University of Cambridge from 1998 to 2005 and professor of sociology in the Asia Research Institute, National University of Singapore. He is currently the Alona Evans Distinguished Visiting Professor of Sociology at Wellesley College, Boston. He edited the *Cambridge Dictionary of Sociology* (2006) and the *New Blackwell Companion to Social Theory* (2008). He is the author of *Vulnerability and Human Rights* (2006) and is the founding editor of the journal *Citizenship Studies*.

Anthony Woodiwiss was Dean of Social Sciences at City University London from 2004 to 2008 and is currently Distinguished Professor in the Department of Sociology at Seoul National University. He is the author of numerous articles and books, including *Globalization, Human Rights, and Labour Law in Pacific Asia* (1998), *Making Human Rights Work Globally* (2003), and *Human Rights* (2005).

Acknowledgements

The idea for this collection was first conceived in 2005. It is in part a product of research and teaching on the sociology of rights that emerged in the Department of Sociology in the Faculty of Social and Political Sciences at the University of Cambridge. In this regard, Darin Weinberg was influential in shaping this early development. Over a much longer period of time we have both benefited from the intellectual environment of sociology at the University of Essex, which has also been a seedbed of ideas on rights. We are indebted to Colin Samson, Anthony Woodiwiss, Ken Plumber, Diane Elson, and Jane Hindley.

The editors would like to acknowledge their gratitude to the contributors to this volume. Their commitment to this project has been crucial, and we would like to thank the authors both for responding positively to the initial call for contributions and for responding promptly to the reviewers' comments. Their patience has also been much appreciated. Warm thanks are also due to Gerhard Boomgarden at Taylor & Francis for his speedy and positive response to the manuscript.

Bryan Turner would like to thank Thomas Cushman (Wellesley College), Anthony Woodiwiss (National University of Seoul), Engin Isin (Open University), John Torpey (City University of New York) and Brian Johnson (former Master of Fitzwilliam College Cambridge) for their encouragement in developing a sociological perspective on rights. Aspects of his chapter were presented at Jeffrey Alexander's cultural sociology seminar at Yale University in 2008. The staff and postgraduates were generous in both criticism and praise.

Rhiannon Morgan would like to thank the sustaining presence of her friends and family at all stages of this project, especially Brendan.

1 Introduction

Human rights research and the social sciences

Rhiannon Morgan

Introduction and overview

In the past few decades, the academic study of human rights has expanded in scope, so that what was once the almost exclusive domain of legal scholars and political philosophers has increasingly come to engage scholars from a wide variety of disciplines, including political science, sociology, anthropology, economics, history, and psychology. The contributions from these disciplines, which are as yet uneven across the social sciences, now make up a substantial body of social scientific research on human rights that both complements and builds upon the extensive scholarship in law and philosophy. The latter have sustained a long-standing interest in human rights, furnishing us on the one hand with countless studies of the legal landscapes of international human rights law and its implementation architecture, and on the other with philosophical explorations on the nature, foundations, and normative function of rights. While, however, we are well attuned to the particular contributions of law and political philosophy to the study of human rights, it is less clear what characterises the social science literature. This volume seeks to demonstrate through its collection of essays the rich contribution that social scientists make to the study of human rights.

The contributors to this volume represent several academic disciplines within the social sciences. Its editors are sociologists, working in a discipline that increasingly recognises a sociology of rights as an emergent sub-field (e.g. Morris ed. 2006; Turner 1993, 2007; Woodiwiss 2005), but that arguably has yet to see the development of a robust research agenda in respect of human rights of the kind that has been seen in political science, international relations (IR), and anthropology. Indeed, in part, this volume aims to draw historically lagging disciplines into the human rights dialogue whilst also enabling enhanced exchanges across the social scientific disciplines. What seems important is that our understanding of human rights benefits from the insights of a range of social scientific disciplines, each concerned with differing issues, engagements, and dilemmas, and employing a range of methods and research techniques. The practices surrounding the entity of 'human rights' are myriad, involving a multiplicity of actors, institutions, and organisations whose actions have a bearing, both positive and negative, on human rights outcomes, and inviting investigation at a number of spatial or geographical levels from the global to the local. Thinking through these practices adequately and completely requires the combined gaze of multiple disciplines, existing in productive tension with one another. The study of human rights should therefore be a project shared across disciplines, if not an inherently interdisciplinary, ecumenical enterprise.

A second basic premise of this volume is that a better understanding of human rights, and especially human rights violations, may support their promotion and protection in practice. A striking feature of contemporary human rights is that in spite of the progress that has been made in the last 50 or so years in elaborating a diverse range of human rights declarations and treaties and in establishing machinery for the implementation of these standards, we face a world in which states persistently find cause to violate the human rights of both citizens and non-citizens, and in which genocidal politics is commonplace. Indeed, not only has there not been a significant reduction in the scale and intensity of human rights violations in the last half century, but arguably the cases of Cambodia, Rwanda, Burundi, the former Yugoslavia, and more recently Darfur, Myanmar, Afghanistan, Iraq, and Gaza point to an increase in the frequency with which they occur. This arguably creates a paradox, and one that the social sciences are well placed to explain as a first step towards remedy. Insofar as the social sciences have the methods and tools to ascertain the political, economic, social and cultural causes of human rights violations, or, equally, to isolate the social and political prerequisites of human rights protection, they can suggest how human rights might better be realised, and therefore make a contribution to their advancement.

It might be assumed that a volume concerned with the social science of human rights is bound to avoid moral evaluations of any kind. A common standard in social science is that normative judgements should be avoided in favour of objective, scientific analysis. A final feature of this book, however, is that it is based on the editorial view that social scientific approaches to the study of human rights are incomplete without normative or critical evaluation, that 'normative neutrality' is potentially constraining to the development of the social science of human rights, and, moreover, that evaluation need not confuse the social scientific analysis of human rights problems. To the extent that this volume figures in human rights education, this approach should enable a kind of learning that engages 'critical intelligence and moral sensitivity together' (Beetham 1995: 8; see also Booth and Dunne 1999).

This introduction is organised in the following way. First, it accounts for the relative lateness of social scientists to address the subject matter of human rights. Second, it discusses the ways that social scientists have responded to the tensions inherent in the social scientific study of human rights. Third, it argues the limitations of a legal approach to human rights research and teaching. Fourth, it explores the principal tasks of a social science of human rights and the extent to which these have been achieved in existing scholarship. Finally, it discusses the chapters in this volume.

Epistemology

It is undeniable that scholarly work on human rights in the social sciences has burgeoned in the past few decades. Yet whilst we now find a proliferating body of literature on the topic of human rights by political scientists, sociologists, anthropologists, and the like, the social sciences historically neglected the study of human rights. There are two main reasons for this. First, the origins of the concept of human rights lie in theology and philosophy, which are 'metaphysical' rather than empirical disciplines, whereas practitioners of the social sciences have thought of themselves as committed to the development of objective and empirical knowledge about reality, obtained through the methods provided by the natural sciences. Emerging in the nineteenth century, in an era profoundly influenced by the achievements of the natural sciences, the social sciences were imbued from their inception with scientific positivism, poised 'to "learn" the truth on the basis of empirical findings, not to invent or intuit it' (Wallerstein 1996: 13). Second, the doctrine of rights as developed in the seventeenth and eighteenth centuries, which saw the justification of rights in the laws of God or nature, is normative, meaning that it prescribes certain forms of conduct as morally appropriate. The social sciences, on the other hand, underpinned as they are by scientific positivism, are both secular and anti-moralistic, and have traditionally sought either to avoid analysis of normative concepts or to be neutral or 'value-free' where values do arise. Contemporary human rights, understood as the body of international and domestic law designed to protect human rights that has developed in the post-World War II period, are a modern and secular version of God-given or natural rights, but they are heir to this normativity in that they are expressive of what 'should' or 'ought' to be in human affairs.

In addition to a generalised myopia in the social sciences towards the study of normative concepts such as human rights, the individual social science disciplines, diversifying gradually from the late eighteenth century to the middle of the twentieth century, have their own subject specific reasons for shunning the issue of rights until late. If we examine the intellectual currents within anthropology, for example, we find a discipline committed to cultural diversity and toleration of difference, and by tradition opposed to the search for and imposition of ethical universals. In 1947, the American Anthropological Association (AAA) submitted a statement to the United Nations (UN) in which it warned against adopting a universal declaration of human rights that did not respect cultural particularities, only rescinding this view in 1999 in a subsequent AAA statement, a 'Declaration of Anthropology and Human Rights' (Engle 2001). In sociology, similarly, we have a discipline for which rights pose a number of difficulties, as outlined in Chapters 3, 8, 9, and 10. Influenced on the one hand by the positivistic traditions of its founding fathers, particularly French positivism as evidenced in the works of Auguste Comte and Émile Durkheim, and on the other by a basic relativism within the sociology of knowledge, sociology has shied away from normative debate. Sociology, moreover, has an ingrained scepticism towards rights inherited from Marx, a foremost critic of rights who believed that liberal rights seemingly established equality whilst in fact disguising unequal property relations (Marx, Karl, 'On the Jewish Question', in Waldron 1987). Sociology has also been hampered by a limited gaze in the sense that the nation state has overwhelmingly formed the basic unit of analysis, whereas contemporary human rights are supra-national in nature. This has led sociologists to focus on the rights of citizenship, which relate to the nature of social membership within modern nation states, and which are tied to a societal rather than a global framework. For its part, scholarship in the law and society tradition has tended to explore 'the politics of rights' within the context of domestic courts and with a focus on social change efforts and activist recruitment (Scheingold 1974; McCann 1994).

In political science, attention to human rights stretches back to the mid-1970s (e.g. Claude 1976), and has also been more sustained, particularly through the work of Jack Donnelly (e.g. 1982, 1986, 1989, 1998, 1999, 2003) and the extensive literature on the determinants of human rights abuses (e.g. Howard and Donnelly 1986; Mitchell and McCormick 1988; Meyer 1996; Davenport 1999; Zanger 2000; Miller 2004). Moreover, studies in related areas of genocide, state terror, and totalitarianism point to a longer legacy of work relevant to an understanding of human rights (e.g. Gurr 1968, 1970; Hibbs 1973). Where the traditional concerns of political science in different political regimes and their behaviours and effects brought political scientists to address human rights sooner than other social science disciplines, in political science we nevertheless also find a discipline influenced not only by positivism but also by a body of classical and contemporary political theory critical of human rights (e.g. Bentham, in Waldron 1987; MacIntyre 1985). In the sub-field of IR, moreover, scholarship has been dominated by realism, a perspective that emphasises power politics and de-emphasises ideas and norms (Donnelly 2000). Two early scholars of IR to take human rights seriously are R. J. Vincent (1986) and David Forsythe (1983, 1989). In *Human Rights and International Relations*, Vincent explores the nature and definition of rights, assesses their contemporary role in international politics, and makes recommendations about policy; notably, he argues that 'as a project for international society, the provision for subsistence rights has a strong claim to priority over other human rights' (1986: 2). Forsythe (1983, 1989) evaluates contemporary human rights law and practice, and has interests in human rights norms as a reflection of political values and as potentially powerful limits on the exercise of power. More recently, Forsythe (2006) has confirmed his cautious optimism for a liberal world order in the longer term, based on the resilience of human rights discourses, the changing nature of state sovereignty, the role of non-governmental organisations in international human rights developments, and the importance of 'soft' law. Realism has also been challenged by the theoretical school of constructivism in IR, which calls attention to the role of ideas in constituting state identities, interests, and behaviour (e.g. Finnemore 1996; Klotz 1995). This school has embraced human rights norms as important determinants of state behaviour, and has, particularly, drawn attention to the role of social movements in socialising states to comply with existing human rights norms (e.g. Keck and Sikkink 1998; Risse, *et al.* 1999; Khagram, *et al.* 2002).

Approaches to social scientific research in human rights

Notwithstanding tensions inherent within the social scientific study of human rights, it is clear that social scientists could not reasonably have overlooked so significant a phenomenon. In the last few decades, we have witnessed with impressive pace and scope the global diffusion of a human rights culture, evidenced in the almost boundless production of international human rights law, which some commentators now describe as being in its fourth generation,[1] and the public adoption of rights discourses worldwide, as people seeking access to social and political resources increasingly frame their claims in the language of human rights. Rights practices and discourses are now universal and multitudinous, such that scholars have written variously of 'the age of rights' (Bobbio 1996), 'the international rights revolution' (Ignatieff 2001a: 5), 'the world's first universal ideology' (Weissbrodt 1988: 1), and 'the rise and rise of human rights' (Sellars 2002). Just why rights have come to occupy so central a position in contemporary global discourse is an interesting question, and one that social scientists might be encouraged to consider in greater detail. In part, it is because they are 'politically agnostic' (Roach Anleu 1999: 202) inasmuch as they can be adopted in support of a variety of interests, regardless of where those interests stand on the political spectrum. Indeed, rights discourses can frame even contradictory interests, as evidenced for example in the case of the pro-life and pro-choice movements, with both sides employing the language of rights to structure their conflicting claims. The language of rights can likewise be assumed by a variety of actors regardless of their position on the political hierarchy, playing as important a role in the emancipatory struggles of social movements as in the practices and 'grammars' (Baxi 2002: 8–9) of governance.

The way around the epistemological tensions for many social scientists has been, following the distinction specified by German sociologist Max Weber (1991: 143–9) between 'value-relevant' and 'value-free' research, to allow themselves to be influenced by values at the point of subject selection, but to remain 'value-free' during the research process and in their pursuit of conclusions. As Carey and Poe (2004a: 4) point out, there is no reason why research selected on the basis of some value judgement need not go on to produce replicable, valid research (see also Landman 2006). A further consideration is whether social scientists should refrain from making moral observations, thereby conflating the empirical and the normative (Galtung 1977). Where scholars have been attracted to a particular topic out of human rights concerns, accounts may inevitably turn towards some normative comment, if only to the extent of censuring some regimes and condoning others. John McCamant (1981: 534) counsels against expanding science 'beyond its usual bounds'. Michael Freeman, on the other hand, (2001: 139) maintains that 'a political science of human rights will flourish only if it is neither narrow nor rigid'. Bryan S. Turner (1993, 1997; Turner and Rojek 2001; this volume, Chapter 10), moreover, argues that sociological accounts of political life and behaviour are incomplete without normative evaluation, and that a sociology of rights requires engagement with moral discourse. He argues that sociologists should attend to the social and economic foundations of universal human rights, thereby providing sociology with a basis to justify their existence, and so with a moral vocabulary to make observations on human rights violations as perpetrated by both state and non-state actors. Distancing himself from the natural law tradition in political philosophy and normative political theory, Turner suggests that a foundationalist conception of human rights might be based upon our ontological frailty, in particular the vulnerability of the body, and in the idea of social precariousness (1993; this volume, Chapter 10). He argues that bodily frailty is a universal feature of human-kind, and one that is unlikely to be disputed cross-culturally (1993: 509).

There is considerable scepticism amongst scholars of human rights, but par-ticularly amongst social scientists, about the value of debating the theoretical foundations of human rights (e.g. Ignatieff 2001b; Landman 2006; Waters 1995). This derives in part from the persistent failures of those in the natural law tradition to establish uncontested foundations of human rights, which has led many to bypass foundational arguments and to appeal instead to the content found in international law (Woodiwiss 2005), the existence of a consensus (Bobbio 1996), or to prudential and historical rather than foundational justifications of rights (Ignatieff 2001b). The reluctance to engage foundational claims also reflects the social scientific preference to theorise the social construction or genealogies of human rights. The social constructionist conception of the nature of human rights posits that ideas of human rights are socially constructed in specific historical circumstances, that is, 'created, re-created, and instanciated by human actors in particular socio-historical settings and conditions' (Stammers 1999: 981). Generally, those aligning themselves with this view of rights are legal positivists (Woodiwiss 2005) or 'realists' in the Benthamite tradition (Dembour 2006: Chapter 3), meaning they reject the idea of human rights existing outside of legal or social recognition, though a social constructionist approach to human rights does also sometimes go hand in hand with some notion of natural rights. Donnelly (2003: 10; 2006), for example, states that 'human rights are, literally, the rights that one has simply because one is human', from which he derives that human rights are equal, inalienable, and universal, whilst also discussing in a number of places various features of the historical and contemporary development of human rights (e.g. 1989; 1999). Whether there is any contradiction in this approach is uncertain; arguably, to the extent that Donnelly (1999: 81) regards the universality of human rights as 'a moral claim about the proper way to organise social and political relations in the contemporary world, not an historical and anthropological fact', this is a perfectly consistent approach to take. In a related discussion, Turner (1997: 566) argues that a dichotomy or opposition between social constructionist and foundationalist accounts of human rights is 'both artificial and unnecessary'. Responding to an objection to his foundationalist account of human rights based on a social constructionist position (Waters 1996), he contends that 'it is perfectly consistent to argue that human rights can have a foundationalist ontology in the notion that human beings are frail and accept the argument that human rights will be constructed in a contingent and variable way according to the specific characteristics of the societies in which they are developed and as a particular outcome of political struggles over interests' (Turner 1997: 566). It might also be added that foundationalist accounts can complement and reinforce social constructionist accounts, for inasmuch as the latter are able to contextualise particular conceptions of human rights, and indeed to expose their inclusions and exclusions, the former can provide the means to critique those exclusions.

The limitations of the legal discourse

One of the unfortunate consequences of positivism in the social sciences has been the domination of human rights research and teaching by the academic discipline of law (Freeman 2001, 2002). Kathleen Pritchard (1989), assessing the nature of human rights teaching at university level in the late 1980s, found that the majority of courses on human rights were offered within law faculties, and that the contribution from political scientists was nominal in spite of a widespread view in the academy that political science would have much to offer the study of human rights. Similarly, UNESCO, assessing the bibliographical contribution of various disciplines to the study of human rights, also in the late 1980s, identified just one interdisciplinary journal devoted exclusively to human rights – Human Rights Quarterly – compared to nine legal journals on the subject (UNESCO 1987: 50).

Today, the legal bias in human rights teaching and publishing is much less pronounced, a change that is reflected in both the growing number of interdisciplinary undergraduate and graduate human rights programmes in the UK, the US, and elsewhere, and the establishment of Human Rights sections within, for example, the American Political Science Association and the International Sociological Association. There are also a number of interdisciplinary journals dedicated to human rights, as well as a considerable number of social science monographs on various substantive aspects of human rights, including truth commissions (e.g. Wilson 2001), different human rights movements (e.g. Brysk 1994, 2001; Foweraker and Landman 1997; Merry 2006), the transmission of human rights norms (e.g. Risse, *et al.* 1999), and selected human rights topics such as labour rights (e.g. Woodiwiss 2003) and migrants rights (Soysal 1994). There has also been a significant increase in the number of interdisciplinary textbooks on human rights (e.g. Freeman 2002; O'Byrne 2003). Nevertheless, the amount of legal literature still outweighs the social science literature.

A vast legal literature need not be unwelcome, and in one sense it is natural that legal scholarship on human rights has mushroomed given the development since the end of World War II of a large body of international and domestic law designated to the protection of human rights. Human rights are, however, complex phenomena that cannot be grasped by legal scholarship alone, which, being 'text oriented' (Freeman 2003), is concerned chiefly with the internal logic, elegance, and coherence of the law (Evans 2003: 157), and is ill equipped to help us understand either the causes or context of human rights violations. It can tell us about the formal mechanisms of implementation that are put in place to monitor states' compliance with human rights legislation, but it is methodologically unable to explore the ways in which social, political, economic, and cultural forces influence its implementation. Nor can it apprise us of the social and political origins of human rights, or access the process of construction of international human rights law. Legal scholars are apt, like the gardeners in W. H. Auden's 'Law, Like Love' ('Law, say the gardeners, is like the Sun'), to regard human rights law in its various forms as 'objective' or 'above politics' (Klug 2005), which is problematic in that they are not inclined, therefore, to hold the law up to scrutiny or to question the political engagements and interests that may lie behind the law. In addition to the 'idolatry' (Ignatieff 2001b) of human rights often found in the legal discourse, the legal literature is inclined towards an excessively positive and optimistic account of the progress made in protecting human rights throughout the world (e.g. Marks and Weston 1998: 114). A particular tendency is to measure advances in human rights in terms of the law, celebrating, in other words, the formal elaboration of human rights norms as equal to their actualisation (Evans 1998: 2; Evans 2003: 158). Yet despite the ever increasing zeal with which the UN and other inter-governmental organisations formally recognise 'new rights of subjects and new rights to objects' (Bobbio 1996: 48), the sobering reality is that governments everywhere regularly and routinely break their commitments as established by international human rights law.

The role of social science

Important though legal scholarship is in enhancing our understanding of the central instruments, interpretation, and application of the law of human rights, it hardly gives us an account of the multiple praxes of human rights as they are attached to their intended bearers, their makers, or their perpetrators. The concerns and interests of the social sciences in human rights, however, extend well beyond those of legal scholars, as do their research techniques. Over and above the descriptive or technical analysis of legal texts and implementation procedures, social scientists are oriented towards a number of interrelated, mutually supportive tasks.

A first and central task for a social science of human rights is of course to specify the social, political, economic, and cultural conditions that explain why human rights violations occur. There is often a striking gap between the ideals of rights as embodied in the vast body of international human rights law drawn up in the period since World War II and the real world of human rights violations as reported daily in our media and the reports of the world's burgeoning non-governmental organisation (NGO) community. This gap is obviously related in part to the limitations of the legal systems in which these rights are embedded, which frequently fail to hold states accountable to the law, but beyond the law and its enforcement mechanisms are a range of social, political, economic, and cultural factors that influence the occurrence of human rights abuses. A major task of social science is therefore to determine these explanatory factors.

To date, political scientists have led this field, providing us in particular with quantitative studies that aim to account for cross-national variations in the realisation of different categories of human rights through the identification of objective conditions that explain why particular rights are abused or realised. Key explanatory variables identified include a range of political factors, with particular attention paid to democracy and democratisation or regime change (e.g. Howard and Donnelly 1986; Mitchell and McCormick 1988; Fein 1995; Davenport 1999; Zanger 2000; Davenport and Armstrong 2004). Findings generally support a negative relationship between democracy or liberalism (Howard and Donnelly 1986) and the violation of human rights, in particular 'life integrity violations' such as torture, arbitrary detention, extrajudicial executions, apartheid, and other repressive activities threatening to the integrity of the mind and body of the person. The relationship between democratisation, in other words the process of moving towards democracy, and human rights violations is less clear, with a few studies suggesting that the development of democracy and the withdrawal of repression are not related in a linear way. Davenport and Armstrong (2004), for example, find that a threshold exists below which there is no effect of democracy on repression, whilst Fein (1995) finds that there is 'more murder in the middle', in other words, that there is 'more conflict mobilized and incentives for repression as democracy is extended before it is fully institutionalized' (1995: 170). Zanger (2000), by contrast, finds that human rights abuses decrease during changes to democracy, particularly during the first year of change.

Economic factors also receive considerable attention in this literature in the form of a country's level of economic development and wealth, the presence of transnational corporations (TNCs), and foreign aid (e.g. Mitchell and McCormick 1988; Meyer 1996; Smith, Bolyard and Ippolito 1999). Findings show that countries enjoying higher levels of income are less likely to employ repressive measures against their citizenry, whereas countries characterised by economic scarcity are more likely to violate personal integrity rights as a result of instability brought about by shortages (Mitchell and McCormick 1988). Studies of the effects of multinational corporations on human rights in developing countries are interesting insofar as corporations replace the nation-state as the primary actor, but they have produced conflicting results. Thus, Meyer (1996) finds the presence of multinational corporations to be positively associated with the observance of not only political and civil rights but also economic, social, and cultural rights, whilst a study employing a different set of measures of human rights practice is unable to replicate his results (Smith, Boyard and Ippolito 1999). Studies evaluating links between foreign aid and human rights seek to understand how human rights affect the behaviour of international actors rather than explain why human rights abuses occur; these tend to focus on the US, and are inconclusive (see Poe 1990). More recently, Barratt (2004) has investigated human rights considerations in the allocation of UK aid. Her findings suggest that human rights considerations are relevant in the first instance, but that amount of aid to selected recipients is influenced by trade links.

Further independent variables tested for a linkage with the human rights practices of nation-states include cultural diversity, population size or pressure, experience of interstate war, and arms transfers (e.g. Henderson 1993; Poe and Tate 1994; Walker and Poe 2002; Lee, *et al.* 2004; Miller 2004). Much of political theory suggests that cultural pluralism presents difficulties for functioning democracy and guarantees of freedom, but Walker and Poe (2002) find no clear relationship between cultural diversity and violations of human rights, a finding that is also supported by Lee, *et al.* (2004). However, Walker and Poe do suggest some support for a probabilistic relationship between societal homogeneity and respect for rights. Population pressure is shown to increase the probability that countries will employ repressive measures (Henderson 1993; Poe and Tate 1994), whilst expectations concerning the experience of international conflict, which scholars hypothesised would compel regimes to resort to political repression to control domestic opposition and maintain order, are also supported by the findings (e.g. Poe and Tate 1994). In the first study to analyse the impact of arms transfers on different categories of human rights, Miller finds arm transfers affecting personal integrity rights and political and civil rights, with little impact on subsistence rights (2004).

This substantial literature represents an important contribution to the social science of human rights, but it is as yet incomplete insofar as: i) there remains a need to introduce a wider range of variables, such as those relating to social conditions within nation-states; ii) consensus has not been reached in relation to the impact of certain variables; and iii) where prescriptions might be made to government policymakers on the basis of existing studies, with few exceptions (e.g. Miller 2004) these relate to variables that cannot be easily controlled by policy-makers or human rights activists, such as democracy and democratisation (Carey and Poe 2004a: 8). For the most part, moreover, this literature focuses on a range of security and personal integrity rights in what Woodiwiss (2003, 2005) has described as 'the American tradition', and fails to pay adequate attention to social and economic rights, which Shue (1980, 1996) describes as 'basic rights', meaning rights that are necessary for the enjoyment of all other rights.[2] Further limitations relate more broadly to the characteristics of quantitative research, which is not to criticise statistical analyses as such but to suggest the need for complementary studies based on qualitative or mixed methods approaches. In particular, it might be said that statistical analyses, in examining relationships between variables, often fail to reveal how what appears to be a relationship is produced (Bryman 2001: 78), even where there is a concern for causality. That is, they do not capture the causal stories through which observed correlations evolve (Yee 1996: 85), which involve an emphasis on processes and interactions and their workings in context, and which belong to the qualitative areas of inquiry (Bryman 2001). In the field of social scientific research on human rights, studies in this mould include a number of studies on the impact of transnational activism on governments' adherence to human rights norms (e.g. Risse, *et al.* 1999; Keck and Sikkink 1998; Brysk 2000; Khagram, *et al.* eds 2002), which is linked to the strategic use of information politics, symbolic politics, leverage politics, and accountability politics on the part of transnational advocacy networks (Keck and Sikkink 1998) and the role of international human rights norms in shaping states' identities and interests (e.g. Thomas 2002). These studies constitute holistic, narrative accounts of interactions and processes based on case study research, though a focus on fewer cases does not prohibit some suggestion of wider patterns.

Another characteristic of statistical analyses on the determinants of human rights abuse is that they seek to make general propositions based on a breadth of cases, and in doing so arguably aim to arrive at a kind of summary or 'conceptual closure' (Flyvbjerg 2001: 84–7) that reduces complexity. Analogously, the abstract universalism of human rights discourse 'speaks in a clear and certain voice' (Freeman 2002: 93) and often ignores the social and cultural particularities and complexities that play an important role in the realisation of human rights. In contrast, an anthropology of human rights takes as central the complexities that arise from the impact of human rights discourse on local social, cultural, and political contexts. Based on close ethnographic engagement with particular human rights experiences and practices, or 'thick description' (Geertz 1993), much of this work is drawn into three edited volumes (Wilson ed. 1997; Cowan, *et al.* eds 2001; Wilson and Mitchell eds 2003), and is important in identifying both the way in which local concerns shape how transnational discourses of human rights are implemented, resisted and transformed in context, and the inappropriateness, ineffectiveness, and 'unsustainability' (Schirmer 1997) of human rights interventions that are decontextualised (e.g. Griffiths 2001; Montgomery 2001; Samson 2001). At the same time, moving beyond crude dichotomies between 'universalism versus relativism' or 'rights versus culture', this literature speaks to the shifting nature of both rights and culture (Merry 2001) in which international human rights law is transformed, for example, via the campaigning efforts of indigenous peoples in and around intergovernmental institutions (Niezen 2003), whilst human rights ideas are extracted from the universal and adapted to national and local settings. This latter process has been termed 'vernacularisation', understood as a dual process of appropriation and translation (Merry 2006). More recently, this rich body of anthropological literature has extended its efforts to produce a volume of ethnographic work based around four themes in the practice of human rights: states of violence, registers of power, conditions of vulnerability, and ambivalence (Goodale and Merry eds 2007).

Critical to the task of understanding the prevalent features characterising the global violation of human rights is the need to map the terrain of key actors in respect of human rights, and to evaluate their impacts on human rights, which may be positive or negative to their protection, though not necessarily in a way that is homogenous within categories of actors. The nation-state has overwhelmingly figured as the principal actor in respect of human rights. The current international legal regime for protecting and promoting human rights emerged as a response to atrocities committed by Nazi Germany, and is statist to the extent that it was devised to contain the destructive capabilities of states claiming the 'monopoly of legitimate power within a given territory' (Weber 1964) and insofar as it privileges states with the primary responsibility for implementing human rights. As a number of commentators have pointed out, however, the culpability of states may not always be evident, whilst the capacity of states to rectify and prevent human rights abuses might also be limited (e.g. Hurrell 1999: 287). Gordon (2002) identifies a process of 'outsourcing' whereby human rights violations are subcontracted to sources outside the state and its institutions, masking the role of the state in the violation of human rights and obfuscating social and legal responsibility (see also Singer 2003). Equally, the role of the state may be altogether absent, as increasingly abuse is recognised as emanating directly from private actors in global civil society (e.g. Brysk 2002; Brysk 2005; Smillie 2004), where global civil society refers to 'patterns of political behaviour by private actors across borders' (Brysk 2005: 16). Recent scholarship shows us that countless violations of human rights are the result of private actors; some, like transnational corporations, exercising delegated authority and others acting entirely autonomously, in the form, for instance, of guerrilla movements, child traffickers, or terrorist organisations (e.g. Brysk 2005; Kaldor 2003; Sell 2003). This raises serious challenges for the human rights community insofar as private authorities are far less accountable than states, and because the current international regime of protection assumes that it is the state that is in need of taming. Equally, if the global violation of human rights is defined as largely derived from the structures and practices of neoliberal globalisation (Evans 1998), then this also problematises an international human rights regime organised around placing restraints on the abusive behaviour of states (Bhaksar 1991; Brown 2004), as does the changing nature of war, which increasingly implicates a range of actors beyond the state (Kaldor 2007). Moreover, whether states possess the capacity to operate as regulators and mediators of private transnational action, or to correct abuses consequent to structural causes, is uncertain. According to a number of commentators, states have been weakened by globalisation to the extent that their capacity to correct human rights abuses may be extremely limited, particularly in the economic and social sphere (e.g. Cox 1997; Symonides 1998; McGrew 1998; Evans 2005). In part, the role of monitoring and publicising human rights abuses and campaigning on specific causes has been taken up by an ever expanding network of NGOs and social movements acting within global civil society, and increasingly focused not solely on the practices of states but on struggles for global reform and global justice. This orientation of the global justice movement reflects a shift in the human rights narrative consequent to the challenges of globalisation, as, arguably, do new strategies involving collaborative activism between civil society actors and amenable governments (Falk 2004).

Closely connected to the task of explaining violations, another core task of social science is to explore the origins and development of human rights, with a view to understanding issues of power and interests in relation to particular conceptions of rights. For social scientists, including those in the foundationalist tradition, rights are not 'texts without authors' (Baxi 2003), but the outcome of political struggles between actors with differing interests and possessed of varying degrees and forms of power and authority located in specific historical settings (Stammers 1993, 1995, 1999; Waters 1996). These struggles need elucidation in order both to reveal the inclusions and exclusions of human rights (Baxi 2002) and to enable critique of dominant conceptions of human rights, a project that becomes particularly important to the extent that the legal discourse presents current conceptions and standards of human rights as both neutral and settled in a previous chapter (Evans 2003), supported by the language of the universality and inalienability of human rights.[3] As Mutua (2002: 4) observes, however, 'the movement is young and its youth gives it an experimental status, not a final truth'. As to its neutrality, moreover, what emerges from various accounts of the historical and contextual nature of human rights is that, far from being dispassionate, power and interests underpin their development, whilst human rights also play a role in sustaining those interests. Written from diverse perspectives, some have focused on the relationship of the human rights project and the exercise of state hegemony (e.g. Falk 1980), and in particular on the promotion of an American conception of human rights as part of a strategy to extend the sphere of US influence (e.g. Evans 1996; Chomsky 1998). Others have focused on the convergence of the project of universal human rights with the requisites and smooth running of the global free market (e.g. Evans 2005). Still others, notably feminist scholars, point to the androcentrism behind human rights, and to the advantages afforded to male-defined interests by the marginalisation of women in the mainstream discourse of human rights (e.g. Ashworth 1999; Peterson and Parisi 1998). Finally, a number of scholars from the Third World link the human rights endeavour in different periods to colonialism and neocolonialism. Thus, Baxi (2002: 29, original emphasis), writing of 'modern' Enlightenment conceptions of human rights, underpinned as they were by the sweeping exclusion of parts of humanity, suggests that 'the foremost historical role performed by these was the justification of the unjustifiable: namely colonialism and imperialism'.[4] Baxi (2002) is more optimistic about the inclusions of what he terms 'contemporary' human rights, whereas, for Rajagopal (2003: 186), the current international legal order 'remains caught up in the discursive formations of colonialism that makes it blind to many types of violence', particularly what he terms 'economic violence' (2003: 231). Similarly, Mutua (2002: xi) points to the 'parallels between Christianity's violent conquest of Africa and the modern human rights crusade'.

Interestingly, few scholars engaging in a critique of human rights actually reject the idea of human rights outright. In part, this might relate to a lack of options. According to Dembour (2006: 251), alternative emancipatory projects are 'typically vague'. More important, however, seems to be the fact that the practices surrounding human rights are incredibly diverse, and while some might be objectionable, others involve a challenge to unjust nodes of political, economic, social, and cultural power. This distinction is drawn by Baxi (2002: 41), who differentiates between a 'politics *of* human rights', which 'deploys the symbolic and cultural capital of human rights to the ends of management of distribution of power in national and global arenas', and an emancipatory 'politics *for* human rights', referring to 'that order of progress which makes the state more ethical, governance progressively just, and power increasingly accountable'. Thus, human rights might be seen to both sustain and challenge power, and we might be drawn to further explore the 'sustaining' and 'challenging' dimensions of human rights (Stammers 1999).[5] The latter is a more common understanding of the human rights project in the popular imagination; it is also present in the robust body of literature on the practices of human rights activism (e.g. Keck and Sikkink 1998; Risse, *et al.* 1999; Gready 2004; Morgan 2004, 2007). This literature tends to suggest an important role for NGOs and social movements in (re)creating and implementing human rights and in contesting unjust practices in the language of human rights, and is influenced by a variety of theoretical approaches, including constructivism in IR (e.g. Keck and Sikkink 1998; Brysk 2000) and social movement theory (e.g. Morgan 2004, 2007). At the same time, the global politics of contestation should not itself be looked upon as wholly benign. Asymmetries exist within networks of NGOs and social movements in terms of access to resources and sites of power, not least between North and South (Sikkink 2002), whilst we might also counsel caution about the status and legitimacy of NGOs as distinct from social movements (Rajagopal 2003).

Suffice to say that the core tasks outlined above do not exhaust what the social sciences might offer to an understanding of human rights. Much has gone unmentioned, not least the need to explore the impacts of high science and technology on human rights, or the challenges posed to human rights by terrorism and counter-terrorism. By the same token, the literature highlighted above does not represent an exhaustive reading of all that currently exists within these bodies of knowledge.

This volume

As the above discussion shows, the contribution of the social sciences to an understanding of human rights is incredibly rich. This volume highlights that contribution by treating as thematic that which might otherwise simply be regarded as multidisciplinarity.

The chapters broadly reflect the agenda and orientations outlined above, though not in a singular way; inevitably, the tasks overlap, and this is reflected within individual chapters. The chapters exemplify the complexity of the human rights terrain, both in respect of the actors, organisations, institutions, structures, and processes that have a bearing on human rights, and the scope, subjects, and objects of human rights. They show a range of situations. A number of chapters are concerned with what is arguably the central priority for a social science of human rights, namely with examining why human rights abuse occurs and explaining the limits of existing human rights provisions. As Todd Landman demonstrates in Chapter 2, empirical political science research has produced a substantial literature directed towards explaining and understanding human rights problems in terms of theories located in rationalist, structuralist and culturalist approaches, comparative methods, and the development of comparable human rights measures, and where the difference between explanation and understanding represents an epistemological and methodological orientation. In Chapter 3, Michael Freeman explores the objective conditions that limit the implementation and effectiveness of the right to health, a right that he maintains has a strong claim to universality (reflecting his stance as a 'natural scholar' according to Dembour's (2006) categorisation of human rights scholars), but which is limited by a range of factors relating to the political economy of health, the politics of health, and social inequality. Similarly, Colin Samson discusses the role of cultural logics in human rights abuse in Chapter 4, and particularly the part played by cultural evolutionism in justifying some of the worst practices and policies of European colonisation and the destruction of indigenous communities and ways of life.

In Chapter 5, sociologist Kate Nash tackles the question of whether human rights are undemocratic. This is a view held in the US in particular, where there is a general prejudice against implementing international human rights in the national political system, yet Nash argues against opposing human rights to democracy. Characterising the international law of human rights as cosmopolitan law – one of the criticisms of which is that it introduces human rights into national polities via the courts rather than those branches of the state that are legitimately charged with making and executing law in the name of the sovereign people – Nash contends that cosmopolitan law may be realised through national legislatures. Drawing on a limited number of examples in the US and the UK, she suggests, however, that greater popular support for human rights might be necessary for such practice to become more widespread. In Chapter 6, Anthony Woodiwiss, another sociologist, claims a role for past and present rights discourse in the production of social divisions and inequalities, and yet defends rights on the basis of their socially constructed constitution, or 'the realisation of the ... system of differences in how rights might be written' (p. 115). Such a view of rights allows not only a role for non-dominant interests and agencies in the construction of human rights – and therefore a range of possibilities with regard to protective outcomes – but also the capacity for local translations and reworking of rights. Rights are therefore 'polyvalent', which is explored by Woodiwiss in the particular context of Japanese labour rights.

Some of these ideas are given further empirical credence in Chapter 7, in which Rhiannon Morgan adopts a social constructionist position on human rights to explore the role of the global indigenous peoples' movement in the recent development of a UN Declaration on the Rights of Indigenous Peoples. A process involving state representatives, UN human rights experts, and the representatives of indigenous peoples' organisations in protracted and difficult negotiations over an approximately 20 year period, the adoption of the UN declaration in September 2007 represents an extraordinary achievement, particularly to the extent that it recognises in Article 3 a right of indigenous peoples to self-determination, a right vehemently opposed by UN member states throughout much of the drafting process. The case study reveals an important role for social movements in the contemporary construction of human rights, while highlighting the potential of a strategy based on the creative manipulation of institutional and legal logics and norms.

In Chapter 8, Judith Blau and Alberto Moncada find much cause for optimism in what they describe as a 'human rights revolution' in progress, which they contend will be 'far more significant, far more comprehensive, and far more transformative than those who in 1948 celebrated the adoption of the UDHR could possibly have dreamed' (p. 151). They argue, too, that the human rights revolution, embodied in the plethora of civil society organisations and movements for which human rights are central, has been accompanied by an ethical turn in philosophy and the social sciences, and a move amongst US sociologists in the direction of adopting a rights-based perspective. The authors argue that human rights 'burst onto the global scene', in large part because 'human rights uniquely address the uncertainties of global capitalism, which all people share' (p. 151). As Gideon Sjoberg demonstrates in Chapter 9, however, the extent to which human rights can at present fully address violations consequent to economic globalisation is complicated by the relative insulation of one of the principal drivers of the global economy, the corporation, from moral accountability. Sjoberg points to the historical and contemporaneous role of corporations in various instances of human rights abuse, and posits that, consistent with a theoretical understanding of human rights as founded on claims made against organised power in order to advance human dignity, corporations must be brought under the human rights mantle, a process necessitating the legal redefinition of corporations.

In the final chapter, sociologist Bryan S. Turner is concerned with the question of whether social theory exists, and argues that if social theory is to be relevant to modern sociology it must be able to throw light on a range of contemporary problems such as the rapid degradation of the environment, the changing nature of warfare, the impacts of neoliberal globalisation, and the growing incivility of the public sphere, which are all situations in which human rights are implicated, at the very least as claims or 'preconditions for reform'. As Turner maps out in the chapter, traditionally sociology has avoided discussion of human rights and justice, in part as a result of its separation from political theory, focusing instead on the social rights of citizenship as distinct from the rights of human beings. Turner argues, however, that a comprehensive sociology of rights must also address the issue of civil liberties and individual human rights, and suggests therefore that for modern sociology to be relevant in this way it must take a more positive view of liberal philosophy, and in particular a concern for human autonomy.

Notes

1 Legal theorists tend to refer to three generations of rights: i) civil and political; ii) economic, social, and cultural rights; and iii) solidarity rights. Solidarity rights are those rights most commonly framed as rights to public goods such as a healthy and sustainable environment, peace, global redistribution of power and resources, and development. Indigenous survival rights are sometimes designated fourth generation rights.
2 The concept of basic rights has been criticised as potentially allowing for the neglect of other human rights essential to a life of dignity (e.g. Donnelly 1989). By the same token, Donnelly (1989, 1998) has convincingly opposed claims that economic, social, and cultural rights are less important than civil and political rights and that the latter should take precedence. These tend to cite in their support a distinction between positive and negative rights (e.g. Cranston 1973). Donnelly argues that some rights are 'relatively positive' and that others are 'relatively negative', but the distinction does not necessarily correspond to the distinction between economic and social rights on the one hand and civil and political rights on the other; the right to vote, for example, requires extensive positive endeavours (1998: 25).
3 Evans (2003: 160) distinguishes between criticism and critique, according to which the former does not disturb the narrative of human rights, whereas the latter 'challenges the uncontested state of human rights in world politics'. Following this distinction, he notes that criticism is found in the legal literature in the form of suggestion concerned with 'refining, polishing, and elaborating accepted norms and standards'.
4 It is worth noting that Baxi (2002) argues strongly against a view of human rights as 'enclosed in originary Western metanarratives' (2002: 27). He sees this view as entailing a number of negative consequences, including a denial of equal discursive dignity to other cultures and civilisations. Equally, Rajagopal (2003) criticises historiographies of the development of human rights in the post-World War II period that displace the role of the Third World (see esp. 174–6).

5 Stammers (1999) suggests that the nature of the relationship between 'sustaining' and 'challenging' dimensions of human rights might lie in degree of institutionalisation, according to which pre-legal claims for human rights can be understood as most likely to represent a challenge to power.

Bibliography

Ashworth, G. (1999) 'The Silencing of Women', in Dunne and Wheeler (eds) *Human Rights in Global Politics*, Cambridge: Cambridge University Press.

Barratt, B. (2004) 'Aiding and Abetting: British Foreign Aid Decisions and Recipient Country Human Rights' in Carey and Poe (eds) *Understanding Human Rights Violations: New Systematic Studies*, Aldershot: Ashgate.

Baxi, U. (2002) *The Future of Human Rights*, Oxford University Press: New Delhi.

—— (2003) 'Politics of Reading Human Rights', paper presented at the Legalisation of Human Rights Conference, University College London, April 2003.

Beetham, D. (1995) 'Introduction: Human Rights and the Study of Politics', in Beetham (ed.) *Politics and Human Rights*, Oxford: Blackwell.

Bhaksar, R. (1991) *Philosophy and the Idea of Freedom*, Oxford: Blackwell Publishing.

Bobbio, N. (1996) *The Age of Rights*, Cambridge: Polity Press.

Booth, K. and Dunne, T. (1999) 'Learning Beyond Frontiers', in Tim Dunne and Nicholas J. Wheeler (eds) *Human Rights in Global Politics*, Cambridge: Cambridge University Press.

Brown, W. (2004) '"The Most We Can Hope For ...": Human Rights and the Politics of Fatalism', *South Atlantic Quarterly* 103: 451–63.

Bryman, A. (2001) *Social Research Methods*, Oxford: Oxford University Press.

Brysk, A. (1994) *The Politics of Human Rights in Argentina: Protest, Change, and Democratization*, Stanford, Cal: Stanford University Press.

—— (2000) *From Tribal Village to Global Village: Indian Rights and International Relations in Latin America*, Stanford, Cal: Stanford University Press.

—— (ed.) (2002) *Globalization and Human Rights*, Berkeley: University of California Press.

—— (2005) *Human Rights and Private Wrongs: Constructing Global Civil Society*, Abingdon, Oxon: Routledge.

Carey, S. C. and Poe, S. C. (2004a) 'Human Rights Research and the Quest for Human Dignity', in Carey and Poe (eds) *Understanding Human Rights Violations: New Systematic Studies*, Aldershot: Ashgate.

—— (2004b) 'The Quest for Human Dignity: The Journey Continues' in Carey and Poe (eds) *Understanding Human Rights Violations: New Systematic Studies*, Aldershot: Ashgate.

Chomsky, N. (1998) 'The United States and the Challenge of Relativity' in Evans (ed.) *Human Rights Fifty Years On: A Reappraisal*, Manchester: Manchester University Press.

Claude, R. (1976) 'The Classical Model of Human Rights Development', in Richard Claude (ed.) *Comparative Human Rights*, Baltimore: John Hopkins University Press.

Cowan, J., Dembour, M-B. and Wilson, R. (eds) (2001) *Culture and Rights: Anthropological Perspectives*, Cambridge: Cambridge University Press.

Cox, R. (1997) 'Democracy in Hard Times: Economic Globalisation and the Limits to Liberal Democracy', in MacGrew (ed.) *The Transformation of Democracy*, Cambridge: Polity Press.

Cranston, M. (1973) *What are Human Rights?*, London: Bodley Head.

Davenport, C. (1999) 'Human Rights and the Democratic Proposition', *Journal of Conflict Resolution* 43(1): 92–116.

Davenport, C. and Armstrong, D. (2004) 'Democracy and the Violation of Human Rights: A Statistical Analysis from 1976–96', *American Journal of Political Science* 48(3): 538–4.

Dembour, M-B. (2006) *Who Believes in Human Rights? Reflections on the European Convention*, Cambridge: Cambridge University Press.

Donnelly, J. (1982) 'Human Rights and Human Dignity', *American Political Science Review* 76 (2): 433–9.

—— (1986) 'International Human Rights: A Regime Approach', *International Organization* 40 (3): 599–642.

—— (1989) *Universal Human Rights in Theory and Practice*, Ithaca: Cornell University Press.

—— (1998) *International Human Rights*, 2nd edn, Boulder: Westview Press.

—— (1999) 'The Social Construction of International Human Rights', in Dunne and Wheeler (eds) *Human Rights in Global Politics*, Cambridge: Cambridge University Press.

—— (2000) *Realism in International Relations*, Cambridge: Cambridge University Press.

—— (2003) *Universal Human Rights in Theory and Practice*, 2nd edn, Ithaca: Cornell University Press.

—— (2006) 'Human Rights' in Drysek, Honig and Phillips (eds) *Oxford Handbook of Political Theory*, Oxford: Oxford University Press.

Dworkin, R. (1977) *Taking Rights Seriously*, London: Duckworth.

Engle, K. (2001) 'From Skepticism to Embrace: Human Rights and the American Anthropological Association from 1947–99', *Human Rights Quarterly* 23(3): 536–9.

Evans, T. (1996) *US Hegemony and the Project of Universal Human Rights*, Basingstoke: Macmillan.

—— (1998) 'Introduction: Power, Hegemony and the Universalization of Human Rights', in Evans (ed.) *Human Rights Fifty Years On: A Reappraisal*, Manchester: Manchester University Press.

—— (2003) 'Universal Human Rights: "As Much Round and Round As Ever Onward"', *International Journal of Human Rights* 7(4): 155–68.

—— (2005) *The Politics of Human Rights: A Global Perspective*, London: Pluto Press.

Falk, R. (1980) 'Theoretical Foundations of Human Rights', in Newburg (ed.) *The Politics of Human Rights*, New York: New York University Press.

—— (1999) 'The Challenge of Genocide and Genocidal Politics in an Era of Globalisation' in Dunne and Wheeler (eds) *Human Rights in Global Politics*, Cambridge: Cambridge University Press.

—— (2000) *Human Rights Horizons: The Pursuit of Justice in a Globalizing World*, New York: Routledge.

—— (2004) 'Human Rights and Global Civil Society' in Gready (ed.) *Fighting for Human Rights*, London: Routledge.

Fein, H. (1995) 'More Murder in the Middle: Life-Integrity Violations and Democracy in the World, 1987', *Human Rights Quarterly* 17: 170–91.

Finnemore, M. (1996) *National Interests in International Society*, Ithaca: Cornell University Press.

Flyvbjerg, B. (2001) *Making Social Science Matter: Why Social Inquiry Fails and How it Can Succeed Again*, Cambridge: Cambridge University Press.

Forsythe, D. (1983) *Human Rights and World Politics*, Lincoln: University of Nebraska Press.

—— (1989) *Human Rights and World Politics*, 2nd edn, Lincoln: University of Nebraska Press.

—— (2006) *Human Rights in International Relations*, 2nd edn, Cambridge: Cambridge University Press.

Foweraker, J. and Landman, T. (1997) *Citizenship Rights and Social Movements: A Comparative and Statistical Analysis*, Oxford: Oxford University Press.

Freeman, M. (2001) 'Is a Political Science of Human Rights Possible?', *Netherlands Quarterly for Human Rights* 2: 123–39.

—— (2002) *Human Rights*, Polity Press: Cambridge.

—— (2003) 'Putting Law in its Place: An Interdisciplinary Evaluation of National Amnesty Laws', paper presented at the Legalisation of Human Rights Conference, University College London, April 2003.

Galtung, J. (1977) *Methodology and Ideology*, Copenhagen: Christian Ejlers.

Goodale, M. and Merry, S. E. (eds) (2007) *The Practice of Human Rights: Tracking Law Between the Global and the Local*, Cambridge: Cambridge University Press.

Gordon, N. (2002) 'Outsourcing Violations: The Israeli Case', *Journal of Human Rights* 1(3): 321–7.

Gready, P. (2004) 'Introduction' in Gready (ed.) *Fighting for Human Rights*, London: Routledge.

Gurr, T. (1968) 'A Causal Model of Civil Strife', *American Political Science Review* 62: 1104–24.

—— (1970) *Why Men Rebel*, Princeton: Princeton University Press.

Henderson, C. W. (1993) 'Population Pressures and Political Repression', *Social Science Quarterly* 74(2): 322–3.

Hibbs, D. (1973) *Mass Political Violence: A Cross-National Causal Analysis*, New York: Wiley.

Howard, R. (1986) *Human Rights in Commonwealth Africa*, Rowman & Littlefield: Totowa, NJ.

Howard, R. and Donnelly, J. (1986) 'Human Dignity, Human Rights, and Political Regimes', *American Political Science Review* 80(3): 801–17.

Howard-Hassmann, R. (2005) 'The Second Great Transformation: Human Rights Leapfrogging in the Era of Globalization', *Human Rights Quarterly* 27(1): 1–40.

Hurrell, A. (1999) 'Power, Principles, and Prudence: Protecting Human Rights in a Deeply Divided World', in Dunne and Wheeler (eds) *Human Rights in Global Politics*, Cambridge: Cambridge University Press.

Ignatieff, M. (2001a) 'Human Rights as Politics', in Gutman (ed.) *Human Rights as Politics and Idolatry*, Princeton: Princeton University Press.

—— (2001b) 'Human Rights as Idolatry', in Gutman (ed.) *Human Rights as Politics and Idolatry*, Princeton: Princeton University Press.

Kaldor, M. (2003) *Global Civil Society: An Answer to War*, Cambridge: Polity.

—— (2007) *New and Old Wars*, Stanford: Stanford University Press.

Keck, M. and Sikkink, K. (1998) *Activists Beyond Borders: Advocacy Networks in International Politics*, Ithaca: Cornell University Press.

Khagram, S., Riker, J. and Sikkink, K. (eds) (2002) *Restructuring World Politics: Transnational Social Movements, Networks, and Norms*, Minneapolis: University of Minnesota Press.

Klotz, A. (1995) *Norms in International Relations: The Struggle against Apartheid*, Ithaca: Cornell University Press.

Klug, F. (2005) 'Human Rights: Above Politics or a Creature of Politics?', *Policy and Politics* 33(1): 3–14.

Landman, T. (2005) 'Review Article: The Political Science of Human Rights', *British Journal of Political Science* 35: 549–72.

—— (2006) *Studying Human Rights*, London and New York: Routledge.

Lee, C., Lindström, R., Moore, W. H. and Turan, K. (2004) 'Ethnicity and Repression: The Ethnic Composition of Countries and Human Rights Violations', in Carey and Poe (eds) *Understanding Human Rights Violations: New Systematic Studies*, Aldershot: Ashgate.

McCamant, J. (1981) 'Social Science and Human Rights', *International Organization* 35(3): 531–2.

McCann, M. (1994) *Rights at Work: Pay Equity Reform and the Politics of Legal Mobilization*, Chicago: University of Chicago Press.

McGrew, A. (1998) 'Human Rights in a Global Age: Coming to Terms with Globalization', in Evans (ed.) *Human Rights Fifty Years On: A Reappraisal*, Manchester: Manchester University Press.

MacIntyre, A. (1985) *After Virtue*, London: Duckworth.

Marks, S. and Weston, B. (1998) 'International Human Rights at Fifty: A Foreword', *Transnational Law and Contemporary Problems* 8: 113–24.

Merry, S. E. (2001) 'Changing Rights, Changing Culture', in Cowan, Dembour and Wilson (eds) *Culture and Rights: Anthropological Perspectives*, Cambridge: Cambridge University Press.

—— (2006) *Human Rights and Gender Violence: Translating International Law into Local Justice*, Chicago: Chicago University Press.

Meyer, W. H. (1996) 'Human Rights and MNCs: Theory Versus Quantitative Analysis', *Human Rights Quarterly* 18: 368–97.

Miller, D. (2004) 'Security at What Cost? Arms Transfers to the Developing World and Human Rights' in Carey and Poe (eds) *Understanding Human Rights Violations: New Systematic Studies*, Aldershot: Ashgate.

Mitchell, N. and McCormick, J. (1988) 'Economic and Political Explanations of Human Rights Violations', *World Politics* 40(4): 476–98.

Morgan, R. (2004) 'Advancing Indigenous Rights at the United Nations: Strategic Framing and its Impact on the Normative Development of International Law', *Social and Legal Studies* 13(4): 481–501.

—— (2007) 'On Political Institutions and the Dynamics of Social Movements: The Case of the United Nations and the Global Indigenous Movement', *International Political Science Review* 28(3): 273–92.

Morris, L. (ed.) (2006) *Rights: Sociological Perspectives*, Abingdon, Oxon: Routledge.

Mutua, M. (2002) *Human Rights: A Political and Cultural Critique*, Philadelphia: University of Pennsylvania Press.

Niezen, R. (2003) *The Origins of Indigenism: Human Rights and the Politics of Identity*. Berkley: University of California Press.

O'Byrne, D. (2003) *Human Rights: An Introduction*. Harlow, Essex: Pearson Education.

Peterson, V. S. and Parisi, L. (1998) 'Are Women Human? It's Not an Academic Question', in Evans (ed.) *Human Rights Fifty Years On: A Reappraisal*, Manchester: Manchester University Press.

Poe, S. C. (1990) 'Human Rights and US Foreign Aid: A Review of Quantitative Studies and Suggestions for Future Research', *Human Rights Quarterly* 12: 499–512.

Poe, S. C., and Tate, N. (1994) 'Repression of Human Rights to Personal Integrity in the 1980s: A Global Analysis', *American Political Science Review* 88(4): 853–72.

Pritchard, K. (1989) 'Political Science and the Teaching of Human Rights', *Human Rights Quarterly* 11: 459–75.

Rajagopal, B. (2003) *International Law from Below: Development, Social Movements and Third World Resistance*, Cambridge: Cambridge University Press.

Risse, T., Ropp, S. and Sikkink, K. (1999) *The Power of Human Rights: International Norms and Domestic Change*, Cambridge: Cambridge University Press.

Roach Anleu, S. (1999) 'Sociologists Confront Human Rights: The Problem of Universalism', *Journal of Sociology* 35(2): 198–212.

Samson, C. (2001) 'Rights as a Reward for Simulated Cultural Sameness: the Innu in the Canadian Colonial Context', in Cowan, Dembour and Wilson (eds) *Culture and Rights: Anthropological Perspectives*, Cambridge: Cambridge University Press.

Scheingold, S. (1974) *The Politics of Rights: Lawyers, Public Policy, and Political Change*, New Haven: Yale University Press.

Sell, S. (2003) *Private Power, Public Law: The Globalization of Intellectual Property Rights*, New York: Cambridge University Press.

Sellars, K. (2002) *The Rise and Rise of Human Rights*, Stroud: Sutton Publishing.

Shue, H. (1980) *Basic Rights: Subsistence, Affluence, and U.S. Foreign Policy*, Princeton: Princeton University Press.

—— (1996) *Basic Rights: Subsistence, Affluence, and U.S. Foreign Policy*, 2nd edn, Princeton: Princeton University Press.

Sikkink, K. (2002) 'Restructuring World Politics: The Limits and Asymmetries of Soft Power', in Khagram, Riker and Sikkink (eds) *Restructuring World Politics: Transnational Social Movements, Networks, and Norms*, Minneapolis: University of Minnesota Press.

Singer, P. (2003) *Corporate Warriors: The Rise of the Privatized Military Industry*, Ithaca: Cornell University Press.

Smillie, I. (2004) 'Climb Every Mountain: Civil Society and the Conflict Diamonds Campaign', in Gready (ed.) *Fighting for Human Rights*, London: Routledge.

Smith, J., Chatfield, C. and Pagnucco, R. (eds) (1997) *Transnational Social Movements and Global Politics: Solidarity Beyond the State*, Syracuse: Syracuse University Press.

Smith, J., Bolyard, M. and Ippolito, A. (1999) 'Human Rights and the Global Economy: A Response to Meyer', *Human Rights Quarterly* 21: 207–19.

Stammers, N. (1993) 'Human Rights and Power', *Political Studies* XLI: 70–82.

—— (1995) 'A Critique of Social Approaches to Human Rights', *Human Rights Quarterly* 17: 488–508.

—— (1999) 'Social Movements and the Social Construction of Human Rights', *Human Rights Quarterly* 21: 980–1008.

Symonides, J. (1998) 'New Human Rights Dimensions, Obstacles, and Challenges: Introductory Remarks', in Symonides (ed.) *Human Rights: New Dimensions and Challenges*, Paris: UNESCO.

Thomas, D. (2002) 'Human Rights in U.S. Foreign Policy', in Khagram, Riker and Sikkink (eds) *Restructuring World Politics: Transnational Social Movements, Networks, and Norms*, Minneapolis: University of Minnesota Press.

Turner, B. S. (1993) 'Outline of a Theory of Human Rights', *Sociology* 27(3): 489–512.

—— (1997) 'A Neo-Hobbesian Theory of Human Rights: A Reply to Malcolm Waters', *Sociology* 31(3): 565–71.

Turner, B. S. and Rojek, C. (2001) *Society and Culture: Principles of Scarcity and Solidarity*, Sage: London.

UNESCO (1987) *Human Rights Documentation, Data Bases and Bibliographies*, Paris: UNESCO Publishing.

Vincent, R. J. (1986) *Human Rights and International Relations*, Cambridge: Cambridge University Press.

Waldron, J. (1987) *Nonsense upon Stilts: Bentham, Burke and Marx on the Rights of Man*, Methuen: London.

Walker, S. and Poe, S. C. (2002) 'Does Cultural Diversity Affect Countries' Respect for Human Rights?', *Human Rights Quarterly* 24: 237–63.

Wallerstein, I. (1996) *Open the Social Sciences: Report of the Gulbenkian Commission on the Restructuring of the Social Sciences*, Stanford University Press: Stanford.

Waters, M. (1996) 'Human Rights and the Universalisation of Interests: Towards a Social Constructionist Approach', *Sociology* 30(3): 593–600.

Wilson, R. A. (ed.) (1997) *Human Rights, Culture & Context: Anthropological Perspectives*, London: Pluto Press.

—— (2001) *The Politics of Truth and Reconciliation in South Africa: Legitimizing the Post-Apartheid State*, Cambridge: Cambridge University Press.

Wilson, R. A. and Mitchell, J. (eds) (2003) *Human Rights in Global Perspective: Anthropological Studies of Rights, Claims, and Entitlements*, London: Routledge.

Woodiwiss, A. (1998) *Globalisation, Human Rights, and Labour Law in Pacific Asia*, Cambridge: Cambridge University Press.

—— (2003) *Making Human Rights Work Globally*, London: Glasshouse Press.

—— (2005) *Human Rights*, Abingdon, Oxon: Routledge.

Yee, A. S. (1996) 'The Causal Effects of Ideas on Policies', *International Organization* 50(1): 67–108.

Zanger, S. (2000) 'A Global Analysis of the Effect of Political Regime Changes on Life Integrity Violations, 1977–93', *Journal of Peace Research* 37(2): 213–33.

2 Political science and human rights

Todd Landman

The relationship between empirical political science and human rights has evolved since its initial period of *engagement* through a period of *ambivalence*, to a more recent era of engagement and *systematic analysis*, albeit with the persistent and narrow focus on government respect for civil and political rights. Described as an 'eclectic progressive' development, the modern form of the discipline started with formal legal-institutional analysis, moved to an almost exclusive focus on individuals (i.e. the 'behavioural revolution' and the rise of rationalism), redis-covered the importance of institutions (the advent of the 'new institutionalism'), while continuously struggling with the question of culture (see Almond 1996; Mair 1996; Landman 2000, 2003, 2008). Arguably, human rights have received more consistent attention in normative political theory than in empirical political science, where arguments for or against human rights have appeared in works that range from the ancient Greek philosophers through to the latest postmodern deconstruction of rights discourse (see Rorty 1993; Douzinas 2000; Ishay 2004). Such debates have sought to examine claims for the existence of (human) rights and whether these were based on appeals to divine sources, nature, human reason, or social construction (Rorty 1993; Mendus 1995; Donnelly 1999).

In contrast, attention to human rights within empirical political science has waxed and waned. The early 'public law' phase of political science at the begin-ning of the twentieth century engaged in comparative constitutionalism and comparative analysis of institutional design in fairly formalistic terms and in ways that highlighted the *de jure* commitment of states to various rights protection at the domestic level (Valenzuela 1988; Landman 2003, 2008). The behavioural revolution that began in the 1930s and 1940s (see Eulau 1996) putatively moved political science away from normative questions and 'value-based' research, and concentrated on observable and measurable attributes of human beings and human societies, while seeking to uncover empirical regularities and providing law-like generalisations that had universal applicability. Where human rights featured in this research tradition if at all was in the focus on political violence and state repression, but this research did not adopt the language of rights to frame its research questions or its policy implications. It did, however, initiate the attempt to measure state and non-state violence in ways that would prove crucial to the development of human rights measures (see below).

The rise and hegemonic dominance of rationalist and realist perspectives displaced in part behaviouralism and its emphasis on social psychological explanations for human behaviour by positing purely economic motives for individual and state choices. In assuming individuals and states to be unitary and intentional actors, rationalist and realist approaches concentrate on utility functions that only relate to the material self-interest of individuals and the material factors that provide the basis for state power on the international stage (e.g. population size, raw materials, technology, etc.) (see e.g. Ward 1995; Mearsheimer 1994–5; Lichbach 1997; Legro and Moravcsik 1999). Human rights are seen as normative concerns and as a set of values that do have explanatory or analytical leverage for providing parsimonious accounts of political events, outcomes, and interactions. For these perspectives, human rights only matter when their pursuit falls in line with other material and geo-strategic interests, or when powerful states back a particular rights issue, such as the abolition of the slave trade in the nineteenth century (Krasner 1993); a state of affairs in which individuals and states engage in a human rights double standard.

The rediscovery of institutions at the domestic and international level revived an interest in human rights as renewed attention to law and its codification of sets of rights are seen as having a possible constraint on individual and state action. This renewed interest in institutions has been coupled with the development of human rights measures, greater attention to comparative method, and the proliferation of human rights norms, actors, and organisations since the mid 1970s (Claude 1976; Landman 2005a). Today, there is a strong community of political science researchers specifically dedicated to the application of the theories and methods in political science to significant human rights problems and puzzles. For example, in 2001 the American Political Science Association established a Human Rights Section, which attracts a steady membership of approximately 420 members per annum and organises panels and papers at its annual conference. The International Political Science Association (IPSA) and the International Studies Association (ISA) have established similar such organisations and groups. In 2002 at its joint sessions in Turin, the European Consortium for Political Research (ECPR) hosted a joint workshop organised by Steve Poe and Sabine Carey on the systematic study of human rights violations. In 2007, the *Journal of Peace Research* published a special issue dedicated to political science analysis of protecting human rights (Hafner-Burton and Ron 2007).

There is thus a growing international community of political scientists dedicated to human rights research. It can largely be described as 'post-behavioural' in the sense that it has an explicit focus on a set of values, but applies the theories and systematic methods of contemporary political science in ways that provide explanation and understanding, and draw larger inferences and policy prescriptions that can help improve the promotion and protection of human rights. The community is engaged in research that is highly consistent with Max Weber's position on values in social scientific research, where research on topics has been influenced by values, but the research process itself has not been so influenced. Rather, it takes the international law of human rights as either explicitly or implicitly setting an international standard against which the practices of states are compared.[1] The gap between the *de jure* commitment of states and the *de facto* realisation of human rights thus forms the primary object of inquiry, while systematic analysis is dedicated to explaining and understanding its cross-national variation using a variety of quantitative and qualitative research designs.

With this brief overview of the evolution in political science and its relationship with human rights in mind, this chapter addresses key themes developed in this volume in two important ways. First, it shows the contribution empirical political science has made to the explanation and understanding of human rights problems through the application of empirical theories located in rationalist, structuralist, and culturalist approaches. Second, it shows how political science has applied comparative methods and developed human rights measures for the analysis of significant human rights problems. Both these contributions are illustrated with numerous examples from the political science literature. The chapter concludes by identifying the many challenges facing the political science of human rights, including greater application of rationalist approaches; synthesis of theoretical approaches; attention to systematic analysis of economic and social rights (including the development of measures); more research on the variation of rights protection in advanced industrial democracies (especially in the 'new' age of terror); and more attention to the principles of case selection in order to maximise the kinds of inferences drawn about human rights problems in the field.

The contribution of empirical political science to human rights

The primary aim and objective of political science is to provide meaningful explanation and understanding of social and political phenomena, which are understood to be a set of observable events, actions, outcomes, conditions, processes, and/or perceptions. For human rights research, such social and political phenomena are those events, actions, outcomes, conditions, processes, and/or perceptions that have either a direct or indirect impact on the realisation of human dignity. For example, macro-events, actions and outcomes such as wars, military coups, and democratic transition have various impacts on the protection of all categories of human rights. They may also include significant micro-events such as individual decisions or acts that constitute violations of particular human rights. Conditions and processes may be underlying socio-economic structures, bureaucratic organisations, and institutional arrangements that either facilitate or hinder the realisation of human dignity. Finally, perceptions may be of rights conditions in general, more abstract notions of attachments to, and orderings of, rights conceptions, or the direct experiences and recollections of personal human rights abuses.

Political science *explanation* involves the process of providing a general account of why such phenomena occur, why certain states of affairs exist, and/or why certain conditions persist. The process of explanation involves observation, specification of either deductive or inductive theory with observable implications, research design, data collection and analysis, and the making of inferences (see King, *et al.* 1994).

Understanding, on the other hand, involves providing a deeper grasp of the meaning of what has happened, what persists, and what changes, where theory and method are used to provide a broader and more holistic interpretation (Flyvbjerg 2001; Brady and Collier 2004; Schram and Caterino 2006). Understood in this way, explanation and understanding represent two ends of an epistemological and methodological continuum that ranges from the deep hermeneutic, thick descriptive and discursive approaches to the formal nomothetic-deductive approaches (see Landman 2006: 59–65), or what Karl Popper (1972) called 'cloud-like' versus 'clock-like' approaches.

Across these different approaches the political science of human rights rests on a number of basic assumptions. First, it assumes by and large that social and political human rights phenomena are observable[2] in ways that can be compared, measured, and examined in systematic ways that minimise bias and maximise making inferences. Second, despite the absence of agreed philosophical foundations for the existence of human rights, it assumes that human rights protection varies across units of observation, such as individuals, sub-national units, groups, states, and regions, and that this variation is susceptible to systematic analysis. Third, it assumes that different research methods are linked to the kind of research questions identified by the human rights scholar. Fourth, and related to the third, it assumes that there are trade-offs in using different methods and levels of analysis, each of which is linked to the types of inferences that can be drawn about the particular human rights research question under investigation. Building on these assumptions, extant studies in human rights have begun to provide a progressive accumulation of knowledge about the patterns in human rights violations, reasons for their variation between and within countries, their relationship with the actions (and inactions) of individuals and states, and deeper questions of what human rights mean to different people around the world.

Empirical theories and human rights

As across many other topics of research, political science research on human rights has made an increasing contribution to empirical theories, including rational approaches, structural approaches, and cultural approaches at the domestic and international levels. The largest volume of political science literature on human rights involves research that uses the 'messy centre' of theorising in comparative politics (Kohli, *et al.* 1995), comprised of macro-structural explanations for variation in human rights protection across many countries, while rationalist and cultural approaches have begun to appear in a number of small-N (or smaller-N) comparative studies.[3] Drawing on the behavioural tradition in the social sciences, global comparative studies of human rights in political science focus on a discrete sets of civil and political rights, or more narrowly, 'personal integrity rights', and the data sets tend to vary across time ($15 \leq T \leq 25$) and space ($150 \leq T \leq 194$), yielding a large total number of observations used for econometric estimation of empirical relationships ($2,250 \leq N*T \leq 4,850$) (Landman 2005a).

Theory is not given a particular emphasis in these studies, but the collection of variables that comprise them has been extensive. The variables most notably include the level, pace, and quality of economic development (e.g. Henderson 1991; Poe and Tate 1994; Poe, *et al.* 1999); the level, timing, and quality of democratisation (e.g. Davenport 1999; Zanger 2000; Davenport and Armstrong 2004; Mesquita, *et al.* 2005); involvement in internal and external conflict (Poe and Tate 1994; Poe, *et al.* 1999); and the size and growth of the population (Henderson 1993; Poe and Tate 1994; Poe, *et al.* 1999). The consensus from these studies is that there are positive and significant effects on the protection of human rights for the level of democracy and its initial period of transition, as well as high levels of economic development. There are negative and significant effects for involvement in civil war and international war, as well as for those countries with large populations.

In addition to these more general variables, there have been further and more specific areas of research conducted that include such variables as foreign direct investment and/or the presence of multinationals (Meyer 1996; 1998; 1999a; 1999b; Smith, *et al.* 1999); the level of global interdependence (Landman 2005b); the proliferation of international human rights law (Keith 1999; Hathaway 2002; Landman 2005b; Neumayer 2005; Hafner-Burton and Tsutsui 2005, 2007); corruption (Landman and Schudel 2007); and income and land inequality (Landman and Larizza 2009). The results of this extended research on human rights are more mixed than the 'first generation' of work and the difference in direction, magnitude, and significance of the different independent variables is a function of variable construction and measurement, model specification and estimation, and in some instances case selection. Nevertheless, this entire tradition of research focuses on the impact on human rights of broad socio-economic change, institutional differentiation and transition, international legal regimes, and particular structural constraints at domestic and international levels of analysis.

Against this focus on macro-patterns, holistic structures, and inter-connections and constraints, rationalist accounts or those heavily influenced by rationalism return to a concern over the micro-foundations for human rights violations. Rational accounts focus on the *intentionality* of individual and state choices, the strategic interaction of state and non-state actors, and the human rights implications of the multiple outcomes of these interactions. Such a focus on intentional choices means that rational accounts concern themselves with dimensions of human rights abuse in which a perpetrator and an act of violation can be identified.[4] The rational turn was slow in moving toward human rights, but in following its general emergence as a dominant paradigm in other research areas in political science, it eventually has been used for the study of human rights problems and puzzles. One of the main positions adopted by rationalist accounts of human rights abuse is that it is possible, and in many ways imperative, to look beyond questions of grievance, moral outrage against injustice, and ideological extremism and to focus on material reasons for why an individual or a state commits human rights violations. From an applied policy perspective, the rational turn has important implications. Indeed, to provide rational explanations for human rights abuse means that rational solutions can be put in place to prevent violations in the future. To this end, two studies in political science stand out as good examples of rational accounts of human rights violations. Wantchekon and Healy (1999) present a classic game theory analysis on the use of torture, while Neil Mitchell (2004) provides a 'principal-agent' model for explaining large-scale atrocities during times of civil war. Both these studies adopt primarily a rational explanatory framework, have important implications, and invite further research either to other sets of rights violations or other political contexts.

Wantchekon and Healy (1999: 597) construct a 'signalling' game that is modelled using three 'ideal' players: the state, the torturer, and the victim. The use of torture by the state is seen as a rational strategy for either *gaining information* or *maintaining social control*. The state balances the benefits of gaining information or establishing social control against the costs of increased international outrage over the use of torture, and carries out its torture through the use of torturers, who are further differentiated into sadists (who enjoy the use of torture for personal reasons), zealots (who actively carry out the state's wishes and obtain results at all costs), and professionals (who deliberate carefully over the use of torture relative to the gains that are likely to be achieved) (ibid. 600). Victims in this signalling game include those that are 'weak and guilty' (i.e. they have information and are willing to reveal it), 'strong and guilty' (i.e. they have information but resist attempts to extract it), 'weak and innocent' (i.e. they do not have information but are likely to make a false confession), and 'strong and innocent' (i.e. they do not have information and are unlikely to make a confession) (ibid. 600). The game also includes payoff structures for the players, preference orderings, and uncertainty, where the resulting game moves through a series of stages and where 'the intensity and scope of torture are much higher under the social control case than under the information extraction case' (ibid. 599). The use of game theory and its application of formal logic to the interaction of states, torturers, and victims found in this study yield important insights into finding the structure of incentives that may reduce state propensity to rely on torture.

In reflecting on the body of cross-national quantitative literature on human rights, Mitchell (2004) argues that much less is known about the micro-foundations for human rights abuse than the general conditions under which human rights violations are committed. In response, he moves away from his own initial work on the cross-national analysis of human rights abuse (e.g. Mitchell and McCormick 1988) to present a principal-agent model that explains different levels of human rights abuse across the cases of the Russian Civil War (high level), the Arab-Israeli War (middle-level), and the English Civil War (low level). The differences he observes across these three cases are explained by the relationship between different *types of principals* (the ideologically 'intolerant' in Russia, the instrumental 'opportunists' in Israel, and Cromwellian 'tolerators' in England) and the *exercise of control over the agents* to whom they have delegated their authority to use violence. While his model accounts for the differences across these three cases, it invites replication for other political contexts in which similar violent conflicts took place (e.g. Sierra Leone, Guatemala, El Salvador, and Peru)[5] and for other sets of human rights abuse, such as economic and social rights violations in which perpetrators can be identified.[6] It also provides insight into the ways in which the structure of incentives can be changed to prevent the worst forms of rights abuse from taking place.

Alongside the macro-structural and rational explanations for the variation in human rights abuse across countries, culturalist approaches have examined the ways in which human rights have been socially constructed (e.g. Donnelly 1999), the ways in which human rights are part of a process of 'norms cascade' in the international arena (e.g. Risse, *et al.* 1999), and how the language of rights and the 'framing' of rights claims account for the relative success of different social movements around the world (Foweraker and Landman 1997; Bob 2005). These accounts recognise that norms and ideas 'matter' for explaining political development and outcomes in the area of human rights, and draw on the proliferation of human rights norms since the 1948 Universal Declaration of Human Rights as evidence of a certain 'language of commitment' (Boyle 1995) that has been constructed through the activities of international governmental and international non-governmental organisations (NGOs) that gather in such global events as the 1993 Vienna Conference.

In *The Power of Human Rights*, Risse, *et al.* (1999) and their contributors present a series of paired comparisons (and one single-country study) of liberalising authoritarian regimes in order to examine the degree to which 'transnational advocacy networks' contribute to the diffusion of international human rights norms and promote domestic policy change. Such networks are seen to create both 'top-down' and 'bottom-up' pressure on authoritarian regimes to undergo political transformations necessary for the full institutionalisation of human rights protection. The paired comparisons provide evidence in support of a 'spiral model' of norms diffusion in which there is a primary role for ideas in shaping state behaviour. The model depicts a progression from initial international consciousness-raising about human rights violations in the target country, followed by regime denial of the atrocities (which is in itself an acknowledgement of human rights norms), concessions by the state to improve the situation, and the ultimate institutionalisation of human rights norms through changes in domestic policy and state behaviour (Risse, *et al.* 1999:17–35). In short, the model shows how the international human rights regime can have an impact on state behaviour, while the inferences from the comparison of the 11 countries remain 'generalizable across cases irrespective of cultural, political, or economic differences' (Risse and Sikkink 1999: 6).

In *The Marketing of Rebellion*, Clifford Bob (2005) places great emphasis on the ways in which the 'framing' of issues and demands by domestically-based social movement organisations explains their relative success or failure in attracting international support from large and influential NGOs. In comparing successful and unsuccessful movements in Nigeria and Mexico, Bob (2005) argues that savvy organisations that match the agenda of international NGOs and expand the framing of their struggle are more likely to attract international attention, financial assistance, and logistical support that raise the profile of the organisation and its demands for change. He shows how the movement for Ogoni people in Nigeria expanded its initial frame of ethnic subordination to one of a more general critique of environmental degradation and human rights abuse to attract the support of organisations such as Greenpeace, Amnesty International and Human Rights Watch. In similar fashion, he shows how the Zapatista movement in Mexico has been successful, despite its initial violent assault on the city of San Cristobal de las Casas, framed itself as a non-violent movement fighting for indigenous rights and resisting the negative externalities of economic globalisation. In both cases, he demonstrates that grievance and the solving of collective action problems is not enough, and that larger questions of awareness-raising through cultural framing provide a crucial variable in accounting for successful mobilisation around domestic human rights concerns.

Finally, survey analysis and public opinion research have begun to explore the degree to which citizen attitudes and perceptions about human rights are in line with the actual human rights situation in countries. This research combines the standards-based indicators of human rights used in the large-N quantitative studies outlined above with random sample surveys that ask questions about respect for human rights, where typical response categories include such terms as 'a lot', 'some respect', 'not much respect', and 'no respect at all' (see Anderson, *et al.* 2005; Richards 2006). The research effort is then to compare the perceptions of the human rights situation to the general trends in the protection of different categories of human rights either for the world (Richards 2006), or broken down for particular regions (Anderson, *et al.* 2005; Richards 2006). The global comparisons reveal that citizens have multiple rights referents when they formulate assessments on the human rights situation in their own countries, and that there is a moderate congruence between public opinion about the human rights situation and the actual human rights situation, which is further differentiated across regions (Richards 2006: 28–31). Across the post-communist states of Central and Eastern Europe there is a high congruence between perceptions of human rights and actual human rights practices, but this congruence tends to be stronger for more highly educated citizens (Anderson, *et al.* 2005). Both studies represent the application of cross-cultural analysis using perceptions as a main subjective variable of interest as it relates to more objective human rights conditions.

This brief excursus on the application of rational, structural, and cultural approaches to the study of human rights shows that each provides a different set of insights into human rights problems through their focus on different aspects of the social world, which are in turn a function of their different ontological and epistemological starting assumptions. But it would be highly rare indeed to find examples of 'pure' approaches in political science. Rather, each of the approaches places emphasis on rational, structural, and cultural variables, while not losing sight of the importance of other variables from competing perspectives. For example, while Mitchell's principal-agent model is primarily a rationalist micro-foundational account of human rights abuse, the prime motivation for his ideal type of the intolerant 'Grand Inquisitor' embodied in Lenin during the Russian Civil War is grounded in ideology and not the type of material interests fundamental to pure rational choice models of human behaviour. There is a thus a melding of rational and cultural assumptions in his model. Similarly, Risse, *et al.* (1999) concede a large role for both the *structure* of power relations in the international human rights arena and the *rationality* of states in calculating the relative costs and benefits associated with making tactical concessions to human rights pressure. Nonetheless, political science research on human rights is contributing to a progressive accumulation of knowledge that is built upon these three theoretical traditions.

Comparative methods and measurement

The second significant contribution that political science is making to the study of rights involves comparative methods and the development of comparable measures of human rights. The study of human rights is inherently comparative since the evolution of human rights norms suggests a universal ideal standard against which country practices, conditions, and perceptions can be compared. The field of comparative politics is based on the assumption that valid comparisons can be made between and among different countries to examine empirically the universal claims for human rights that have been made normatively (Landman 2002). The methods available as outlined in the previous section of this chapter on the theoretical contribution of political science to human rights include the comparison of many countries, the comparison of few countries, and single-country studies. Each of these comparative methods carries with it different assumptions, strengths, weaknesses, and suitable research questions that can be addressed adequately. In addition, systematic political science research of this kind has created a demand and consequent supply of human rights measures, which also have their associated strengths and weaknesses. This section of the chapter discusses the contribution that political science has made to comparative method and measurement in the study of human rights.

Comparative methods provide ways in which to compare similarities and differences across countries to arrive at a series of generalisations about particular human rights problems. As outlined above, there are three general comparative methods available to social scientists of human rights: global comparisons of many countries, few-country comparisons, and single-country studies. The trade-offs associated with these methods involve the degree to which each can make broad ranging empirical generalisations at different levels of theoretical and conceptual abstraction (Mair 1996; Landman 2000, 2002, 2003, 2005b, 2008). Global comparisons tend to make empirical generalisations using concepts and constructs at a fairly high level of abstraction. Few-country comparisons tend to limit their generalisations and lower the level the abstraction in analysing human rights problems across a selection of countries. Single-country analysis tends to limit further its empirical generalisations and concentrates on the contextual particularities of the single case under investigation, but can be constructed in such a way so as to contribute to larger theoretical and empirical problems.

In the discussion above on the structural approaches to human rights research in political science, we saw that global comparative analysis typically involves the use of large and complex data sets comprised of variables that have been operationalised quantitatively and have been specified in such a way that they can be measured over time and across space. With such a large number of observations (typical time and space combinations exceed 4,000 such observations), global comparisons make empirical generalisations about relationships between and among variables that have associated degrees of statistical significance. The main strengths of this kind of analysis include statistical control to rule out rival explanations, extensive coverage of cases, the ability to make strong inferences, and the identification of 'deviant' cases or 'outliers'. The large number of observations means that there are sufficient degrees of freedom to add control variables and robustness tests to eliminate the possibility of spuriousness[7], while the types of inferences that are made tend be of a general nature as outlined above.

But global analysis also has a number of weaknesses, including data availability, validity and reliability of rights and other measures, and its limited application to human rights problems. First, until very recently, there had been a dearth of cross-national data on human rights practices. There are still only five major sources of human rights measures available for global comparative analysis, all of which are limited ordinal 'standards-based' scales of human rights practices (see also Landman 2004). The 'political terror scale' (Mitchell, *et al.* 1986; Poe and Tate 1994; Gibney and Dalton 1996; Gibney and Stohl 1998), the Freedom House civil and political liberties scales (Gastil 1978, 1980, 1988, 1990; http://www. freedomhouse.org), and the torture scale (Hathaway 2002) measure a narrowly defined set of civil and political rights, while the Cingranelli and Richards human rights data set (http://www.humanrightsdata.com) includes measures of civil and political rights, worker rights, and women's economic and social rights. Second, despite the development of measures of human rights for cross-national quantitative analysis, there are serious questions remaining about the validity and reliability of these measures, which code qualitative information typically found in Amnesty International and/or US State Department human rights country reports into quantitative scales. Third, global comparative analysis cannot address a whole range of important research questions in the human rights field, since many such topics are not susceptible to quantitative methods. Even if they are, global quantitative analysis provides generalisations that need greater specification and in-depth research that can only be carried out on smaller samples of countries (Landman 2005a).

It is precisely because of the limitations and weaknesses of global comparative analysis that many human rights scholars carry out their analyses on a smaller selection of countries. Comparing few countries achieves control through the careful selection of cases that are analysed using a middle level of conceptual abstraction. Studies using this method are more intensive and less extensive since they encompass more of the nuances specific to each case. The outcomes that feature in this type of comparison are often seen to be 'configurative', i.e. the product of multiple causal factors acting together. Such comparisons tend to make generalisations that are less broad using concepts and constructs that have been analysed in greater depth across the countries that have been selected for analysis.

The comparison of the similarities and differences across a small number of countries is meant to uncover the empirical relationship between the presence of key explanatory factors and the presence of an observed outcome. The isolation of these explanatory factors and the determination of their relationship to the observed outcome can be achieved through adopting two distinct types of research design: 'most similar systems design' and 'most different systems design' (Przeworski and Teune 1970; Skocpol and Somers 1980; Faure 1994; Landman 2000, 2002, 2003, 2008). Most similar systems design (MSSD) compares different outcomes across similar countries. Comparing countries that share a host of common features allows for the isolation of those factors that may account for an outcome. Most different systems design (MDSD) compares countries that share very few features and then focuses on those factors common across the countries that may account for an outcome. In the examples of political science research discussed above, Bob (2005) compares the same outcome (i.e. successful attraction of international support for a domestically based movement) across the two very different cases of Nigeria and Mexico (MDSD), while Mitchell compares different levels of atrocity across similar instances of civil war (MSSD).

Both MSSD and MDSD seek to identify a relationship between explanatory factors and outcomes by comparing different outcomes across similar countries or similar outcomes across different countries. Both the Bob (2005) and Mitchell (2004) examples seek to identify the overall relationship between the presence and absence of the studies' explanatory variables and their dependent variables through the focused comparison of few countries. Of the two research designs, MSSD is slightly more robust, since it allows for the presence of different outcomes across the countries under investigation to vary. In contrast, MDSD does not allow for the presence of different outcomes, and thus has no variance in the dependent variable (a form of selection bias). MDSD thus establishes a concomitance of explanatory factors and outcomes since it does not allow for 'negative' instances of the outcomes being examined (see Mahoney and Goertz 2004). Moreover, there are a finite number of outcomes of interest in the world that limits the number of countries this framework of analysis can include in any one comparison.

The comparison of few countries suffers from two major methodological weaknesses. First, such studies may identify a large number of explanatory variables whose full variation far exceeds the number of countries under investigation. This problem is commonly labelled 'too many variables, not enough countries' (Dogan and Pelassy 1990; Collier 1991; Hague, *et al.* 1992), or 'too many inferences and not enough observations' (King, *et al.* 1994). Second, the intentional selection of cases rather than a random selection can seriously undermine the types of inferences that can be drawn. This problem is known as selection bias, and occurs in comparative politics through the non-random choice of countries for comparison, or the deliberate selection by the comparativist (Collier 1995: 462). Both the Bob (2005) and Mitchell (2004) are excellent examples of few country comparisons, but they both illustrate a need to extend the analysis to new cases. For Mitchell (2004), it would be good to see if the principal-agent model applies to countries that are not in civil war and to categories of human rights that go beyond political killings. For Bob (2005) it would be good to see instances in which a domestic-based movement without adequate framing was nonetheless successful in attracting outside support or instances in which adequate framing did not lead to garnering such support.

With regard to human rights measures, few-country comparisons can use quantitative and qualitative data to show the variation in human rights protection and human rights outcomes both across cases and over time. For example, Foweraker and Landman (1997) use events-based and standards-based data across the cases of Brazil, Chile, Mexico and Spain to examine the relationship between social movements and citizenship rights. Brockett (2005) uses comparative historical analysis and time-series events-data on social protest and patterns of state repression in El Salvador and Guatemala. The comparative analysis shows how state violence in Guatemala virtually eliminated a popular rural movement while in El Salvador similar levels of state violence did not. Finally, Risse, *et al.* (1999) do not use time-series data but instead compare long histories across 11 different countries and trace the processes involved in the cascade of global norms, the changing tactics of states, and in the case of many countries in the volume, the internalisation of human rights norms.

The field of human rights research is full of single-country studies. By definition, they focus on countries with particularly problematic human rights records and include official reports from international governmental (IGOs) and non-governmental organisations (INGOs), domestic commissions and NGOs, journalistic and descriptive accounts, and research monographs. The *Nunca Más* (CONADEP 1984) report from Argentina and the *Nunca Mais* (Dassin 1986) report from Brazil are classic examples of such descriptive accounts of human rights abuse under conditions of authoritarianism, and as discussed above, truth commissions often publish their findings for the general public, such as the South African Truth and Reconciliation Commission and the *Comisión de Verdad y Reconciliación* in Peru (Truth and Reconciliation Commission, CVR). On balance, however, these descriptive accounts are not grounded in any one discipline, and they rarely make larger inferences from the intensive examination of the individual case. The descriptive accounts do, however, serve as the foundation for research monographs, which are grounded in one or more disciplines and tend to locate the country study in a broader set of theoretical and empirical questions relevant to the study of human rights.

Beyond their pure descriptive function, single-country studies can make significant and valuable contributions to the study of human rights, including establishing new classifications, the generation of hypotheses and their use as 'crucial cases' for testing hypotheses (see Eckstein 1975; George and Bennett 2005; Gerring 2006, Landman 2008: Chapter 5). There are several examples where the development of new classifications has advanced scholarship in describing, understanding, and explaining patterns of human rights abuse, such as the notion of the 'authoritarian' regime based on Spain and the expanded idea of the 'bureaucratic-authoritarian' regime based on Argentina (Linz 1964; O'Donnell 1973; Collier 1979); the idea of patron-client relations and their permeation of state organisation identified in Latin America and their extension to Africa

(Clapham 1982; Bratton and van der Walle 1997; Haynes 2002); the specification of new forms of warfare that move beyond more traditional understandings of conflict and that have grave consequences for human rights (Kaldor 1999; Gilbert 2000; Münkler 2005); and the concept of 'uncivil' movements developed in Latin America that 'travels' for subsequent comparative studies (Payne 2000).

As 'plausibility probes' (Eckstein 1975: 108), single-country studies explicitly (or implicitly) suggest that a hypothesis generated in one country ought to be tested in a larger selection of countries (Lijphart 1971: 692). For example, Hawkins (2002) tests hypotheses generated in the Chilean case about the relationship between international human rights pressure and regime change in the additional cases of Cuba and South Africa. Certain 'rule-oriented' factions within the Chilean military became influenced by outside human rights pressure, which ultimately led to gradual concessions by the regime and the transition to democracy; a similar process took place in South Africa but not in Cuba, since there are not significant fissures in the ruling elite that would be susceptible to the influence of international human rights pressure.

Finally, single-country studies are useful if they act as 'crucial' cases drawn from theoretical expectations and propositions about the world. These include 'most likely' and 'least likely' (Eckstein 1975: 118), which can confirm or inform existing theories about the occurrence of particular social and political phenomena relevant to human rights. Least likely case studies select a country where theory suggests an outcome is not likely to occur. If the outcome is observed, then the theory is infirmed, since it suggested such an outcome should not be obtained in that particular country. Most likely case studies apply a reverse logic to least likely studies by selecting countries where theory suggests the outcome is definitely meant to occur. If the outcome is not observed, then the theory is infirmed. The task of the analyst is thus to explain these so-called unexpected events and/or 'non-events' in particular cases through identifying those factors that have led to a different outcome than the one that is expected given the assumptions and pre-dictions of a particular theory.

Single-country studies thus serve larger comparative purposes if they lead to new classifications of social phenomena, generate new hypotheses about important empirical relationships, and provide critical tests of extant theories. Human rights abuses take place across a huge range of different social, economic, and political contexts, and single-country studies provide the richness of contextual description and the analysis of new institutional, cultural, and behavioural phenomena. Like the few country comparisons, single-country studies have used different com-binations of qualitative and quantitative data on human rights to provide the base of evidence for advancing larger political science arguments. The biggest advances in the measurement of human rights have arguably taken place through the analysis of single countries, where new techniques for coding and analysing multiple sources of human rights information have produced extensive and robust event-based data sets for countries such as Guatemala, Peru, El Salvador, East Timor, Sierra Leone, Colombia, and South Africa (see Ball, *et al.* 2000; Ball, *et al.* 2003; Guzmán, *et al.* 2007). These data efforts have also been accompanied by extensive qualitative research, such as the 30 *estudios en profundidad* carried out by the Peruvian Truth and Reconciliation Commission (see the Final Report and Landman 2006: Chapter 7).

Summary

This chapter has shown that political science has overcome its historical ambivalence about human rights and has been actively developing a significant sub-discipline of research on human rights that has produced studies at all levels of analysis and across all types of theoretical approaches. These developments in the discipline have been facilitated by the establishment of specialist research and teaching divisions within the major professional political science associations in the US, Europe, and internationally. While many academic programmes in human rights in the US and Europe are multi-disciplinary and inter-disciplinary, the 'political science of human rights' (Landman 2005a) is now becoming a rich tradition in and of itself. This chapter has shown that this burgeoning field of research is making significant contributions to the study of human rights problems in terms of theory, comparative methods, and the development of comparable human rights measures.

Despite the many contributions that the political science has made, however, there are a number of remaining challenges that the discipline needs to address, including greater attention to theory, methods, and measurement, as well as greater attention to particular parts of the world. In theoretical terms, more work is needed on developing rationalist approaches to human rights in general and in developing analyses that take into account the insights and assumptions of structural and cultural approaches. Lichbach's (1997) notion of the 'socially embedded unit act' is one such attempt to show how the intentional choices of individuals are embedded in larger structural and institutional contexts and influenced by significant sets of ideas, norms, and beliefs. Such a theoretical construct seems particular apt for the study of human rights since it captures the individual and contextual aspects of any human rights event and will be applicable to all categories of human rights.

Methodologically, greater attention is needed among those studies that compare few countries or that carry out single country studies on the principals of selection. The choice of cases cannot be arbitrary nor can it be the function of the gravity of the human rights situation. Rather, choosing cases must reflect the logic of inference and how it relates to case selection in the ways outlined in this chapter. What kind of case has been chosen? Why is it important? Is it a typical case? Does it present a particular puzzle for human rights? Is it a least likely or most likely case? And how does any answer to the research question investigated through the case provide deeper insight and a larger set of inferences for human rights policymaking?

In terms of measurement, existing indicators are still biased towards standards-based scales of civil and political rights, while more attention is needed on the development of events-based measures and the use of socio-economic and administrative statistics on all categories of human rights (UNDP 2006). For ideological and methodological reasons, civil and political rights have received far greater attention in political science than economic and social rights, yet research on human rights is beginning to show the interrelationships between these different sets of rights (Landman and Larizza 2009) and the discipline is beginning to provide creative ways of measuring economic and social rights that take into account the ability of states and their willingness to engage in their progressive realisation (Cingranelli and Richards 2007). More work is needed on the 'agents' who violate economic and social rights and the fiscal capacity of states to invest in the promotion and protection of civil and political rights (see Holmes and Sunstein 1999).

Finally, more research is needed on the variation in human rights protection across well developed democracies. Too often, the political science of human rights has a North to South focus and risks being ethnocentric, patronising, and prescriptive, while existing measures are too crude to differentiate the human rights performance of OECD countries. Particularly now, in the age of terror, where advanced liberal democracies are beginning to undermine hard fought and long cherished rights traditions through a roll back of laws protecting individuals from prolonged detention without charge and torture (either at home or through the policy of extraordinary rendition), human rights scholarship in political science needs to provide explanations for the variation of response among advanced democracies to threat from international terrorism (see Brysk and Shafir 2007; Landman 2007a, 2007b; Moeckli 2008). There are rational, structural, and cultural reasons for these differences in response, and the research topic is itself ripe for comparative analysis of the kinds that have already been done for other topics in the field of human rights.

Notes

1 This field of research does risk falling into the problem of 'legalisation' of human rights, where the international law of human rights is used uncritically as an agreed upon baseline against which state performance is measured (see Meckled-Garcia and Cali 2005).
2 Even though much of what constitutes human rights practices, violations, and conditions, may not be directly observable, there have been many developments in statistics in the use of multiple sources, data matching, and modelling to estimate patterns of human rights abuse for certain categories of human rights (see Ball, *et al.* 2000; Ball, *et al.* 2003; Guzmán, *et al.* 2007 and http://www.benetech.org).
3 One exception is Poe's (2004) examination of the applicability of the Most-Starr (1989) model of conflict to the area of human rights abuse, which remains under researched to date.
4 In the language found in the international instruments and documents on human rights, the two dimensions of relevance for rationalist accounts are the state obligation to *respect* (i.e. the state must refrain from interference in the exercise of the right) and to *protect* (i.e. possible third party violations of human rights) civil, political, economic, social, and cultural rights in which it is possible to identify a perpetrator for violations.
5 There are also data sets on the atrocities for these conflicts that have been made available through the truth commissions that investigated them (see Ball, *et al.* 2003; Brockett 2005; Landman 2006) that would be particularly apt for replicating Mitchell's model.

6 Since the appearance of Mitchell's 2004 book, he and Sabine Carey have been globalising the model to examine the cross-national variation in militia groups in the world.

7 Recent methodological developments have provided a set of statistical techniques to control for the possible confounding influence of variables that do not vary much over time, such as those for political institutions, income inequality, and population size (see Plümper and Troeger 2007 and for application to human rights, Landman and Larizza 2009; Landman and Schudel 2007).

Bibliography

Abouharb M. R. and Cingranelli, D. L. (2007) *Human Rights and Structural Adjustment*, Cambridge: Cambridge University Press.

Anderson, C. J., Paskeviciute, A., Sandovici, M. E. and Tverdova, Y. V. (2005) 'In the Eye of the Beholder?: The Foundations of Subjective Human Rights Conditions in East-Central Europe', *Comparative Political Studies* 38(September): 771–98.

Ball, P. B., Asher, J., Sulmont, D. and Manrique, D. (2003) *How many Peruvians have died?*, Washington, DC: American Association for the Advancement of Science (AAAS). Available online at http://shr.aaas.org/hrdag/peru/aaas_peru_5.pdf

Ball, P. B., Spirer, H. F., and Spirer, L. (eds) (2000) *Making the Case: Investigating Large Scale Human Rights Violations Using Information Systems and Data Analysis*, Washington DC: American Association for the Advancement of Science.

Bob, C. (2005) *The Marketing of Rebellion: Insurgents, Media, and International Activism*, Cambridge: Cambridge University Press.

Brady, H. and Collier, D. (eds) (2004) *Rethinking Social Inquiry: Diverse Tools, Shared Standards*, Lanham: Rowman and Littlefield.

Bratton, M. and van de Walle, N. (1997) *Democratic Experiments in Africa: Regime Transitions in Comparative Perspective*, Cambridge: Cambridge University Press.

Brockett, C. (2005) *Political Movements and Violence in Central America*, Cambridge: Cambridge University Press.

Brysk, A. and Shafir, G. (2007) *National Insecurity and Human Rights: Democracies Debate Terrorism*, Berkeley: University of California Press.

Cingranelli, D. and Richards, D. (2007) 'Measuring Government Effort to Respect Economic and Social Human Rights: A Peer Benchmark', in Hertel and Minkler (eds) *Economic Rights: Conceptual, Measurement and Policy Issues*, Cambridge: Cambridge University Press.

Clapham, C. (ed.) (1982) *Private Patronage and Public Power: Political Clientelism in the Modern State*, London: Pinter.

Claude, R. P. (1976) 'The Classical Model of Human Rights Development' in Claude (ed.) *Comparative Human Rights*, Baltimore and London: Johns Hopkins University Press.

Collier, D. (ed.) (1979) *The New Authoritarianism in Latin America*, Princeton, NJ: Princeton University Press.

—— (1991) 'New Perspectives on the Comparative Method', in Rustow and Erickson (eds) *Comparative Political Dynamics: Global Research Perspectives*, New York: Harper Collins.

—— (1995) 'Translating Quantitative Methods for Qualitative Researchers: The Case of Selection Bias', *American Political Science Review* 89(2): 461–6.

CONADEP, (1984) *Nunca Más (Never Again): A Report by Argentina's National Commission on Disappeared People*, Buenos Aires.

Dassin, J. (ed.) (1986) *Torture in Brazil, A Report by the Archdiocese of São Paulo*, New York: Vintage Books.

Davenport, C. (1999) 'Human Rights and the Democratic Proposition', *Journal of Conflict Resolution* 43(1): 92–116.

Davenport, C. and Armstrong, D.A. (2004) 'Democracy and the Violation of Human Rights: A Statistical Exploration from 1976 to 1996', *American Journal of Political Science* 48(3): 538–4.

Dogan, M. and Pelassy, D. (1990) *How to Compare Nations: Strategies in Comparative Politics*, 2nd edn, Chatham, NJ: Chatham House.

Donnelly, J. (1999) 'The Social Construction of Human Rights' in Dunne and Wheeler (eds) *Human Rights in Global Politics*, Cambridge: Cambridge University Press.

Douzinas, C. (2000) *The End of Human Rights*, Hart Publishing.

Eckstein, H. (1975) 'Case-study and Theory in Political Science', in F. I. Greenstein and N. S. Polsby (eds) *Handbook of Political Science, Vol. 7: Strategies of Inquiry*, Reading, MA: Addison-Wesley.

Eulau, H. (1996) *Micro-Macro Dilemmas in Political Science: Personal Pathways through Complexity*, Norman, OK: University of Oklahoma Press.

Faure, A. M. (1994) 'Some Methodological Problems in Comparative Politics', *Journal of Theoretical Politics* 6(3): 307–22.

Flyvbjerg, B. (2001) *Making Social Science Matter*, Cambridge: Cambridge University Press.

Forsythe, D. (2000) *Human Rights in International Relations*, Cambridge: Cambridge University Press.

Foweraker, J. and Landman, T. (1997) *Citizenship Rights and Social Movements: A Comparative and Statistical Analysis*, Oxford: Oxford University Press.

Gastil, R. D. (1978), *Freedom in the World: Political Rights and Civil Liberties 1978*, Boston: G. K. Hall.

—— (1980) *Freedom in the World: Political Rights and Civil Liberties*, Westport, CT: Greenwood Press.

—— (1988) *Freedom in the World: Political and Civil Liberties 1986–87*, New York: Freedom House.

—— (1989) *Freedom in the World: Political and Civil Liberties 1988–89*, New York: Freedom House.

—— (1990) 'The Comparative Survey of Freedom: Experiences and Suggestions', *Studies in Comparative International Development* 25: 25–50.

George, A. L. and Bennett, A. (2005) *Case Studies and Theory Development in the Social Sciences*, Cambridge, MA: MIT Press.

Gerring, J. (2006) *Case Study Research: Principles and Practice*, Cambridge: Cambridge University Press.

Gibney, M. and Dalton, M. (1996), 'The Political Terror Scale', in Cingranelli (ed.) *Human Rights and Developing Countries*, Greenwich, CT: JAI Press.

Gibney, M. and Stohl, M. (1998), 'Human Rights and US Refugee Policy', in Gibney (ed.) *Open Borders? Closed Societies?: The Ethical and Political Issues*, Westport, WT: Greenwood Press.

Gilbert, P. (2003) *New Terror, New Wars*, Edinburgh: Edinburgh University Press.

Guzmán, D., Guberek, T., Hoover, A. and Ball, P. (2007) 'Missing People in Casanare', Palo Alto: The Benetech Initiative. Available online at http://www.hrdag.org/resources/publications/casanare-missing-report.pdf (accessed 28 August 2008).

Hafner-Burton, E. and Ron, J. (2007) 'Special Issue on Human Rights', *Journal of Peace Research* 44(4).

Hafner-Burton, E. and Tsutsui, K. (2005) 'Human Rights in a Globalizing World: The Paradox of Empty Promises', *American Journal of Sociology* 110(5): 1373–1411.

—— (2007) 'Justice Lost! The Failure of International Human Rights Law to Matter Where Needed Most', *Journal of Peace Research* 44(4): 407–25.

Hague, R., Harrop, M. and Breslin, S. (1992) *Political Science: A Comparative Introduction*, New York: St Martin's Press.

Hathaway, O. (2002) 'Do Treaties Make a Difference? Human Rights Treaties and the Problem of Compliance', *Yale Law Journal* 111: 1932–2042.

Hawkins, D (2002) *International Human Rights and Authoritarian Rule in Chile*, Lincoln: University of Nebraska Press.

Haynes, J. (2002) *Politics in the Developing World: A Concise Introduction*, Malden, MA: Blackwell.

Henderson, C. (1993) 'Population Pressures and Political Repression', *Social Science Quarterly* 74: 322–3.

Holmes, S. and Sunstein, C. R. (1999) *The Cost of Rights: Why Liberty Depends on Taxes*, New York: W.W. Norton.

Ishay, M. (2004) *The History of Human Rights: From Ancient Times to the Globalization Era*, Berkeley: University of California Press.

Kaldor, M. (1999) *New and Old Wars: Organized Violence in a Global Era*, Cambridge: Polity.

King, G., Keohane, R. O., and Verba, S. (1994) *Designing Social Inquiry: Scientific Inference in Qualitative Research*, Princeton, NJ: Princeton University Press.

Kohli, A., Evans, P., Katzenstein, P. J., Przeworski, A., Rudolph, S. H., Scott, J. C. and Skocpol, T. (1995) 'The Role of Theory in Comparative Politics: A Symposium', *World Politics* 48: 1–49.

Krasner, S. (1993) 'Sovereignty, Regimes and Human Rights', in Rittberger and Mayer (eds) *Regime Theory and International Relations*, Oxford: Oxford University Press, pp. 139–67.

Landman, T. (2000) *Issues and Methods in Comparative Politics: An Introduction*, London: Routledge.

—— (2002) 'Comparative Politics and Human Rights', *Human Rights Quarterly* 43(4): 890–923.

—— (2003) *Issues and Methods in Comparative Politics: An Introduction*, 2nd edn, London: Routledge.

—— (2004) 'Measuring Human Rights: Principle, Practice, and Policy', *Human Rights Quarterly*, 26 (November): 906–31.

—— (2005a) 'Review Article: the Political Science of Human Rights', *British Journal of Political Science* 35(3): 549–72.

—— (2005b) *Protecting Human Rights: A Global Comparative Study*, Washington DC: Georgetown University Press.

—— (2006) *Studying Human Rights*, London: Routledge.

—— (2007a) 'The United Kingdom: The Continuity of Terror and Counterterror' in Brysk and Shafir (eds) *National Insecurity and Human Rights: Democracies Debate Terrorism*, Berkeley: University of California Press.

—— (2007b) 'Imminence and Proportionality: The US and UK Responses to Global Terrorism', *California Western International Law Journal* 38(1): 75–106.

—— (2008) *Issues and Methods in Comparative Politics: An Introduction*, 3rd edn, London: Routledge.

Landman, Todd and Larizza, Marco (2009) 'Inequality and Human Rights: Who Controls What When and How,' *International Studies Quarterly*, forthcoming.

Landman, T. and Schudel, C. W. (2007) 'Corruption and Human Rights', working paper prepared for the International Council for Human Rights Policy, Geneva. Online. Available online at http://www.ichrp.org/paper_files/Landman_and_Schudel_2007.pdf

Legro, J. and Moravcsik, A. (1999) 'Is Anybody Still a Realist?' *International Security* 24(2): 5–55.

Lichbach, M. (1997) 'Social Theory and Comparative Politics', in Lichbach and Zuckerman (eds) *Comparative Politics: Rationality, Culture, and Structure*, Cambridge: Cambridge University Press.

Lijphart, A. (1971) 'Comparative Politics and Comparative Method', *The American Political Science Review* 65(3): 682–93.

—— (1975) 'The Comparable Cases Strategy in Comparative Research', *Comparative Political Studies* 8(2): 158–77.

Linz, J. J. (1964) 'An Authoritarian Regime: Spain', in Allardt and Rokkan (eds) *Mass Politics*, New York: Free Press.

Mahoney, J. and Goertz (2004) 'The Possibility Principle: Choosing Negative Cases in Comparative Research', *American Political Science Review* 98(4): 653–9.

Mair, P. (1996) 'Comparative Politics: An Overview', in Goodin and Klingemann (eds) *The New Handbook of Political Science*, Oxford: Oxford University Press.

Mearsheimer, J. J. (1994–5) 'The False Promise of International Institutions', *International Security* 19(3): 5–49.

Meckled-Garcia, Saladin and Çali, Ba‚sak. (eds) (2006) *The Legalisation of Human Rights: Multi-disciplinary Perspectives on Human Rights and Human Rights Law*, London: Routledge.

Mendus, S. (1995) 'Human Rights in Political Theory', *Political Studies*, 43 (Special Issue): 10–24.

Mesquita, B. B., Cherif, F. M., Downs, G. W. and Smith, A. (2005) 'Thinking Inside the Box: A Closer Look at Democracy and Human Rights', *International Studies Quarterly* 49(3): 439–58.

Meyer, W. H. (1996) 'Human Rights and MNCs: Theory vs. Quantitative Evidence', *Human Rights Quarterly*, 18 (2): 368–97.

—— (1998) *Human Rights and International Political Economy in Third World Nations: Multinational Corporations, Foreign Aid, and Repression*, Westport, CT: Praeger.

—— (1999a) 'Confirming, Infirming, and Falsifying Theories of Human Rights: Reflections on Smith, Bolyard, and Ippolito Through the Lens of Lakatos', *Human Rights Quarterly* 21(1): 220–8.

—— (1999b) 'Human Rights and International Political Economy in Third World Nations: Multinational Corporations, Foreign Aid, and Repression', *Human Rights Quarterly* 21(3): 824–30.

Mitchell, C., Stohl, M., Carleton, D. and Lopez, G. (1986) 'State Terrorism: Issues of Concept and Measurement', in Stohl and Lopez (eds) *Government Violence and Repression: An Agenda for Research*, New York, Greenwood Press.

Mitchell, N. (2004) *Agents of Atrocity: Leaders, Followers, and the Violation of Human Rights in Civil War*, London: Palgrave.

Moeckli, D. (2008) *Human Rights and Non-Discrimination in the War on Terror*, Oxford: Oxford University Press.

Most, Benjamin A., Starr, Harvey (1989) *Inquiry, Logic and International Politics*, Columbia, SC: University of South Carolina Press.

Münkler, H. (2005) *The New Wars*, Cambridge: Polity Press.

Neumayer, E. (2005) 'Do International Human Rights Treaties Improve Respect for Human Rights?', *Journal of Conflict Resolution* 49(6): 925–53.

O'Donnell, G. (1973) *Economic Modernization and Bureaucratic Authoritarianism*, Berkeley, CA: Institute of International Studies.

Payne, L. (2000) *Uncivil Movements: The Armed Right Wing and Democracy in Latin America*, Baltimore: Johns Hopkins University Press.

Plümper, T. and Troeger, V. (2007) 'Efficient Estimation of Time Invariant and Rarely Changing Variables in Panel Data Analysis with Unit Effects', *Political Analysis* 15: 124–39.

Poe, S. C. (2004) 'The Decision to Repress: An Integrative Theoretical Approach to Research on Human Rights and Repression', in Sabine Carey and Steven C. Poe (eds) *Understanding Human Rights Violations: New Systematic Studies*, Aldershot: Ashgate. 16–42.

Poe, S. C. and Tate, C. N. (1994) 'Repression of Human Rights to Personal Integrity in the 1980s: A Global Analysis', *American Political Science Review* 88: 853–72.

Poe, S. C., Tate, C. N. and Keith, L. C. (1999) 'Repression of the Human Right to Personal Integrity Revisited: A Global Cross-National Study Covering the Years 1976–93', *International Studies Quarterly* 43: 291–313.

Popper, K. (1972) 'Of Clouds and Clocks: An Approach to the Problem of Rationality and Freedom in Man' in Popper (ed.), *Objective Knowledge: An Evolutionary Approach*, Oxford: Clarendon Press.

Przeworski, A. and Teune, H. (1970) *The Logic of Comparative Social Inquiry*, New York: Wiley.

Richards, D. 'What do Citizens Mean When They Say "Human Rights": A Comparative Examination of the Formation of Citizen Attitudes about, and Understandings of, Human Rights', paper presented at the Annual Meeting of the American Political Science Association, Philadelphia, August–September 2006.

Risse, T., Ropp, S. C. and Sikkink, K. (eds) (1999) *The Power of Human Rights: International Norms and Domestic Change*, Cambridge: Cambridge University Press.

Risse, T. and Sikkink, K. (1999) 'The Socialization of International Human Rights Norms into Domestic Practices: Introduction', in Risse, Ropp and Sikkink (eds) *The Power of Human Rights: International Norms and Domestic Change*, Cambridge: Cambridge University Press.

Rorty, R. (1993) 'Human Rights, Rationality, and Sentimentality', in Shute and Hurley (eds) *On Human Rights: The Oxford Amnesty Lectures*, New York: Basic Books.

Schram, S. and Caterino, B. (eds) (2006) *Making Political Science Matter: Debating Knowledge, Research, and Method*, New York: New York University Press.

Skocpol, T. and Somers, M. (1980) 'The Uses of Comparative History in Macrosocial Inquiry', *Comparative Studies in Society and History* 22: 174–97.

Smith, J., Bolyard, M. and Ippolito, A. (1999) 'Human Rights and the Global Economy: A Response to Meyer', *Human Rights Quarterly* 21: 207–19.

Valenzuela, A. (1988) 'Political Science and the Study of Latin America', in Mitchell (ed.) *Changing Perspectives in Latin American Studies: Insights from Six Disciplines*, Stanford, CA: Stanford University Press.

Wantchekon, L. and Healy, A. (1999) 'The "Game" of Torture', *Journal of Conflict Resolution* 43(5): 569–609.

Ward, H. (1995) 'Rational Choice Theory', in Marsh and Stoker (eds) *Theories and Methods in Political Science*, London: Macmillan.

Zanger, S. C. (2000) 'A Global Analysis of the Effect of Regime Changes on Life Integrity Violations, 1977–93', *Journal of Peace Research* 37(2): 217–33.

3 The right to health

Michael Freeman

Overview

Health is a strong candidate for the status of a universal value. Almost everyone would choose good health over ill health, if everything else were equal. International law recognises a human right to health. The most authoritative statement of this right is found in Article 12 (1) of the International Covenant on Economic, Social and Cultural Rights. This states that everyone has a right to 'the highest attainable standard of physical and mental health'. This formulation of the right has been criticised by some philosophers on the ground that it does not help us to perform the unavoidable task of deciding health priorities in circumstances of scarce resources. I argue that philosophical critics of human rights often miss their mark for lack of an adequate sociology of law. I support this argument with an analysis of the work of the UN Special Rapporteur on 'the right to health', who has the task of interpreting international law in such a way that its intention can be implemented so far as possible. This analysis shows that law, philosophy and sociology each has characteristic strengths and weaknesses in their treatment of human rights, and that only an interdisciplinary approach can provide us with an adequate understanding of the concept. I conclude that the human right to health is a vague and complex idea, with a morally valid core, and that both its theoretical understanding and its practical implementation require a philosophically and sociologically informed approach to international law.

Introduction: health, human rights and sociology

Health is a strong candidate for the status of a universal value. Almost everyone would choose good health over ill health, if everything else were equal. Yet many millions of people around the world suffer from preventable, serious ill health. Every year more than ten million children die of preventable illness (Hunt 2003b: 4). This is surely morally unacceptable. In 1946 the World Health Organization (WHO) proclaimed that '[t]he enjoyment of the highest attainable standard of health is one of the fundamental rights of every human being' (Hunt 2003a: 6). The International Covenant on Economic, Social and Cultural Rights (ICESR), adopted by the United Nations in 1966, incorporated this right into international law. Article 12 (1) of the Covenant says that state parties 'recognize the right of everyone to the highest attainable standard of physical and mental health'.

Sociologists have traditionally taken little interest in human rights, although this is beginning to change (Turner 1993, 2006; Morris 2006; Woodiwiss 1998, 2003, 2005). This neglect may seem surprising, since the struggles for, and violations of, human rights are social processes that have powerful effects on the lives of many millions of people. Much sociology – concerning, for example, class, race, ethnicity, gender and sexuality – seems to overlap with the terrain of human rights. However, the Cold War moved the concept to a legal utopia, apparently containing little for sociologists to study. In the real world, massive human rights violations were taking place, but, if sociologists analyzed them at all, they did so with familiar categories, such as class struggle, capitalism, socialism, authoritarianism, totalitarianism, and national liberation movements.

Sociology's neglect of human rights had deep philosophical roots. The concept of human rights derives from that of 'natural rights', which derived in turn from the philosophy of natural law. The concept of natural rights reached the peak of its influence in the French Revolution. However, the disorders of the Revolution led several thinkers to reject the idea of natural rights on the ground that it subverted social order, and natural-law philosophy was undermined by new, 'scientific' modes of thought. In France the philosophy of natural rights was challenged by the science of society. The origins of sociology, therefore, lie in the rejection of natural rights.

A sociology of rights was developed by T. H. Marshall, but these were rights of citizenship, not human rights. Sociology confined its attention to 'society' in the form of the nation-state (Turner 1993: 490). The discipline of public health, developed from responses to the social and medical ills of nineteenth-century industrial capitalism, concerned itself with the well-being of the people without using the language of rights. After the Second World War the UN introduced the concept of 'human rights' by universalizing that of citizens' rights. Gradually, the processes of 'globalization' diffused the idea of human rights. However, the boundaries between international law and sociology remained intact. The idea of a human right to health brought together the concept of public health with that of human rights.

The human right to health was nevertheless neglected until recently. This neglect was probably caused in part by the different socialization and institutionalization of health and human rights professionals. The WHO has been the principal site at which health, human rights and sociology have converged. Its 1978 Declaration of Alma-Ater stated that public health required action, not only by health professionals, but also by a variety of other social agents (Mann, *et al.* 1994: 2–3).

Concern with health can raise human rights and sociological issues in several ways:

1 Human rights violations can cause bad health: torture is an obvious example.
2 Health policies can be implemented in ways that violate human rights, by, for example, unjustified discrimination.
3 Health may be a precondition for the enjoyment of human rights.

4   Health challenges the idea of human rights because resources are usually scarce, and consequently the relation between a right to health and health priorities must be problematic.

5   'Health' is both a natural and a socially constructed phenomenon, and thus raises problems about 'common humanity' and cultural diversity.

6   Sociology can help us to make sense of the right to health, since bad health is to a significant extent socially constructed. The UN Committee on Economic, Social and Cultural Rights has recognized that the social obstacles to the implementation of the right to health are formidable (United Nations Committee on Economic, Social and Cultural Rights 2000: 4–5, 8–11).

7   Public health has begun to adopt a human rights approach, emphasizing the need to respect human rights while promoting public health (Mann, *et al.* 1994: 8–9).

There are, therefore, social conditions of the realization of the right to health. Sociology can contribute to our understanding of this right by identifying those conditions. Before it can do that, however, we must achieve a reasonably precise conception of what 'the right to health' means. This is firstly a concept of international law, and it is there that we must begin our quest for its meaning.

The right to health in international law

The expression 'the right to health' is shorthand for a complex idea. It is *not* the right to be healthy, since no government can guarantee that. The UN Special Rapporteur on the right to health admits that it is an 'exceedingly vague' norm, which allows grey areas and good-faith disagreements, but it includes the right to be free from coercive medical treatment, to health care without arbitrary discrimination, and to the conditions conducive to the highest attainable standard of health (Hunt 2003a: 8–9, 11, 23; 2003b: 6; 2004c: 6; 2005d: 10–12, 15). Virginia Leary has pointed out that rights in constitutions, international declarations and treaties are usually expressed in succinct language, and that the implications of this language are realized only gradually. Civil and political rights have been developed by a substantial national and international jurisprudence, which economic and social rights have lacked. Where the meaning of human rights is unclear, it is interpreted by independent experts on treaty monitoring committees and by Special Rapporteurs, who engage in dialogue with governments, inter-governmental and non-governmental organizations (NGOs), academic experts, and others (Leary 1994: 2–3). The UN Commission on Human Rights has acknowledged that the full realization of this right remains a distant goal and that, for many, especially the poor, this goal is becoming increasingly remote (United Nations Commission on Human Rights 2003: 1).[1]

In seeking to clarify the meaning of the right to health, and to encourage its implementation, the Special Rapporteur has accorded priority to its association with poverty and discrimination. Human rights promise minimum standards for everyone, and this justifies prioritizing the needs of the worst-off. The emphasis on non-discrimination entails priority for those known to be victims of discrimination, such as women, indigenous peoples and those who suffer from stigmatized conditions, such as mental illness and disability (Hunt 2003a: 11–19, 22; 2003b: 20; 2003c: 5–9; 2004a: 19–20; 2004c: 12; 2005a: 12–16; 2005c: 18, 21; 2005d: 5, 9; 2006a: 5, 14–17). By interpreting his brief in this way, the Special Rapporteur converts a human right into a set of policy priorities.

States that are parties to the ICESR have legal obligations that include the following: to prevent and reduce disease; minimize the risk of accidents; ensure equal access to health services for all; ensure the dissemination of health information; prohibit traditional practices harmful to health; protect the health of vulnerable groups, especially to reduce infant and maternal mortality, as well as gender-based violence; provide culturally appropriate health care; and ensure equal access of all to the social determinants of health. These obligations are to realize the right to health *progressively*, but states have 'core' obligations to provide minimum levels of enjoyment of the right without discrimination, and these are to be implemented immediately (United Nations Committee on Economic, Social and Cultural Rights 2000: 9–13). States are always obliged to fulfil their core obligations, and, beyond those, are obliged to use the maximum of their available resources. They are obliged to adopt the budgets necessary to fulfil the right. If a state lacks the resources to fulfil its core obligations, the nature of its obligation is unclear, although it would be vulnerable to criticism on human rights grounds if it 'wasted' resources through, for example, corruption. The right to health is multi-dimensional so there is no single indicator of its fulfilment (United Nations Committee on Economic, Social and Cultural Rights 2000: 14–15; Hunt 2005c: 11–12, 16; 2005d: 13–14; 2006a: 19; 2006b: 11–14). Rich states have obligations not to harm the health of people in other countries, to prevent third parties from doing so, and to assist poor countries. The precise nature of the duty to assist is also unclear, and controversial (United Nations Committee on Economic, Social and Cultural Rights 2000: 12, 14; Hunt 2003a: 9; 2004a: 18; 2004b: 5, 8–9; 2005a: 19; 2005d: 16; 2005f: 15–16; 2006c: 6).

The right-to-health approach differs from the public health tradition in emphasizing the worst-off, non-discrimination and participation. The Special Rapporteur argues that the right *empowers* the disadvantaged, because it is based on international norms, the obligations of states, international monitoring, and the accountability of states. Consequently, policies based on the right are likely to be more effective, inclusive and equitable (Hunt 2003a: 19; 2003b: 15, 23; 2004a: 14, 20, 22; 2004c: 7; 2005a: 10–11, 21; 2005d: 11, 15; 2006b: 8). These claims depend on a strong set of normative and empirical assumptions about the effectiveness and equity of rights-based health policies, which need to be spelled out and substantiated.

Philosophers and sociologists have ignored the social processes by which human rights law has been interpreted, whereas lawyers make normative and empirical claims without the requisite supporting argument and evidence. The UN Special Rapporteur has recognized the need for research into the social conditions of the realization of the right to health, although he seems less aware of the normative assumptions supporting his choice of priorities (Hunt 2003a: 11; 2006a: 17).

Rights, obligations and resources

The law, sociology and philosophy of the right to health converge on questions raised by the scarcity, availability and distribution of resources. The Special Rapporteur claims that policies based on the right to health are likely to be more 'equitable'. This links the *right* to health with a conception of *justice*. The Universal Declaration of Human Rights says that recognition of human rights is the 'foundation' of justice. This suggests that human rights specify some *minimal* conditions, upon which a more elaborate system of justice might be built. The Commission on Human Rights, however, interprets the right to health as entailing the obligation of states to devote the *maximum* of their available resources to realize, progressively, for everyone, the highest attainable standard of health (United Nations Commission on Human Rights 2003). This is a *maximal* rather than a minimal requirement, limited only by the availability of resources.

James Griffin denies that there is a human right to the highest attainable standard of health, and that it is even a reasonable social goal. Societies are justified in balancing the good of health with other social goals. He concedes, however, that there is a right to 'the health care necessary for our functioning effectively as agents' (Griffin 2000: 22, 25–6). The so-called Limburg Principles, adopted by a conference of experts in 1986, require that priority be given to meeting minimal, essential needs, thereby narrowing the gap between the UN and Griffin's conception of the right (Limburg Principles on the Implementation of the International Covenant on Economic, Social and Cultural Rights). Onora O'Neill argues that the best possible health policy requires decisions about *priorities*. The language of human rights, she says, is unhelpful in guiding such decisions. By contrast, focusing on *obligations* enables us to compare obligations to provide health with those to provide other social goods (O'Neill 2002: 42–3). She is, however, mistaken in implying that an emphasis on human rights rules out attention to obligations, for the UN Special Rapporteur holds that the power of the human rights approach is precisely its emphasis on the obligations of states (Hunt 2006c: 5–10). He has also admitted that selecting *priorities* and making *trade-offs* are part of 'the inescapable reality of policy-making' (Hunt 2006a: 16; 2006b: 12, 14). It is not clear, however, how a human right to 'health' is related to the choice of health priorities.

It is often said that poor countries lack the resources necessary to implement economic and social rights, but some health-improvement policies are fairly inexpensive, and costs are lower in poor countries. Some poor countries have good health records. Costa Rica, for example, had, in 2004, a GDP per capita of US$9,481 and life expectancy at birth of 78.3, whereas the USA had a GDP per capita of US$39,676 and life expectancy of 77.5 (United Nations Development Programme 2006). Bad health hinders development, so investment in health may be part of a sound development strategy. Poor countries waste resources on corruption, bureaucracy, repression and military expenditures, and external agents, such as international financial institutions and multinational corporations, also undermine the efficient use of resources for the improvement of health (Leon and Watt 2001: 5–6; Sen 2001: 340; Leary 1994: 17; World Health Organization 2001; Hunt

2004b). Normatively, therefore, the right to health assumes the availability and just distribution of resources. Empirically, the relation between resources and successful health policies is not straightforward, and requires detailed investigation.

The political economy of health

Because fulfilment of the right to health demands substantial resources, an adequate normative theory requires an appropriate political economy. The concept of human rights does not entail endorsement of any particular economic system. Nowadays, the human rights movement works, for pragmatic reasons, within the framework of global capitalism. International law imposes human rights obligations primarily on *states*, but the UN assumes that the right to health may be delivered by some form of public-private partnership (United Nations Commission on Human Rights 2003: 2). Capitalism is not designed to fulfil the right to health, but it can generate the resources that can be used to improve health. Politics mediates between economic systems and health outcomes. The available evidence therefore justifies the reticence of human rights advocates about the relative merits of different economic formations. Sociologists working within the Marxist tradition have doubted whether the liberal discourse of rights can address the social inequalities that lead to inequalities in health (Benton 2006: 25–9). This view is mistaken, as the 'right to health' includes the right to the social conditions of health. Leftist sociologists often assume that health equality is the proper goal of health policy. This, however, is not always so. For example, in most countries women live longer than men. Since the causes of this inequality are almost certainly biological, and not social, it is not unjust, and a policy to achieve equality by reducing the life expectancy of women would be egalitarian but unjust (Wikler 2002: 52–3).

Although not all health inequalities are unjust, the social inequalities produced by capitalism may threaten the implementation of the right to health. Global health has improved in recent years, but economic globalization is probably increasing health inequalities. Neoliberal economic ideology, structural adjustment programmes, the weakening of the state, the reduction of aid, the debt burden and trade liberalization all increase health inequality (Coburn 2003: 339, 351; Leon and Watt 2001: 1–3, 7; Gershman, *et al.* 2003: 171–2; Bambas and Casas 2003: 323; Labonte 2003: 476, 478–9; Hunt 2005c: 12). Yet the evidence suggests that equality is more conducive than inequality to economic growth and poverty reduction (Gershman, *et al.* 2003: 168). The World Bank and the International Monetary Fund (IMF) recognize that investment in 'human capital' (including health and education) might be an effective means to promote development (Gershman, *et al.* 2003: 174–6, 183; Braveman 2003: 314). Human rights activists and scholars have recently turned their attention to the relations between the international trade system and human rights (Dine and Fagan 2006; Hunt 2004b). Trade liberalization can increase resources available for health, but this tends to benefit the rich more than the poor (Hunt 2003b: 11; 2004b: 5–8, 14–15, 19). International trade agreements can limit the capacity of governments to regulate multinational corporations for the sake of public health. The Agreement on Trade-Related Aspects of Intellectual Property

Rights (TRIPS) hinders the ability of developing countries to meet their health obligations. The General Agreement on Trade in Services (GATS) encourages the movement of health professionals from poor to rich countries. Powerful states also use bilateral treaties to impose terms of trade that may harm the right to health. Our understanding of the relations between international trade and human rights is still limited, but the liberal, human rights approach can be the basis for criticizing certain forms of capitalism (Navarro 1999: 219–10; Labonte 2003: 490–5; Hunt 2003a: 20–1; 2003b: 18, 20–1; 2004b: 5–6, 11–13; 2005a: 14–15, 20; 2005c: 14–15; 2005f: 11, 19; Anderman and Kariyawasam 2006).[2]

Traditionally, the concept of human rights was developed to limit the power of governments over individuals. It did not enter the realm of economics. Because the human right to health is relatively resource-hungry, it requires a supportive political economy. Consequently, the right is a basis for a critique of the existing global economic system.

Health justice

The right to health responds to the problem of scarce resources by prioritizing the worst-off and the principle of non-discrimination. This presupposes a theory of health justice that it does not make explicit. Theories of justice have either ignored the distribution of health, or limited their concerns to the distribution of health care. Health justice is, however, about the distribution of *health*, not of health care *per se*. Evidence suggests that social development contributes more than improvements in health care to increases in life expectancy (House and Williams 2003: 97; Levins 2003: 372; Graham 2003: 531). The normative theory of health justice, therefore, must incorporate a sociology of health distribution in order to identify the causes of just and unjust health distributions.

Right-to-health advocates cannot reasonably assume that health justice is unproblematic. They must show, for example, that the right to health should 'trump' the utilitarian principle of maximizing health. The WHO and the World Bank have adopted the concept of the 'quality-adjusted life year' (QALY), which measures health outcomes as the number of years saved, adjusted for quality. This carries the utilitarian implication that we should maximize the production of QALYs. This would, however, discriminate against the chronically ill, the elderly and the poor, since the allocation of resources to their health problems would probably be QALY-inefficient. We could, for example, produce more QALYs by allocating resources to the treatment of 40-year-olds in Japan, where life expectancy is 82.2 years, than to 40-year-olds in Sierra Leone, where life expectancy is 41.0. This would, however, offend the priority given by the right to health to the poor and to non-discrimination (Anand and Peter 2004: 7; Sen 2004a: 27; Kamm 2004: 233; Brock 2004: 210–12; United Nations Development Programme 2006). It is not clear whether or not this conceptual problem has led to unjust health policies.

It is often said that health priorities should be decided in a 'cost-effective' way. This might be given a utilitarian interpretation, and thus be subject to anti-utilitarian objections. Utilitarian calculations are, however, not always inappropriate. If we had to choose between producing ten QALYs and producing one, all other things being equal, we should choose the former. Nevertheless, such calculations can leave dilemmas unresolved. It would be very difficult for a utilitarian to decide how we should choose between saving ten lives and making 1,000 more comfortable. QALY-utilitarianism cannot always determine priorities (Brock 2004: 210–12; Kamm 2004: 227). One way of combining right-to-health and utilitarian intuitions is to give priority to raising the worst-off to a minimum standard of health, and then allow utilitarian criteria to enter into the allocation of any health resources that might remain.

Right-to-health theorists might be attracted by Rawls's 'difference principle', which specifies that priority should be given to the worst-off (Rawls 1972: 75). This raises several problems, however. Firstly, it is empirically uncertain how health should be distributed so that the health of the worst-off is as good as possible. Secondly, we have to decide whether we should give priority to those who are worst-off in health or in 'primary goods': rights, liberties, opportunities, powers, income, wealth, and a sense of one's own worth (Rawls 1972: 92). This dilemma reflects the disagreement between those who hold that health justice is an autonomous field and those who believe that it must derive from a general theory of justice. Thirdly, Rawls's theory is more egalitarian than the human rights approach because it prohibits any inequality that does not benefit the worst-off, whereas the rights approach requires the equal right either to the essential minimum or to the highest attainable standard, both of which leave the degree of permissible inequality unclear. Fourthly, the Rawlsian principle of prioritizing the worst-off may not reflect all our strong intuitions. For example, if everyone had poor health, but there was a way to improve the health of some, but not all, this improvement might be justified even though it did not benefit the worst-off. Fifthly, the Rawlsian approach might be less plausible if the resources required to help the worst-off were very great, the probability of improving their condition very low and/or their probable improvement slight, whereas the better-off could be improved greatly at much lower cost (Daniels, *et al.* 2004: 74–6, 79; Peter 2004: 102; Kamm 2004: 228–35; Brock 2004: 212–16). Finally, the Rawlsian theory is open to the objection that it specifies just outcomes, and ignores just procedures. The coercive redistribution of bodily organs, for example, might lead to greater distributive justice in health, but would offend just health procedures (Dworkin 2000: 205–9, 218–10; O'Neill 2002: 41; Brock 2004: 207–8; Leon and Watt 2001: 8; Peter 2004: 98–9; Anand 2004: 15–16; Pogge 2004: 149; Sen 2004a: 24; Kamm 2004: 226). Some variant of Rawls's theory might, however, have a utilitarian justification, as there is evidence that improving the health of the worst-off has a 'trickle-up' effect: the discipline of public health originated in the belief that improving the health of the poor would promote the good of society.

Libertarians argue that individuals are responsible for their own health, and that it is unjust to compel those who make healthy choices to pay for those who make unhealthy choices. Some hold that public resources should be allocated only to involuntary health risks, such as those arising from infectious diseases, and not to those resulting from voluntary decisions, such as smoking. The question of personal responsibility for health raises intractable metaphysical problems about free will. Empirically, strong correlations between social class and health behaviours suggest that such behaviours are socially caused as well as individual choices: childhood poverty, for example, strongly *predicts* poor adult health behaviour. When unhealthy behaviours have been 'chosen', their persistence can be caused by the biology, as well as the sociology and psychology, of addiction. Thus, we do not have to deny personal responsibility to acknowledge the social causes of the ill health that results from behavioural 'choices' (Wikler 2002: 47–51; 2004: 111–12, 117–19; Marmot 2004: 49–50).

Daniel Wikler has pointed out some morally unattractive consequences of the personal-responsibility doctrine. The principle that everyone should bear the cost of their choices assumes that the choices are 'bad' (e.g. smoking). It seems unjust, however, that someone who chooses to be a firefighter should bear the cost of any consequent injuries. The principle also seems unduly harsh: smokers should perhaps bear some cost of their choice, but we might hesitate to impose a death sentence (without a fair trial) by withholding medical treatment. It also entails a questionable form of discrimination: upper-class American smokers, for example, are less likely to contract cancer, and are likely to live longer if they do contract it, than low-status Americans. Wikler also argues that making health professionals into moral judges would introduce arbitrariness into medical practice: treatment according to need is widely regarded as more appropriate. The importance of behavioural choice in causing ill health is also sometimes exaggerated: one US study concluded that unhealthy choices accounted for only 15 per cent of differences in health outcomes. Insofar as behavioural choices do affect health, justice may require that appropriate health education be disseminated to all (Wikler 2004: 124–5; 2002: 47, 51–4). The sociology of health therefore challenges the ethic of individual responsibility by showing that social class explains health behaviours and outcomes better than 'choice' does (Popay, *et al.* 2003: 338; Beauchamp 2003: 269; Bambas and Casas 2003: 329–2; Barry 2005: 86–7; Daniels, *et al.* 2004: 80, 82; Marmot 2004: 49).

The right to health requires a theory of health justice, but such theories are subject to reasonable disagreement about causal relationships, ethical judgements and even metaphysical beliefs. There may be a consensus that there is at least a human right to the minimum standard of health necessary for 'a life of dignity', resources permitting, but the right to 'the highest attainable standard' begs complex questions of health justice (Sen 2004a: 22, 31; Brock 2004: 216–18, 221).

The sociology of health justice

Equal rights do not produce equal outcomes, and the legalization of rights does not necessarily 'empower' the poor. Sociology helps us to understand why legal norms are not reflected in social reality. The rich are generally healthier than the poor. They have healthier diets, not only because they make healthier choices, but also because healthy choices are usually more expensive than unhealthy ones. Even when health services are formally available to all, the better-off get better health treatment. Social class correlates with social confidence, which correlates in turn both with knowledge of, and willingness to exercise, social rights (Davey Smith, *et al.* 2001: 91; Barry 2005: 71–8, 285, Note 21). It has been suggested that low-status persons have less work autonomy, and consequently lower self-esteem, more anxiety about job insecurity, more stress and worse health. Low status usually entails less political influence, so that public policies fail to address the social causes of health inequalities. The correlation between socio-economic status and health exists, however, even for those in the high socio-economic strata, and cannot be explained by access to health care. The explanation is indeed unclear. In many countries race or ethnicity is strongly associated with the social disadvantages that are associated with poor health. Although socio-economic status can explain much of the health inequality between racial or ethnic groups, race and ethnicity have been found to have independent effects (Kunitz 2001: 161; House and Williams 2003: 94, 103–6; Graham 2003: 532; Krieger 2003: 441; Geronimus 2003: 543–7; Kearney 2003: 580–5).

There is evidence that in developed countries national income inequality correlates with poor average health. The changing structure of employment is increasing income inequality by creating more two-earner and more no-earner households. This will probably increase illness within, and health inequalities between, families, not only by reducing incomes, but also by creating tensions that lead to domestic violence and neglect of health (Graham 2003: 523, 532–3, 536; Lanata 2001: 137–43, 147–8). Families are said to be more able to cope with difficult social conditions that cause ill health if they can appeal to social support networks, or if they have 'social capital'. There are, however, good and bad forms of social capital, as social support communities can be mobilized for different purposes, from caring for the vulnerable to the commission of crimes. There is nevertheless evidence that lack of social capital is associated with poor health (Turner 2004: 3–35; Lanata 2001: 140, 148; Wallack 2003: 594–5, 598, 603; Lynch 2003: 360–1; Marmot 2004: 52; Daniels, *et al.* 2004: 72; Kunitz 2001: 161–7). The social capital approach to health has been criticized, not only because the evidence is mixed, but because the concept itself is unclear, and is unduly influenced by an uncritical interpretation of the Tocquevillian and Durkheimian traditions in sociology that give a strong, positive value to community. Doubts have been expressed about the view that social cohesion promotes health equality on the ground that capitalism distributes social cohesion unequally by social class. It has been suggested that *social mobilization* rather than *social capital* produces health improvements. We lack a method for testing whether the Durkheimian, social-cohesion explanation of health distribution or the Marxist class explanation is the more powerful (Kunitz 2001: 160–1; Muntaner, *et al.* 2003: 287–8, 292; Wallack 2003: 599–602; Leon and Watt 2001: 11; Muntaner and Lynch 1999: 60–1, 67–71).

The evidence of relations between income inequality and health is, however, conflicting. Income inequality apparently affects health inequality through mediating variables. Countries that have relative equality of incomes *and* pro-poor health policies are likely to have relative health equality. Social democracy makes people healthier and reduces health inequalities. Reducing social inequality would therefore probably reduce health inequality, but reducing health inequality directly might also reduce social inequality (Kunitz 2001: 161; House and Williams 2003: 94, 103–6; Graham 2003: 525, 531–2, 537; Krieger 2003: 441; Geronimus 2003: 543–7; Kearney 2003: 580–5; Coburn 2003: 335–8; Levins 2003: 370; Moss 2003: 505–8; Bhatia 2003: 570; Wallack 2003: 596; Lynch 2003: 357; Barry 2005: 78–81, 84–5, 91–4). There are two kinds of causal model of health outcomes. The first is the medical model, according to which the pathogens are microbes, viruses or malfunctioning cellular reproduction. The second is the social model, according to which social inequalities are the most important determinants of health. This model challenges current medical and public health preoccupations with health care services and unhealthy behaviours. Biomedical approaches claim to be 'scientific' and non-political, but, in ignoring the social causes of health, they are politically conservative (Popay, *et al.* 2003: 396; Raphael 2003: 463; Raphael and Bryant 2003: 420; Bambas and Casas 2003: 323, 325, 328).

While social democracy provides relatively good solutions to the problems of health justice in nation-states, the human right to health requires global solutions. O'Neill criticizes the idea of human rights because she believes it assumes that only states have the corresponding obligations. This won't do, she argues, because failed or rogue states are unable or unwilling to secure health justice for their citizens, and most states are too self-interested to provide health justice for citizens of other states. The most effective agents of health justice may be different actors – such as international institutions, NGOs or multinational corporations (MNCs) – in different situations. However, if failed and rogue states are the problem, NGOs and MNCs are hardly plausible solutions in the absence of successful state-building (O'Neill 2002: 37, 40–4; Johri and Barry 2002: 33–4; Barry and Raworth 2002: 58; Wikler 2002: 47). Which agents of health justice are the most effective is an *empirical* question, and O'Neill is mistaken to believe that human rights theory is committed to statist answers if these are empirically incorrect. International law does have a statist tradition, but even international law may not hold that *only* states have right-to-health obligations (Hunt 2006c: 19–21). Sociologists have recently begun to study health social movements, bringing together medical sociology and the relatively well-developed literature on social movements (Brown and Zavestoski 2005a). Thomas Olesen, for example, has employed a combination of social-constructionist and structural theories to analyze a successful transnational campaign against the attempt by pharmaceutical companies to fight a South African law designed to provide inexpensive access to HIV/AIDS medicines (Olesen 2006). This analysis provides some confirmation of the thesis, proposed by Risse, Ropp and Sikkink, that particular interactions between national NGOs, international NGOs and governments can, sometimes, achieve human rights victories (Risse, *et al.* 1999).

Thomas Pogge has argued that rich states are partly responsible, causally, for global poverty, and are consequently responsible, morally, for alleviating it (Pogge 2002). Those who benefit from an injustice, knowing it to be so, may also have an obligation to rectify it, even if they have not caused it. If those who have such obligations fail to fulfil them, it is not clear who, if anyone, has the 'back-up' obligations. Those who have right-to-health obligations may well have competing obligations. Neither the rights nor the obligations approach offers a determinate theory of international health obligations. There is no doubt that corrupt and incompetent governments cause ill health. However, these governments are recognized by international law, and are often aided – politically, militarily and financially – by the rich and powerful governments. Policies of the rich countries – such as lending to dictators, bribing government officials, attracting health professionals from poor countries, and restricting immigration – all have a causal impact on the global distribution of health. Pogge's causal theory of moral obligation entails that rich societies and international institutions have obligations to implement the requirements of international health justice (Barry and Raworth 2002: 57; Sreenivasan 2002: 80–1; O'Neill 2002: 40; Barry 2005: 74; Johri and Barry 2002: 33; Gershman, *et al.* 2003: 160; Daniels, *et al.* 2004: 87–8; Pogge 2002: 73–4; 2004: 139).

The burden of global health inequality is carried disproportionately by women. Discrimination against women leads not only to physical violence, but also to greater exposure to deadly diseases, such as HIV/AIDS. In some countries there are 'missing' females – a number substantially less that would be expected statistically – caused by gender-discriminatory abortion and infanticide, malnutrition, higher morbidity, lack of access to health services, and maternal mortality. The evidence indicates that cuts in government expenditure required by structural adjustment programmes disproportionately harm the health of women. The UN Special Rapporteur has also pointed out that international trade agreements may have a disproportionately harmful effect on the health of women (World Health Organization 2001; Mann, *et al.* 1994: 10–11; Östlin, *et al.* 2003: 137–9, 144, 146; Hunt 2004b: 16).

The human right to health raises questions of global justice, which in turn require us to understand global structures of inequality that have an impact on the distribution of health. These are the 'formidable' social obstacles to the realization of the right to health noted by the UN Committee on Economic, Social and Cultural Rights. We should remember that these structures kill millions of children every year. The right to health thus gives rise to urgent moral and sociological challenges.

The politics of health

The explanation of health violations and inequalities can be too 'sociological' and insufficiently political. The policies of governments and political conflicts have a significant impact on the global distribution of health. Violent conflict not only kills; it undermines health services, and creates severe mental-health problems. Resources allocated to conflict may be diverted from health programmes (Hunt 2005a: 7–8; 2005c: 7, 12, 18). There is a consensus that 'good governance' and democratic institutions are necessary to realize the right to health, and that corruption is, in many countries, a barrier to its realization. This may be broadly true, but the precise nature of the truth requires further analysis: China, for example, has an average life expectancy of 71.9, while India has one of 63.6, which suggests that 'democracy' is not the only variable that explains health outcomes (United

Nations Development Programme 2006).[3] The political economy of international aid also has a significant impact on health in poor countries (United Nations Commission on Human Rights 2003: 4; World Health Organization 2001).

The conceptualization of 'health' may itself be political. Vincanne Adams argues that the Chinese government imposes its political control on the Tibetan people partly by implementing a secular, modernizing health policy that is alien to traditional Tibetan culture. 'Health' for traditional Tibetans is a *moral* concept, and consequently attacks on their culture and on their health are intertwined. China adopted this policy partly to gain international recognition, but, because of the close connection between culture and health among the Tibetans, it has been counter-productive. 'Health', on this account, is not an 'objective' or 'scientific' concept, but is politically contested with political consequences (Adams 2004).

The UN requires that health policies be culturally acceptable, as well as consistent with other human rights, but the implications of this requirement have not been fully developed. Sen distinguishes between the subjective and objective dimensions of health. Medical anthropologists emphasize the subjective experience of suffering, influenced by culture. This view is limited, because subjective health status correlates poorly with health status determined by scientific criteria. To privilege the subjective view would turn a problem into a solution by endorsing misperceptions of health. However, what it means to be 'really' healthy is not culture-independent, and thus the subjective point of view should be taken into account. Therefore, the 'ontology' of health is embedded in the universalism/relativism duality, as 'health' itself has both objective and subjective aspects (United Nations Committee on Economic, Social and Cultural Rights 2000: 4; Sen 2004b: 265–6).[4]

Health is also political because improving the health of the worst-off is likely to impose short-term costs on the most powerful, even if it brings long-term benefits. Power determines priorities and distributions, and consequently determines the extent to which the right to health is fulfilled. Government policies and civil society mobilization have protected the poor to some extent when structural adjustment programmes have been imposed on developing countries. Even in developed countries governments' tax and welfare policies can reduce the impact of social and economic developments, such as recession and unemployment, on health. Political policies mediate the connections between the social causes of health and their health effects (Peter 2004: 96; Muntaner and Lynch 2003: 66; World Health Organization 2001; Bhatia 2003: 559; Beauchamp 2003: 267–8; Gershman, *et al.* 2003: 161, 173; Graham 2003: 533–4; Raphael 2003: 59, 73; Östlin, *et al.* 2003: 147; Hofrichter 2003: xviii; Sreenivasan 2002: 84).

The social and economic policies of governments may be more important than their health-care policies in improving health. Indeed, national health services contribute little or nothing to *class* differences in health. Improving health may increase health inequality: for example, reducing smoking improves the overall level of health, but benefits the rich more than the poor.

The status and distribution of health is therefore deeply rooted in its social structure. Political policies nevertheless can make a significant difference. Attention to the politics of health guards against the temptation of sociological determinism.

The role of empirical research

The UN Special Rapporteur holds that the implementation of the right to health requires 'impact assessment' of health and other policies, and *indicators* of the 'progressive realization' of the right. Impact assessments would contribute to evidence-based policy-making on health, thereby connecting law to the social sciences. Impact assessments could tell us the distributional effects of policy on poor and marginalized groups. Information should therefore normally be disaggregated on the basis of age, gender, race, ethnicity, rural/urban residence and socio-economic status. Impact assessments, however, raise formidable problems. They are costly, and may be incomplete indicators of the fulfilment of the right to health (Hunt 2003a: 19–20; 2003b: 8–11; Hunt and MacNaughton 2006). They would have to be designed in a field in which theory, empirical knowledge, methodology and data are all uncertain (Krieger 2003: 430; Leon and Watt 2001: 2, 7; World Health Organization 2001; Gwatkin 2001: 218–15, 229, 243–4; Marmot 2004: 48–9; Daniels, *et al.* 2004: 71–2; Hunt 2003b: 7, 23 Note 6). Measuring 'health' raises complex problems, and the solutions are likely to be controversial. Life expectancy, infant mortality and maternal mortality are all significant, but all refer to *mortality*, and do not directly measure health between birth and death. There are many forms of ill health, and each admits of degrees, which are not easy to measure precisely (Leon 2001: 8–9; Murray, *et al.* 2001: 195–6). The concept of 'health inequality' can also be measured in different ways: for example, as the ratio between the worst and the best, or the difference between them, or in other ways.

The concept of the 'progressive realization' of the right to health seems to assume that states of health can be compared and ranked, so that we can tell whether the realization of the right to health is improving overall in a particular country or not. Health is, however, multi-dimensional, and the dimensions may not be commensurable. Consequently, such ranking comparisons may not always be possible. Health may improve in some respects and worsen in others. The idea of a right to health does not help to choose between policies, each of which has winners and losers (Sen 2004a: 22–3; Leon and Watt 2001: 10–11; Davey Smith, *et al.* 2001: 88–9; Marmot 2004: 44–6; Murray, *et al.* 2001: 207–8). Norway, for example, has a higher average life expectancy at birth than Portugal (79.3 compared with 77.2), but maternal mortality per 100,000 live births is five in Portugal compared with 16 in Norway (United Nations Development Programme 2006).

Public health analysts often consider that it is important to measure health inequalities among *social groups*, defined by conventional sociological categories, such as income, education, occupation, gender, race and ethnicity. This approach has, however, been criticized on the ground that it assumes, falsely, that health within these groups is the same. A better measure of health inequality, therefore, is said to be that between the best-off *individual* and the worst-off individual. There are, however, good arguments for investigating group inequalities. Firstly, some group inequalities – such as those associated with race or gender – may violate reasonable principles of justice. Secondly, group inequalities may indicate social explanations of health outcomes. Strong correlations between social and health indicators suggest explanations, although the causal links between the social factors and the health consequences may be more elusive (Anand 2004: 19–20; Peter 2004: 99; Marmot 2004: 43–4; Murray, *et al.* 2001: 210; Anand and Hanson 2004: 184). However health inequality is measured, total or average improvements in health might be achieved while health inequality remained the same or even increased. It is not clear whether improvements in health combined with increased health inequality would or would not constitute progressive realization of the right to health. The distribution of health can be made more egalitarian in many ways, but 'the right to health' does not always tell us which we should prefer (Anand 2004: 19; Murray, *et al.* 2001: 203–6, 213).

Time also plays a part in the causation of ill health. Explanations of health often identify contemporaneous associations, such as socio-economic status and health. The causes of many non-communicable diseases, however, develop over many years. For some diseases, information about the sufferers' *childhood* social environment may be more significant than their current circumstances. The study of 'life courses' shows how social, psychological and behavioural factors tend to interact, cluster and lead to cumulative health inequalities. Empirical research supports Turner's view that the human body is the locus of social experiences of support, threat and damage over the life course (Leon 2001: 60–1, 70, 73–4; Marmot 2004: 55; Popay, *et al.* 2003: 388; Murray, *et al.* 2001: 214–15; Leon and Watt 2001: 13; Braveman 2003: 310, 315, 317; Graham 2003: 526–8; Lynch 2003: 360; Levins 2003: 370–5; Moss 2003: 511; Krieger 2003: 438–9, 442).

Two issues that have been neglected in the sociology of health are mental health and injuries (Leon and Watt: 12).[5] Mental health problems in developing countries have been particularly neglected. Poverty is a cause, not only of physical illness, but of depression, other mental disorders and suicide. Economic insecurity, lack of education and hopelessness can all cause mental illness. Women are more likely than men to suffer mental illness from these causes. Mental illness leads to disability, and consequently hinders social and economic development. Many common mental disorders are, however, treatable. Since many of the causes of mental health problems are social rather than medical, the solutions too are social rather than medical (Patel 2001: 247–59).

There is evidence that injuries are increasing globally, although there are problems of data collection and interpretation in this field, in part because injuries are very heterogeneous. The economic cost of injuries is probably very great, but very difficult to estimate precisely.[6] Social groups that suffer more ill health also suffer more injuries. The poor suffer more from natural disasters, because their social conditions make them more vulnerable to such events. The number of injuries can be reduced significantly by well-designed public safety policies. Among the causes of the number of injuries is the political powerlessness of the poor. Also, the heterogeneity of injuries means that responsibility for them is fragmented, and thus a coherent policy of injury reduction becomes less likely (Zwi 2001: 263–75). Woodiwiss has argued that concern with injuries and work-related illnesses connects the right to health with the rights of workers (Woodiwiss 2003).

The concept of the human right to health requires the monitoring of the 'progressive realization' of the right, so that governments can be held accountable for the fulfilment of their right-to-health obligations. The UN Special Rapporteur has endorsed the methodology of health impact assessments as a means to this end, but the methodological problems of measuring the realization of this right are formidable. However, if priority is given to the worst violations, problems of measurement and accountability may be eased.

Health improvement strategies

The sociology of health suggests a distinction between *ameliorative* and *structural* health-improvement strategies. Ameliorative strategies would address proximate causes of ill health, such as smoking, but leave structural causes, such as educational inequalities, untouched. However, the sociology of health cannot specify the specific policies that are needed. The wording of the Universal Declaration of Human Rights is here more helpful than the idea of a 'right to health'. The Declaration does not explicitly include a right to health, but, in Article 25, says that everyone has the right to a *standard of living* adequate for health. 'Standard of living' is an important intermediate variable between social structure and health, and one that is to some extent subject to political control (Geronimus 2003: 549; Krieger 2003: 436; Bhatia 2003: 564; Kearney 2003: 584, 587). The UN Special Rapporteur emphasizes the role of 'civil society' in implementing the right to health. Sociology and social movements can combine to determine the social causes of ill health and health inequality, and to combat them. In this struggle, there is likely to be a tension between the roles of social movements and health professionals, for the latter have expert knowledge, while the former may have a broader view of popular needs and more independence of governments and other power-holders. The Special Rapporteur has recommended that human rights education should form part of the training of health professionals, and this could help to 'democratize' the health professions (Beauchamp 2003: 279; Bhatia 2003: 562–72; Hunt 2005c: 13–14; Graham 2003: 538; Krieger 2003: 435; Geronimus 2003: 550–1; Brown and Zavestoski (eds) 2005a; Olesen 2006).

The human right to health: conclusions

The human right to health is paradoxical. On the one hand, good health is one of the least controversial human values. On the other hand, the UN's Special Rapporteur on the right to health has admitted that it is extremely vague, allows grey areas, and good faith disagreements, and the Human Rights Commission acknowledged that its realization remained a distant goal, and, for many, especially the poor, was becoming *increasingly* remote.

James Griffin and Onora O'Neill have criticized the right for ignoring obligations, making excessive demands on public policy and failing to guide the selection of priorities. The first of these criticisms has no merit, as the human rights approach emphasizes the obligations of governments and powerful non-governmental actors, as well as the role of civil society. The other criticisms do have merit because the idea of a right to 'the highest attainable standard' of health is useless in deciding priorities. The Special Rapporteur identifies poverty and discrimination as his priorities. This could be justified by several reasonable theories of justice, but the logical path from the human right to the choice of priorities is unclear. The Rapporteur concedes that trade-offs are an inescapable part of real-world policy-making, but it is difficult to reconcile human rights with trade-offs.

Philosophical criticisms of human rights are sometimes too legalistic and insufficiently sociological. The meaning of human rights is constructed continuously through complex social processes. The UN Special Rapporteurs play a crucial role in these processes, not only because of their official status as 'independent experts', but because they consult a wide range of professional, governmental and civil society actors. The work of Special Rapporteurs is therefore a kind of practical test of the theoretical criticisms made by philosophers. Special Rapporteurs are usually lawyers, but their social role is diplomatic. The strength of this role is that it combines the idealism of international human rights law with the pragmatism of diplomacy. Its weakness is that it usually does not involve a training in social science. Sociology can contribute in two ways to the analysis of these social agents of human rights: it can describe and evaluate their social roles, and it can assess the validity of the social understandings with which they perform them.

The Special Rapporteur on the right to health has three main objectives: 1) to raise the profile of the right to health; 2) to clarify what the right to health means; and 3) to identify ways of operationalizing the right. He claims that the right to health can improve health policies and contribute to the realization of global justice (Hunt 2003a: 5). He admits, however, that his ability to investigate complaints is hampered by extremely limited resources. He has, through numerous reports, sought to reconcile the idea of a 'right to health' with a realistic sense of priorities in policy-making, and, if the impact of this work is uncertain, this is to a large extent the result of the unwillingness of governments to fund international human rights rather than defects in the concept itself (Hunt 2005b: 3; 2005e: 18; 2005g: 4).

The UN human right to health is the right to 'the highest attainable standard' of health care and of the underlying determinants of health. Is this a reasonable aim of normative health justice? The empirical sociology of health suggests that social equality is one of the most important determinants of health. Sociology thereby reveals what international human rights law conceals and philosophy fails to reveal: that the 'right to health' requires radical social transformation. This might be justified by some of the more egalitarian theories of justice, but it is more utopian than human rights lawyers usually admit. The interpretation of the right includes the right of everyone to participate in the determination of their own health care. The participation of the socially marginalized in the design and delivery of health policies intended to benefit them may make such policies more effective, but it begs questions about the compatibility of 'rights' and the outcomes of democratic decision-making processes (Brown and Zavestoski 2005b; Donnelly 2003: 185–94).

Since the human right to health includes the right to the social determinants of health, its meaning depends on the development of an adequate sociology of health, which we do not now have, and which is always likely to be contested. Since all rights require justification by a convincing theory of justice, the right to health lies in a highly contested field. Here lies the paradox of the right to health. Health is a universal value. If everyone has the right to a life of dignity, a right to health seems justified. Making this right reasonably determinate has, however, so far proved to be a formidable problem of social theory and practice. The human right to health illustrates a common feature of the concept of human rights: it combines strong intuitive appeal and sense of urgency (millions of children die unnecessarily) with implications that are philosophically and sociologically complex and controversial. Human rights scholarship must bear in mind the moral imperative, while sorting out the normative and empirical complexities that underlie this imperative.

Notes

1 In March 2006 the UN General Assembly decided to replace the Commission with the Human Rights Council.
2 For analysis of a successful campaign to limit the harmful effects of TRIPS, see Olesen (2006).
3 For the effect of conflict, democracy and other factors on health, see Ghobarah, *et al.* (2004).
4 Brown and Zavestoski (2005b) argue that emphasizing illness-as-experience as opposed to illness-as-scientific-fact has been an important feature of health social movements.
5 Woodiwiss (2003) addresses the question of injuries to some extent through a sociology of labour rights.
6 Woodiwiss (2003: 5) cites the claim by the International Labour Organization that more than two million people die each year from work-related injuries or illnesses, three times the number of people who die in wars.

Bibliography

Adams, V. (2004) 'Equity of the Ineffable: Cultural and Political Constraints on Ethnomedicine as a Health Problem in Contemporary Tibet', in Anand, *et al.* (eds) *Public Health, Ethics, and Equity*, Oxford: Oxford University Press.

Anand, S. (2004) 'The Concern for Equity in Health', in Anand, *et al.* (eds) *Public Health, Ethics, and Equity*, Oxford: Oxford University Press.

Anand, S. and Hanson, K. (2004) 'Disability-Adjusted Life Years: A Critical Review', in Anand, *et al.* (eds) *Public Health, Ethics, and Equity*, Oxford: Oxford University Press.

Anand, S. and Peter, F. (2004) 'Introduction', in Anand, *et al.* (eds) *Public Health, Ethics, and Equity*, Oxford: Oxford University Press.

Anand, S., Peter, F. and Sen, A. (eds) (2004) *Public Health, Ethics, and Equity*, Oxford: Oxford University Press.

Anderman, S. and Kariyawasam, R. (2006) 'TRIPS and Bilateralism: Technology Transfer in a Development Perspective', in Dine and Fagan (eds) *Human Rights and Capitalism: A Multidisciplinary Perspective on Globalisation*, Cheltenham: Edward Elgar.

Bambas, A. and Casas, J. A. (2003) 'Assessing Equity in Health: Conceptual Criteria', in Hofrichter (ed.) *Health and Social Justice: Politics, Ideology and Inequity in the Distribution of Disease: A Public Health Reader*, San Francisco: Jossey-Bass.

Barry, B. (2005) *Why Social Justice Matters*, Cambridge: Polity Press.

Barry, C. and Raworth, K. (2002) 'Access to Medicines and the Rhetoric of Responsibility', *Ethics and International Affairs*, 16(2): 57–70.

Beauchamp, D. E. (2003), 'Public Health as Social Justice', in Hofrichter (ed.) *Health and Social Justice: Politics, Ideology and Inequity in the Distribution of Disease: A Public Health Reader*, San Francisco: Jossey-Bass.

Benton, T. (2006) 'Do We Need Rights? If So, What Sort?', in Morris (ed.) *Rights: Sociological Perspectives*, London: Routledge.

Bhatia, R. (2003) 'Swimming Upstream in a Swift Current: Public Health Institutions and Inequality', in Hofrichter (ed.) *Health and Social Justice: Politics, Ideology and Inequity in the Distribution of Disease: A Public Health Reader*, San Francisco: Jossey-Bass.

Braveman, P. A. (2003) 'Measuring Health Inequalities: The Politics of the World Health Report 2000', in Hofrichter (ed.) *Health and Social Justice: Politics, Ideology and Inequity in the Distribution of Disease: A Public Health Reader*, San Francisco: Jossey-Bass.

Brock, D. W. (2004) 'Ethical Issues in the Use of Cost Effectiveness Analysis for the Prioritisation of Health Care Resources', in Anand, *et al.* (eds) *Public Health, Ethics, and Equity*, Oxford: Oxford University Press.

Brown, P. and Zavestoski, S. (eds) (2005a) *Social Movements in Health*, Malden, MA: Blackwell.

—— (2005b) 'Social Movements in Health: An Introduction', in Brown and Zavestoski (eds) *Social Movements in Health*, Malden, MA: Blackwell.

Coburn, D. (2003) 'Income Inequality, Social Cohesion, and the Health Status of Populations: The Role of Neo-Liberalism', in Hofrichter (ed.) *Health and Social Justice: Politics, Ideology and Inequity in the Distribution of Disease: A Public Health Reader*, San Francisco: Jossey-Bass.

Daniels, N., Kennedy, B. and Kawachi, I. (2004) 'Health and Inequality, or, Why Justice is Good for Our Health', in Anand, *et al.* (eds) *Public Health, Ethics, and Equity*, Oxford: Oxford University Press.

Davey Smith, G., Gunnell, D. and Ben-Shlomo, Y. (2001) 'Life-course Approaches to Socio-economic Differentials in Cause-specific Adult Mortality', in Leon and Watt (eds) *Poverty, Inequality and Health: An International Perspective*, Oxford: Oxford University Press.

Dine, J. and Fagan A. (eds) (2006) *Human Rights and Capitalism: A Multidisciplinary Perspective on Globalisation*, Cheltenham: Edward Elgar.

Donnelly, J. (2003) *Universal Human Rights in Theory and Practice*, 2nd edn, Ithaca, NY: Cornell University Press.

Dworkin, R. (2000) 'Justice in the Distribution of Health Care', in M. Clayton and A. Williams (eds) *The Ideal of Equality*, Basingstoke: Macmillan.

Geronimus, A. T. (2003) 'Addressing Structural Influences on the Health of Urban Populations', in Hofrichter (ed.) *Health and Social Justice: Politics, Ideology and Inequity in the Distribution of Disease: A Public Health Reader*, San Francisco: Jossey-Bass.

Gershman, J., Irwin, A. and Shakow, A. (2003) 'Getting a Grip on the Global Economy: Health Outcomes and the Decoding of Development Discourse', in Hofrichter (ed.) *Health and Social Justice: Politics, Ideology and Inequity in the Distribution of Disease: A Public Health Reader*, San Francisco: Jossey-Bass.

Ghobarah, H.A., Huth, P. and Russett, B. (2004) 'Comparative Public Health: The Political Economy of Human Misery and Well-Being', *International Studies Quarterly* 48(1): 73–94.

Graham, H. (2003) 'From Science to Policy: Options for Reducing Health Inequalities', in Hofrichter (ed.) *Health and Social Justice: Politics, Ideology and Inequity in the Distribution of Disease: A Public Health Reader*, San Francisco: Jossey-Bass.

Griffin, J. (2000) 'Discrepancies Between the Best Philosophical Account of Human Rights and the International Law of Human Rights', *Proceedings of the Aristotelian Society* 101: 1–28.

Gwatkin, D. R. (2001) 'Poverty and Inequalities in Health within Developing Countries: Filling the Information Gap', in Leon and Watt (eds) *Poverty, Inequality and Health: An International Perspective*, Oxford: Oxford University Press.

Hofrichter, R. (ed.) (2003) *Health and Social Justice: Politics, Ideology and Inequity in the Distribution of Disease: A Public Health Reader*, San Francisco: Jossey-Bass.

House, J. S. and Williams, D. R. (2003) 'Understanding and Reducing Socioeconomic and Racial/Ethnic Disparities in Health', in Hofrichter (ed.) *Health and Social Justice: Politics, Ideology and Inequity in the Distribution of Disease: A Public Health Reader*, San Francisco: Jossey-Bass.

Hunt, P. (2003a) *Report of the Special Rapporteur on the Right of Everyone to the Enjoyment of the Highest Attainable Standard of Physical and Mental Health*, United Nations Commission on Human Rights, 13 February 2003, E/CN.4/2003/58.

—— (2003b) *Interim Report of the Special Rapporteur of the Commission on Human Rights on the Right of Everyone to Enjoy the Highest Attainable Standard of Physical and Mental Health*, United Nations General Assembly, 10 October 2003, A/58/427.

—— (2003c) *Neglected Diseases, Social Justice and Human Rights: Some Preliminary Observations*, Health and Human Rights Working Papers Series No. 4, December 2003.

—— (2004a) *Report of the Special Rapporteur on the Right of Everyone to the Enjoyment of the Highest Attainable Standard of Physical and Mental Health*, United Nations Commission on Human Rights, 16 February 2004, E/CN.4/2004/49.

—— (2004b) *Report of the Special Rapporteur on the Right of Everyone to the Enjoyment of the Highest Attainable Standard of Physical and Mental Health, Addendum, Mission to the World Trade Organization*, United Nations Commission on Human Rights, 1 March 2004, E/CN.4/2004/49/Add.1.

—— (2004c) *Report of the Special Rapporteur of the Commission on Human Rights on the Right of Everyone to the Enjoyment of the Highest Attainable Standard of Physical and Mental Health*, United Nations General Assembly, 8 October 2004, A/59/422.

—— (2005a) *Report of the Special Rapporteur on the Right of Everyone to the Enjoyment of the Highest Attainable Standard of Physical and Mental Health, Addendum, Mission to Mozambique*, United Nations Commission on Human Rights, 4 January 2005, E/CN.4/2005/51/Add.2.

—— (2005b) *Report of the Special Rapporteur on the Right of Everyone to the Enjoyment of the Highest Attainable Standard of Physical and Mental Health, Addendum, Summary of Cases Transmitted to Governments and Replies Received*, United Nations Commission on Human Rights, 2 February 2005, E/CN.4/2005/51/Add.1.

—— (2005c) *Report of the Special Rapporteur on the Right of Everyone to the Enjoyment of the Highest Attainable Standard of Physical and Mental Health, Addendum, Mission to Peru*, United Nations Commission on Human Rights, 4 February 2005, E/CN.4/2005/51/Add.3.

—— (2005d) *Report of the Special Rapporteur on the Right of Everyone to the Enjoyment of the Highest Attainable Standard of Physical and Mental Health*, United Nations Commission on Human Rights, 11 February 2005, E/CN.4/2005/51.

64   *M. Freeman*

— (2005e) *Report of the Special Rapporteur on the Right of Everyone to the Enjoyment of the Highest Attainable Standard of Physical and Mental Health, Addendum, Mission to Romania*, United Nations Commission on Human Rights, 21 February 2005, E/CN.4/2005/51/Add.4.

— (2005f) *Report of the Special Rapporteur of the Commission on Human Rights on the Right of Everyone to the Enjoyment of the Highest Attainable Standard of Physical and Mental Health*, United Nations General Assembly, 12 September 2005, A/60/348.

— (2006a) *Report of the Special Rapporteur on the Right of Everyone to the Enjoyment of the Highest Attainable Standard of Physical and Mental Health, Addendum, Mission to Uganda*, United Nations Commission on Human Rights, 19 January 2006, E/CN.4/2006/48/Add.2.

— (2006b) *Report of the Special Rapporteur on the Right of Everyone to the Enjoyment of the Highest Attainable Standard of Physical and Mental Health*, United Nations Commission on Human Rights, 3 March 2006, E/CN.4/2006/48.

— (2006c) *Report of the Special Rapporteur on the Right of Everyone to the Enjoyment of the Highest Attainable Standard of Physical and Mental Health*, United Nations General Assembly, 13 September 2006, A/61/338.

Hunt, P. and MacNaughton, G. (2006) *Impact Assessments, Poverty and Human Rights: A Case Study Using The Right to the Highest Attainable Standard of Health*, submitted to UNESCO 31 May 2006.

Johri, M. and Barry, C. (2002) 'Health and Global Justice', *Ethics and International Affairs* 16(2): 33–4.

Kamm, F. M. (2004) 'Deciding Whom to Help, Health-Adjusted Life Years and Disabilities', in Anand, *et al.* (eds) *Public Health, Ethics, and Equity*, Oxford: Oxford University Press.

Kearney, G. (2003) 'Minnesota's Call for Action: A Starting Point for Advancing Health Equity Through Social and Economic Change', in Hofrichter (ed.) *Health and Social Justice: Politics, Ideology and Inequity in the Distribution of Disease: A Public Health Reader*, San Francisco: Jossey-Bass.

Krieger, N. (2003) 'Theories for Social Epidemiology in the Twenty-First Century: An Ecosocial Perspective', in Hofrichter (ed.) *Health and Social Justice: Politics, Ideology and Inequity in the Distribution of Disease: A Public Health Reader*, San Francisco: Jossey-Bass.

Kunitz, S. J. (2001) 'Accounts of Social Capital: The Mixed Health Effects of Personal Communities and Voluntary Groups', in Leon and Watt (eds) *Poverty, Inequality and Health: An International Perspective*, Oxford: Oxford University Press.

Labonte, R. (2003) 'Globalization, Trade, and Health: Unpacking the Links and Defining the Public Policy Options', in Hofrichter (ed.) *Health and Social Justice: Politics, Ideology and Inequity in the Distribution of Disease: A Public Health Reader*, San Francisco: Jossey-Bass.

Lanata, C. (2001) 'Children's Health in Developing Countries: Issues of Coping, Child Neglect and Marginalization', in Leon and Watt (eds) *Poverty, Inequality and Health: An International Perspective*, Oxford: Oxford University Press.

Leary, V. (1994) 'The Right to Health in International Human Rights Law', *Health and Human Rights: An International Journal*, 1 (1). Available online at http://www.hsph. harvard.edu/fxbcenter/V1N1leary.htm (accessed 28 August 2008).

Leon, D. A (2001) 'Common Threads: Underlying Components of Inequalities in Mortality Between and Within Countries', in Leon and Watt (eds) *Poverty, Inequality and Health: An International Perspective*, Oxford: Oxford University Press.

Leon, D. A. and Watt, G. (2001) 'Poverty, Inequality, and Health in International Perspective: A Divided World?', in Leon and Watt (eds) *Poverty, Inequality and Health: An International Perspective*, Oxford: Oxford University Press.

Leon, D. and G. Watt (eds) (2001) *Poverty, Inequality and Health: An International Perspective*, Oxford: Oxford University Press.

Levins, R. (2003) 'Is Capitalism a Disease? The Crisis in U.S. Public Health', in Hofrichter (ed.) *Health and Social Justice: Politics, Ideology and Inequity in the Distribution of Disease: A Public Health Reader*, San Francisco: Jossey-Bass.

Limburg Principles on the Implementation of the International Covenant on Economic, Social and Cultural Rights. Available online at http://www.unimaas.nl/bestand.asp?id=2453 (accessed 28 August 2008).

Lynch, J. W. (2003) 'Income Inequality and Health: Expanding the Debate', in Hofrichter (ed.) *Health and Social Justice: Politics, Ideology and Inequity in the Distribution of Disease: A Public Health Reader*, San Francisco: Jossey-Bass.

Mann, J. M., Gostin, L., Gruskin, S., Brennan, T., Lazzarini, Z. and Fineberg, H. V. (1994) 'Health and Human Rights', *Health and Human Rights: An International Journal* 1(1). Available online at http://www.hsph.harvard.edu/fxbcenter/V1N1mannetal.htm (accessed 28 August 2008).

Marmot, M. (2004) 'Social Causes of Social Inequalities in Health', in Anand, *et al.* (eds) *Public Health, Ethics, and Equity*, Oxford: Oxford University Press.

Morris, L. (ed.) *Rights: Sociological Perspectives*, London: Routledge.

Moss, N. E. (2003) 'Socioeconomic Disparities in Health in the United States: An Agenda for Action', in Hofrichter (ed.) *Health and Social Justice: Politics, Ideology and Inequity in the Distribution of Disease: A Public Health Reader*, San Francisco: Jossey-Bass.

Muntaner, C. and Lynch, J. (1999) 'Income Inequality, Social Cohesion, and Class Relations: A Critique of Wilkinson's Neo-Durkheimian Research Program', *International Journal of Health Services* 29(1): 59–81.

Muntaner, C., Lynch, J. W. and Davey Smith, G. (2003) 'Social Capital and the Third Way in Public Health', in Hofrichter (ed.) *Health and Social Justice: Politics, Ideology and Inequity in the Distribution of Disease: A Public Health Reader*, San Francisco: Jossey-Bass.

Murray, C. J. L., Frenk, J. and Gakidou, E. E. (2001) 'Measuring Health Inequality: Challenges and New Directions', in Leon and Watt (eds) *Poverty, Inequality and Health: An International Perspective*, Oxford: Oxford University Press.

Navarro, V. (1999) 'Health and Equity in the World in the Era of "Globalization"', *International Journal of Health Services* 29(2): 215–16.

Olesen, T. (2006) '"In the Court of Public Opinion": Transnational Problem Construction in the HIV/AIDS Medicine Access Campaign, 1998–2001', *International Sociology* 21(5): 5–30.

O'Neill, O. (2002) 'Public Health or Clinical Ethics: Thinking beyond Borders', *Ethics and International Affairs* 16(2): 35–45.

Östlin, P., George, A. and Sen, G. (2003) 'Gender, Health, and Equity: The Intersections', in Hofrichter (ed.) *Health and Social Justice: Politics, Ideology and Inequity in the Distribution of Disease: A Public Health Reader*, San Francisco: Jossey-Bass.

Patel, V. (2001) 'Poverty, Inequality, and Mental Health in Developing Countries', in Leon and Watt (eds) *Poverty, Inequality and Health: An International Perspective*, Oxford: Oxford University Press.

Peter, F. (2004) 'Health Equity and Social Justice', in Anand, *et al.* (eds) *Public Health, Ethics, and Equity*, Oxford: Oxford University Press.

Pogge, T. W. (2002) 'Responsibilities for Poverty-Related Ill Health', *Ethics and International Affairs* 16(2): 71–9.

—— (2004) 'Relational Conceptions of Justice: Responsibilities for Health Outcomes', in Anand, *et al.* (eds) *Public Health, Ethics, and Equity*, Oxford: Oxford University Press.

Popay, J., Williams, G., Thomas, C. and Gatrell, A. (2003) 'Theorizing Inequalities in Health: The Place of Lay Knowledge', in Hofrichter (ed.) *Health and Social Justice: Politics, Ideology and Inequity in the Distribution of Disease: A Public Health Reader*, San Francisco: Jossey-Bass.

Raphael, D. (2003) 'Toward the Future: Policy and Community Actions to Promote Population Health', in Hofrichter (ed.) *Health and Social Justice: Politics, Ideology and Inequity in the Distribution of Disease: A Public Health Reader*, San Francisco: Jossey-Bass.

Raphael, D. and Bryant, T. (2003) 'The Limitations of Population Health as a Model for a New Public Health', in Hofrichter (ed.) *Health and Social Justice: Politics, Ideology and Inequity in the Distribution of Disease: A Public Health Reader*, San Francisco: Jossey-Bass.

Rawls, J. (1972) *A Theory of Justice*, Oxford: Oxford University Press.

Risse, T., Ropp, S. C. and Sikkink, K. (1999) *The Power of Human Rights: International Norms and Domestic Change*, Cambridge: Cambridge University Press.

Sen, A. (2001) 'Economic progress and health', in Leon and Watt (eds) *Poverty, Inequality and Health: An International Perspective*, Oxford: Oxford University Press.

—— (2004a) 'Why Health Equity?', in Anand, *et al.* (eds) *Public Health, Ethics, and Equity*, Oxford: Oxford University Press.

—— (2004b) 'Health Achievement and Equity: External and Internal Perspectives', in Anand, *et al.* (eds) *Public Health, Ethics, and Equity*, Oxford: Oxford University Press.

Sreenivasan, G. (2002) 'International Justice and Health: A Proposal', *Ethics and International Affairs* 16(2): 81–90.

Turner, B. S. (1993) 'Outline of a Theory of Human Rights', *Sociology* 27(3): 489–512.

—— (2004) *The New Medical Sociology: Social Forms of Health and Illness*, New York: W. W. Norton.

—— (2006) *Vulnerability and Human Rights*, University Park, PA: The Pennsylvania State University Press.

United Nations Commission Human Rights (2003) Resolution 2003/28, 22 April 2003, E/CN.4/2003/RES/2003/28.

United Nations Committee on Economic, Social and Cultural Rights (2000) *General Comment No. 14, Substantive Issues Arising in the Implementation of the International Covenant on Economic, Social and Cultural Rights, Article 12, The Right to the Highest Attainable Standard of Health*, E/C.12/2000/4.

United Nations Development Programme (2006) *Human Development Report 2006: Beyond Scarcity: Power, Poverty and the Global Water Crisis*, New York: United Nations Development Programme.

Wallack, L. (2003) 'The Role of Mass Media in Creating Social Capital: A New Direction for Public Health', in Hofrichter (ed.) *Health and Social Justice: Politics, Ideology and Inequity in the Distribution of Disease: A Public Health Reader*, San Francisco: Jossey-Bass.

Wikler, D. (2002) 'Personal and Social Responsibility for Health', *Ethics and International Affairs* 16(2): 47–55.

—— (2004) 'Personal and Social Responsibility for Health', in Anand, *et al.* (eds) *Public Health, Ethics, and Equity*, Oxford: Oxford University Press.

Woodiwiss, A. (1998) *Globalisation, Human Rights and Labour Law in Pacific Asia*, Cambridge: Cambridge University Press.

—— (2003) *Making Human Rights Work Globally*, London: The GlassHouse Press.

—— (2005) *Human Rights*, London: Routledge.

World Health Organization (2001) *Macroeconomics and Health: Investing in Health for Economic Development*, report of the Commission on Macroeconomics and Health, Geneva: World Health Organization.

Zwi, A. (2001) 'Injuries, Inequalities, and Health: From Policy Vacuum to Policy Action', in Leon and Watt (eds) *Poverty, Inequality and Health: An International Perspective*, Oxford: Oxford University Press.

4 Indigenous peoples' rights

Anthropology and the right to culture

Colin Samson

Mankind has opted for monoculture; it is in the process of creating a mass civilization, as beetroot is grown in mass. Henceforth, man's daily bill of fare will consist of this one item.

(Claude Levi-Strauss 1973: 44)

... a world millions of years in the making, vanished into the voracious, insatiable maw of an alien civilization.

(Frederick Jackson Turner, quoted by Kirkpatrick Sale 1991: 46)

... all this wreckage, all this waste, humanity reduced to a monologue, and you think that all that does not have its price?

(Aimé Césaire 1955 (2000): 74)

A handful of ashes

Well after a string of political commentaries on the vanishing worlds of American Indians in nineteenth-century North America, Claude Levi-Strauss mourned the displacement of peoples situated on even more remote frontiers. Returning to Europe with only 'a handful of ashes' (Levi-Strauss 1973: 48), *Tristes Tropiques* is his contemplative farewell to the Indians in Brazil. The peoples of the savannahs, river estuaries and plains of South America found the lands that sustained them and the worlds they created from these lands were the edges of another world. Their efforts to protect themselves, as elsewhere in the Americas, rarely halted the intrusions. Even within the last 40 years, Amazonian Indians such as the Yanomamö have been uprooted from their lands by Brazilian government policies, including military actions, and their numbers have been substantially diminished by the exported diseases of miners, loggers and farmers (see Chagnon 1992; Rabben 1998; Survival International 2000).

Territorial invasions by European colonizers as well as agents of the states established by these colonizers have dramatically affected indigenous beliefs, practices, forms of social organisation, and economic and religious connections to land. Numerous indigenous groups around the world have protested that poverty, previously unknown illnesses, environmental degradation and social and psychological dysfunction are all related to *ongoing* activities of these states. In international conferences, many indigenous leaders have also raised the alarm over the loss of languages, religions, and family life that made them distinct as peoples. In the words of Matthew Coon Come, the former Chief of the Assembly of First Nations, on his mission to Europe in 2003, aboriginal peoples in Canada were being pushed towards, 'social, political and cultural extinction' (Assembly of First Nations 2003). More recently, even Coon Come's more moderate successor, Phil Fontaine (2007) remarked that:

> Many of our communities have reached the breaking point. The anger and frustration are palpable. People are so tired and fed up with this type of existence, especially when all around them is a better life and hope. Living without hope is perhaps the worst aspect of life for so many of Canada's First Nations. The lack of hope plays out in so many ways, desperation breeds abuse, suicide, crime, civil disobedience.

Through international organisations like the Inter-American Commission on Human Rights and the United Nations (UN), such state policies as the geographical displacement of indigenous peoples and coercive cultural assimilation are now being treated as human rights matters. International human rights instruments such as Article 27 of the International Covenant on Civil and Political Rights and the International Labour Organization's Convention No. 169 on indigenous peoples stipulate that all minorities shall not be prevented from enjoying their own culture and prescribe governments to take affirmative steps to protect indigenous cultures and redress injustices. In the 46 articles of the 2007 UN Declaration on the Rights of Indigenous Peoples International, indigenous peoples are treated as more than national minorities, as having collective rights to their lands, languages, religions, and laws, as well as rights to determine their own political status (United Nations 1994).

These international actions challenge the hitherto unquestioned sovereignty of states, many of which control indigenous groups and their territories by mere assertion and expose the corresponding extension of state law over them as simply by *fiat*. Equally important, the indigenous quest for culturally specific rights disputes the universalism upon which Western political, legal and social administrations have been articulated. The positive call for recognition of indigenous ways of life is also a call to cease the suppression of practices that differ substantially from those of dominant populations. Countries as diverse as Canada, Brazil and Botswana have all relatively recently arrested hunter-gatherers for hunting within their own territories, and these and other states have not shied away from military action to suppress the aspirations of indigenous peoples. Until recently, the education of indigenous children in many parts of the world was explicitly designed to destroy their languages, cosmologies, and ways of life. More diffuse processes of cultural hegemony through the spread of communications technologies and entertainment industries are also means by which indigenous ways of life may be affected, but these are generally not targets for human rights campaigns. Indigenous rights campaigners are not only trying to stop the destruction of what are seen as unique and distinct ways of life, they are actively promoting their maintenance, and perhaps even, phoenix-like resuscitation.

State policies that diminish indigenous distinctiveness raise the question of the right to culture, a right already enshrined in various international instruments, but one that is met with a marked ambivalence by many governments. In turn, the right to culture for indigenous peoples brings anthropology to centre stage. Anthropologists have studied indigenous peoples as part of their endeavour to understand the range of human societies; they are often called upon to provide expert advice, act as brokers in rights claims cases, and they are assumed to have a particular professional authority over indigenous peoples and their place in the world. Culture has been the profession's central organising theoretical concept, and not incidentally, much of the work of anthropologists has taken place under the authority of the state. Anthropology is therefore situated on the interstices between the state and non-Western peoples.

Cultural fluidity and the right to culture

Over the last 20 years, the profession of anthropology has radically reformulated the concept of culture and the research technique of ethnography, which provided evidence of culture. James Clifford (1986, 1988), among others, argued that ethnography was a composition forged from disparate sources in the anthropologists' encounters with non-European subjects. According to Clifford, anthropologists frame and narrate events, and the choice of inclusion and exclusion is a complex interplay of the personality of the anthropologist and modernist expectations of contrast between the worlds of the Western professional and the native. Clifford (1986: 6) believes that in creating images of non-Europeans anthropologists and other travellers were 'artisanal, tied to the worldly work of writing'. The individual subjects of study embodied specific attributes representative of the culture as a whole. The whole could be deduced from the parts. Each subject became representative of a whole spectrum of ideas and practices that added up to something known as culture.

For Clifford, the concept of culture was too rigid to recognise the many interconnections and mutual influences between peoples throughout the course of history. This necessarily meant looking at ways in which groups invented and reinvented, combining imported cultural influences in unpredictable ways. The Mashpee Wampanoag court case in the US in the 1970s was a case in point. In this case, the Mashpee tried to prove continuous existence as a tribe in order to satisfy the conditions for a land claim with attached rights as Indian peoples. The individuals bringing the case identified themselves as Mashpee, but such identification was deemed by the court to be largely symbolic because their distinctive forms of belief and social organisation had been attenuated over the centuries. Reflecting the Western narrative of culture as whole and continuous, the court decided that the specifically 'tribal' connections of those claiming to be Mashpee were too tenuous to merit Federal recognition. As Clifford (1988: 338) points out, 'metaphors of continuity and "survival" do not account for complex historical processes of appropriation, compromise, subversion, masking, invention, and revival'.

The concepts of authenticity and culture used against the Mashpee have been a staple of Federal Indian policy. For example, blood quantum has long been the gold standard of Federal recognition of Indian peoples in the US (see Miller 2003: 113–22). Historically, of course, indigenous peoples have not defined themselves in the biological terms of race, and the Mashpee that testified in the court case covered by Clifford certainly did not. Several American Indian literary figures emphasize a certain indigenous transcendent sensibility, which is both open and tied to values and identifications that are starkly non-European. Pulitzer Prize winning Kiowa author N. Scott Momaday's (1976) memoir, *The Names*, for example, describes both the indigenous and the European dimensions of the author's ancestry, accepting discordance and discontinuity and never contriving to compose some picture of bounded authenticity. Many indigenous peoples are open to the idea that *some* extraneous ideas and practices can be imported without any diminution of their uniqueness. In the Americas, for example, instead of taking Christianity or science as literally true, indigenous peoples often selectively used them as enriching or useful to their own non-European way of life (see Dowd 1992: 2; Jahner 1994). If we consider the circumpolar region especially, one finds close intercultural contact and borrowings over long periods of history, at the same time that 'Europe remained shut in upon itself' (Levi-Strauss 1973: 332; see also Burch 2005). Besides all this, the notion of an absolute zero point of cultural authenticity is itself absurd to all but the most ardent racists.

However, for many groups that regard themselves as indigenous peoples today, indigeneity is synonymous with attachments to land, and it is the externally orchestrated (often forced) alteration of this relationship that appears to seriously threaten their distinct existence. The loss of interconnection between territory, subsidence, livelihood and cultural practices are in almost all cases the results of impositions that do not enrich a peoples' experience. Among many of the world's indigenous peoples, descents into community-wide trauma and dysfunction have been precipitated by removal from lands. Cases that are too numerous to mention have been documented over the last few decades by the non-governmental organisation (NGO), Survival International. However, there are, of course, individuals who regard themselves as indigenous and may live in urban settings, and may be highly successful and fulfilled in non-indigenous pursuits, but these people are generally not regarded as priorities for specific culturally based human rights.

What is not in doubt is the resilience of indigenous attachments to land. Even in the US where aggressive policies of Indian removal and assimilation were pursued, land still plays a key role in the contemporary identities of indigenous peoples – in the transmission of their histories and in the perpetuation of activities that give them meaning. For example, the Western Shoshone in Nevada have recently taken the US government to international courts and the UN for the confiscation of their lands for nuclear waste storage, military testing and mining (see Kuletz 1998;

Bonvillain 2001: 303–4). The actions of the US government have deprived the Western Shoshone of using what are recognised as *their* lands for cultural and religious activities. The extraordinary lengths the Western Shoshone have gone to reflects a desire to maintain a worldview that does not separate the health of people from the health of all living entities. A report by the Inter-American Commission on Human Rights in 2002 found the US in violation of international law. In the *Dann* case, the US was charged with violating rights of property (by extinguishing underlying title through confiscation) and not attending to due process of law. The close connection between retention of territory and cultural continuity was recognised by the court. As Gómez (2003: 131) states:

> The Inter-American Court of Human Rights has similarly recognized that for indigenous communities the relation with the land is not merely a question of possession and production but has a material and spiritual element that must be fully enjoyed to preserve their cultural legacy and pass it on to future generations.

All this implies that the rights to cultural and religious differences are now deemed human rights dependent upon the retention of indigenous land bases. Confiscation of land cannot, in this legal framework, be treated as simply a prerogative of the state, to which indigenous peoples must adapt.

Significantly, state coercion like that used against the Western Shoshone is a factor that Clifford and many other anthropologists of the globalisation age often minimise. If cultural change is carefully separated from the social, political and economic processes that brought it about, then there are few impediments within the discipline of anthropology to shift attention to groupings such as ethnicities, diasporas, migrants, and refugees as well as NGOs, corporations and internet users purely in terms of contemporary identity (see, for example, Lewellen 2002: 92–5). The emphasis moves from peoples who have maintained a certain degree of continuity and towards those who are caught up in different types of global flux. In this light, the right to culture, especially as a collective right, can be depicted as archaic at best and a form of repressive ethno-nationalism at worst. As Jane Cowan (2006: 10) tells us, 'that very same notion of a "right to culture" that helped indigenous peoples to claim autonomy within nation-states was also being deployed by Ulster Protestant Orangemen marching through Catholic neighbourhoods of Northern Ireland'.

A right to culture can be further derided because the indigenous leaders who are claiming such rights must do so within a political system that is conceptually alien and is designed by their antagonists in the state who wish to restrict their autonomy. This is an important observation, but it is not the fault of the indigenous peoples that this is the case. The arrival of indigenous leaders onto the national or international scene usually takes place only after abrupt changes have been made to the indigenous relationship to the land. As Baines (1999: 218) perceptively comments with reference to the Waimiri-Atroari peoples in Brazil:

After having been incorporated into the settlements directed by the administration where the process of colonization of their discourse was consolidated, there was no longer any possible resistance outside the definitions prescribed by the administration.

However, instead of leading to proposals for different political protocol and the abandonment of state privileges in rights adjudication, we find in some observers cheerful predictions of new evidence of indigenous resistance through these 'definitions prescribed by the administration'. For others, a kind of grim fatalism foretelling only cultural homogeneity prevails. Hence, it is argued that the process of claiming itself can lead to the transformation of indigenous petitioners and their communities. 'These goals of human rights,' anthropologist Ronald Niezen (2005: 44)tells us, 'lead to the convergence of human societies.' The arid *realpolitik* of Niezen suggests that the future can only be sameness.

The long frontier of cultural evolution

Somewhere here there is an echo of cultural evolutionism. While those chroniclers of globalised identities and hybridity rarely invoke evolution as a dynamic of history, they posit other unseen forces such as the market, communications and simply 'globalisation', all of which scarcely have any human driving force behind them. They are simply inevitable realities. Whereas liberals and utilitarians of the nineteenth century argued for human nature as *a priori* egoistic and gain-seeking, values that fit well with industrial capitalism, the new vogue is to propound a kind of fluid and adaptable human nature which also fits remarkably well with the social arrangements effected by the activities of powerful institutions.

In the older anthropological formulations, the main frame for understanding change was cultural evolutionism (see Bidney 1996: Chapter 7; Stocking 1968: Chapter 6; Berkhofer 1978: 49–55; Nisbet 1969), all cultures were conceived in modernist terms as largely whole and bounded with underlying continuities of self and group. Whether the explanations were phrased in terms of ecological accident or European cultural and biological superiority (see Arnold 1996: Chapter 5), change towards a more European set of ideas and practices was frequently the presumed fate of indigenous peoples who found themselves in the path of European territorial colonisation. Fuelled by the Enlightenment, Europeans generally saw themselves as highly dynamic and ever improving, while non-Europeans were perceived as rather static, tradition-bound, and in comparison to themselves, backwards.

These ideas were refined under colonialism and gained nuance through the experiences of colonial occupation. Throughout the twentieth century, the professionalising discipline of anthropology created its knowledge bases under the auspices of European colonial rule. It was not, therefore, altogether coincidental that British anthropologists provided much of that nuance. In early twentieth-century Australia, A. R. Radcliffe-Brown's refinement of the 'genealogical method' was employed while his Aborigine subjects were under brutal police detention on islands hundreds of miles from their homelands. Radcliffe-Brown's published books and reports never mentioned how he obtained his data. He was honoured as Australia's first Professor of Anthropology (see Lindqvist 2007: 112–16). Although there were exceptions, many anthropologists working in Africa, figures such as Bronislaw Malinowski (1945: 138–50) for example, offered professional advice to assist 'indirect rule'. Malinowski's student Lucy Mair taught colonial cadets, produced colonial policy recommendations to make policies more amenable to the native populations, and became a Lecturer and then Reader in Colonial Administration at the London School of Economics (Colson 1986). Towards Africa, these anthropologists displayed a kind of tragic paternalism (Owusu 1979: 150). Sociologists also, as Frantz Fanon (1965: 37) has pointed out in the Algerian context of the 1950s, aided colonialism by passing on 'discoveries' from studies of Arab gender roles that could assist the French in their efforts to assimilate the 'backward' indigenous population.

It is important to remember that cultural evolutionism was not just a theory, but a call to action. Up to the end, it dignified the civilising mission by which British occupation of large swathes of the globe was united (see Elkins 2005: 5) and appears in the rhetoric of manifest destiny under which generations of European settlers swept across North America (see Horsman 1981). Until the 1990s, the idea that aboriginal peoples in Canada did not comprise 'organised societies', and therefore could not legitimately claim land rights was invoked in successive Supreme Court rulings (see Asch 1992). In territories such as Canada and, most notably, Australia, the British reasoned from their assumptions that indigenous peoples were primitive, that the land was therefore *terra nullius*.

The convenient view allied to this – that upon contact with Europeans, the peculiarities of indigenous cultures and perhaps the people also, would disappear – was common among European observers of cultural contact. This was particularly true of North America in the nineteenth century when a broad range of politicians, scientists and cultural figures predicted that the American Indian was destined for extinction. The painter George Catlin criss-crossed the Americas in order to make portraits of peoples that he and others thought would surely die out within a short period of time. In 1832, he dramatically wrote that 'phoenix-like, they may rise from "the stain on a painter's palette" and live again upon canvass, and stand forth for centuries yet to come, the living monuments of a noble race' (Catlin 1989: 11). By the end of the century, the verdict was similar. The process by which Indians degenerated from a living to a dead but noble race was not obscure to the many historians such as Frederick Jackson Turner who believed that ultimately, the demise of the American Indian was a necessary if unfortunate aspect of a process of progressive and universal historical development. 'The disintegrating forces of civilization,' Turner (1961: 45) observed, 'entered the wilderness. Every river valley and Indian trail became a fissure in Indian society, and so that society became honeycombed.'

A question then arises regarding exactly how the evolutionary process fissured and honeycombed Indian society. On the whole, this politically sensitive issue was finessed as an abstract force of history, rather than as purposeful human calculation.

It is plain from reading American frontier writers and contemporary anthropologists that European settlement and the consequent strangulation of the subsistence base of the Indians precipitated the decline of these distinct societies. The actions that affected this decline, however, were often cited as ultimately caused by the more impersonal human will to progress. The very universalism by which these abstract processes were thought to operate prevented European colonists, and those who narrated their heroism, from recommending intervention to stop the destruction. Anthropologists among others obtained Native American remains for ethnological study as part of this process, and much still remains to be done to return bones to the families and communities that were robbed (see, for example, Zimmerman 1997). Some anthropologists, while still adhering to an evolutionism which depicted their subjects below them in the hierarchies of civilisation, notably Frank Cushing and Lewis Henry Morgan, had close associations with Indians and were advocates for Indians vis-à-vis some US policies (see Strong 2004: 347).

A common way to justify evolutionary ideas was to conceive of indigenous peoples, especially hunter-gatherers, as not contemporaries of Europeans (see Brody 2001: 125), but as mere objects of transformation without any specific rights. Despite the fact that they lived healthy, productive and meaningful lives well outside the comfort zones of European expansion, colonisers in such places as the Kalahari (Gall 2002), the Sahara (Fleming 2003), and the Arctic (Brody 2001) made incessant demands that indigenous populations should either relocate or abandon their ways of life and take up sedentary lifestyles, more environmentally suited to temperate climates. All this was justified as an evolutionary advance. However, unlike biological evolution, as Nisbet (1969: 164) points out, cultural evolution did not permit variation, and perhaps this holds a clue to why colonisers were so insistent upon change. In fact, as Brody (2001: 269) has pointed out, such absolutism fuelled the violence and aggression of colonists.

How convenient then that after the critiques of the concept of culture in the 1980s, the anthropological frame shifted to looking at group identity as 'historically contingent and contested and collective identities as friable, imagined and emergent' (Wilson 2000: 21), or as Clifford (1988: 10) put it, identity 'must always be mixed, relational and inventive'. With few places under *formal* colonial occupation at the close of the twentieth century and the global frontier diminished to only a handful of remote locations, coercion suddenly vanished as a context, evolutionism was buried amid a few blushes, and a new postcolonial order of cultural fluidity in a globalised world was posited as the context for anthropological study.

In the fervour to create distance from the earlier notions that non-European cultures were static, anthropologists sidelined continuity and transformation, regardless of how it arose, and transformation was cited as an example of the constant dynamism and flux in the world. An example, perhaps an extreme one, can be drawn from a wide-ranging text on applied anthropology in Canada. Discussing the effects of the James Bay hydroelectric developments on the Cree, Edward Hedican (1995: 152–3) is scornful of the idea that any 'cultural heritage' has been lost as a result of the projects. This, he points out, would imply a static Cree culture: '[s]houldn't the Cree change like anyone else, rather than be locked in a temporal-cultural setting of flint-tipped arrows and birch-bark canoes?' The author (1995: 153) goes on to describe the Cree as having experienced 'cultural *enhancement* ... making a *constructive leap* from one *stage* to another' (my emphasis). As it happens, this *constructive leap* is widely associated with threats to the health of the Cree people because it leads to environmental destruction and loss of habitats of the animals that comprise sources of nutrition and vitality (Adelson 2000: 110). Not incidentally, the Cree have filed complaints at the UN over Canada's development of this mega-project and its failure to abide by the terms of the treaty permitting it (see Niezen, 2003: 149–57). Most of the change experienced by Northern peoples such as the Cree is not the result of some voluntary movement towards new cultural articulations, but made possible by the assumption that such people have no rights to remain distinct, especially if it means retaining their land.

Nonetheless, such externally driven change has rarely created the uniformity that policymakers and colonisers required. Instead of making the target populations' grateful beneficiaries of various improvements, social engineering led to morgues, hospitals and slums, as the indigenous casualties were no longer able to maintain stable orientations in the world. The dismantling of what were organised and vibrant societies left individuals, families and whole communities at the mercy of dominant societies, many of whose members regarded them contemptuously as recipients of the state munificence that was nearly always required in order to prevent wholesale extinction.

The means of cultural change: the Innu of Labrador-Quebec

The Innu of the Labrador-Quebec peninsula in what is now Canada are currently a severely traumatised people. From 1975 to 1995, more than half of all deaths in Innu communities were of people aged under 30; this was the case for only five per cent of Canadians and four per cent of Newfoundlanders. Conversely, while at least 80 per cent of Canadian and Newfoundland deaths were over 60, only a quarter of Innu deaths were in this age range – ages to which people are expected to live in G-8 countries (Samson 2003: 230). These figures are consistently higher than those gathered to compare aboriginal and non-aboriginal mortality in Canada. The prospects for those who survive to become future generations also look bleak. According to a 2004 study, 35 per cent of Innu youth in one village display learning difficulties associated with Foetal Alcohol Syndrome (Philpott, *et al.* 2004). Innu also suffer very high rates of hitherto unknown diseases such as diabetes, heart disease and obesity, associated with radical changes of diet and reductions in physical activity (Samson and Pretty 2006).

Until relatively recently the Innu lived as permanent nomadic hunters in the boreal forests and tundra of the Subarctic. With the aid of Roman Catholic missionaries, the Canadian authorities settled them in a series of villages in Labrador and Quebec in the 1950s and 1960s. Before the onslaught of this aggressive assimilation campaign, they were considered by almost all observers to have experienced a long period of unbroken cultural attachments. For example, only a generation before settlement, anthropologist Frank Speck (1935: 20) remarked:

The culture has continued largely in its original pattern – hunting and wandering .... Radical change would only ensue upon change of their culture base, *eg.* from hunting-nomadism to agriculture, to pastoral life, or to civilized employment.

Although some of Speck's analysis was couched in the cringingly racist framework of cultural evolutionism, it is important to separate this universalistic ethnocentrism from his observations on the ground with the Innu – that their pattern of activities had not changed significantly over a long period of time. Comparing the Jesuit narratives of Innu life compiled by Father Paul Le Jeune and other Jesuits in the early seventeenth century with his own observations in the 1930s, geographer Väino Tanner (1947: 628) came to remarkably similar conclusions:

> one gets the impression that the Gulf Indian groups were living under conditions remarkably similar to those of the Labrador peoples of the present day – the same winter wanderings of small family groups living on the edge of subsistence and avoiding other groups during their migrations.

Basing his interpretation on a summer of fieldwork in the 1950s among the Innu in the interior regions of Lac St. Jean and Mistassini, whom he referred to as 'Naskapi', Julius Lips (1947: 387) pointed out that the 'Naskapi have always been, and always want to remain, a people of hunters'. This was so because hunting was the social, economic and political foundation of their society. Lips (ibid.), too, imagines a fairly unbroken cultural timeline, noting that:

> today, just as at the time when the first white man appeared in their region, their form of economy has remained the same, namely the hunt for moose and caribou and the trapping of fur-bearing animals: beaver, otter, fisher, lynx, muskrat, mink and marten.

While access to trade goods and technologies may have altered life for the Innu, what remained basically the same were the annual cycles of hunting and fishing, and the variations upon them made necessary by contingencies such as weather conditions, availability of animals and sickness. The same held for technologies. The canoe, toboggan and snowshoe, caribou and birch-bark conical tent, the four-sided hunting bow – all Innu creations – remained in constant use until well into the twentieth century (Tanner 1947: 639–41), and the Innu snowshoe is still the best footwear for use in the forests of the Labrador-Quebec peninsula. Tanner based his conclusions also on the reports and diaries of others spending time with the Innu in the eighteenth and nineteenth centuries. His conclusions were similar to Speck's in regard to change:

> In spite of great changes in the equipment of the Montagnais the main characteristics of their ancient culture as a whole are still there; the changes are mostly in details and have certainly been of practical use in their hunting life. (Tanner 1947: 641)

Change had occurred, according to Tanner, and this had been of practical benefit to the Innu, but the 'main characteristics' of their way of life remained. Since then, the mobile hunting practices of the Innu have not been abandoned altogether. Encroachments by Europeans, and the policies of the British and French colonial authorities, and, most recently, the Canadian state, have caused them only to cease nomadic life on a permanent basis. The opinion of most *Tshenut* (older Innu) with whom I have spoken in the two Labrador villages over the last 12 years is that hunting is a preferable way to live. It is quite clear to them that the change from hunting to welfare, from nomadic to village life was involuntary. Part of the reason for their preference for cultural stability lies in the nature of hunting. As Brody (2001) has argued, while agriculturists have demanded territorial expansion (ironically a form of nomadism) because they have needed ever more land that they continuously transform for growing populations, the opposite is the case for hunters. While agriculturists have been natural belligerents and colonists, hunters have depended on fixed and relatively bounded lands with which they have intimate connections. According to Brody (2001: 89, 117):

> Hunters do not make intensive efforts to reshape their environment. They rely, instead, on knowing how to find, use and sustain that which is already there ... the central preoccupation of hunter-gatherer economic and spiritual systems is the maintenance of the natural world as it is.

Canadian state policies of settlement of nomadic populations in the mid-twentieth century were a means by which peoples with a mobile lifestyle within a relatively large territory were reduced (literally) to being sedentary residents in social units designed by and for agriculturists. The establishment of villages was a most effective means of fissuring Innu society since it placed them in an alien environment, which was incompatible with maintaining their largely stable economy, social organisation and religion. Instead, wage labour and education were promised, but with endemic social dysfunction and an economy that relies almost solely on relatively few manual jobs, the fruits of these have never been realised. The administrative documents of the time reveal that, along with schooling, 'economic rehabilitation' through wage labour was a centrepiece of the Canadian authorities' plans to settle the Innu in villages (Samson 2003: 166).

The process was given an impetus by intrusions that simply made it harder for the Innu to hunt and use the land. As European settlement gradually grew in scale in the twentieth century (although it began in the previous century), trappers and settlers extended themselves into areas used by the Innu for fishing, hunting and trapping (see Tanner 1947: 608, 637; Zimmerley 1975: 177). This was particularly the case in the Lake Melville area where the Innu settlement of Sheshatshiu is situated adjacent to the North West River and Happy Valley-Goose Bay settler townships that now serve as hubs for military and resource extraction industries. In regard to the influx of European trappers in the Lake Melville area in the 1930s, Tanner (1947: 637) relates that:

The Indians of course regard this intrusion as an injustice, but they resign themselves to it as their fate, afraid of 'the law', and the law, as elsewhere is dictated by the majority with the 'right of the strong.'

'The law', then, became an instrument of dispossession of land, and correspondingly, as Tanner (ibid.) observes, 'in this way I can imagine that the old social structure of the Montagnais has been loosened and changed'. Slightly later, the existing displacement by trappers was augmented by the vigorous assimilation campaign waged by the Newfoundland government and various orders of missionaries that culminated in the government-sponsored creation of villages in Quebec and Labrador. These villages acted as the main fulcrum of sedentarisation.

Within the government-built villages, schools became vital instruments for enforced cultural change (Samson 2003: 185–221). Honigmann (1964: 356) appreciated this well when he observed 'the teacher represents an agent of change whose object is often to train the child with skills resembling those which are useful or appreciated in the society outside the North'. Similar processes of induced change through education occurred across the Far North (Darnell and Hoem 1996). In his 1976 introduction to Frank Speck's 1915 ethnological study of Innu (known then as Montagnais-Naskapi) religion, J. E. Michael Kew (Speck 1977: xii) observes that the 1967 Churchill Falls hydro-development and the 1972 James Bay dam complex would usher in the death knells of the Cree and Innu cultures. Churchill Falls, 'began the destruction of the northeastern Naskapi territory', while at the same time:

> Those few Crees of Mistassini, Rupert House, and Fort George, holding precariously to a life of hunting and trapping, struggling for a few brief months each winter to maintain the balance through hunting, dreaming and propitiating the souls of bear and beaver, will become fewer and fewer. *Soon their world, the world Speck tells us about, will be gone forever.* [My emphasis.]

Speck (1935: 245) himself had much earlier projected the disappearance of the Naskapi. Fusing his observations on the animist Innu religion with cultural evolutionism, at the end of his work he left his readers with hunters that would 'disappear from their haunts'. Mega-projects are one means by which 'disappearance' can be engineered. After Speck's time, the placement of extractive industries in Innu territories would accelerate the degradation of hunting territories (Samson 2003: 87–111).

In addition to the vicissitudes of cultural encounter just discussed, there are situations in which 'ancient ways of life, after being hastily covered up by official initiative, forge ahead, slowly and surely' (Levi-Strauss 1973: 198). Just as Levi-Strauss discovered beautifully polished stone pestles among the cheap enamel plates and spoons in Brazil, so one can now find meticulously worked Innu snowshoes amid cheap manufactured boots, a re-emergence of painstakingly constructed canoes of Innu design as well as factory-built boats, and caribou stew alongside take-away fried chicken.

... And returning to the right to culture

The Innu are illustrative of many indigenous peoples that have been placed in situations in which they have simply had little choice but to acquiesce to the overwhelming power of their colonisers. As the connection with the land is argu- ably the most important element of the Innu way of life, and hence changes to those connections precipitate overwhelmingly negative social changes, their access to it is a crucial factor. However, the process of land usurpation has continued through the confiscation of parts of Innu territories for mining, logging, roads and hydroelectric power generation. Not having ceded their lands by treaty, Innu political bodies – significantly even these were created and are funded by the state – are currently negotiating with the state through the Comprehensive Land Claims system. This process is a latter-day treaty system by which the aboriginal party must relinquish their usufruct ownership over the land in exchange for specific self-government rights and cash compensation (Samson 1999). If they do not participate in the system, lands can be simply seized, subject to 'consultation'. Echoing treaty negotiations in the US centuries earlier, corporations have been entering into joint venture negotiations with individual Innu, who then collaborate in the appropriation of parcels of land for specific resource extraction businesses. Such land, allegedly under collective Innu ownership, is then alienated, enriching the corporations and a handful of Innu families. This process is almost always divisive among peoples with a deep communitarian ethos.

Given these pressures, it is not surprising that over time, the identities of Innu

Figure 1 Shushep Mark and youth assistants with canoe under construction in a workshop in Sheshatshiu, Labrador, Canada. Photo: Colin Samson, 2006.

Figure 2   Author with Shushep Mark outside newly built Euro-Canadian settler's cabin where the Kenemau River empties into Lake Melville. This area has been used by Shushep and his family for several generations. It is the site of Innu gatherings for excellent salmon fishing and is near a burial site. Photo: Jules Pretty, 2004.

individuals and families, especially those favoured by resource extraction industries, will come to more closely resemble the models of assimilation established by the state. That is, such individuals will still retain some symbolic indigeneity, but will increasingly be living according to principles, and driven by motives, that are alien to those which have guided their actions until recent times. Others, of course, will be so demoralised that they either leave or, as is very common among the Innu, fall into a pattern of self-destructive behaviour within the impoverished villages.

Meanwhile, facts are created on the ground, and as with a number of other currently colonial situations, the passage of time becomes a weapon used by authorities wishing to limit indigenous rights and to absorb them and their lands into the cultural and political order of the state, or by the same token, as postcolonial fragments in an ever changing world. This is the case, for example, in Western Sahara, where the Sahrawi people's quest for a distinct identity within a Sahrawi state is simply worn down by demoralised waiting in refugee camps. The longer the de facto occupation of most of their territories by Morocco and its settlers lasts, the less distinct they become from the Moroccan population, the more their oral tradition, collectivism, desert lifestyle and cultural peculiarities atrophy

(Shelley 2003: 200–1). These pressures build upon those such as sedentarisation, previously exerted by Spain, the colonial occupier until 1975.

What is currently being contested as a question of human rights is not some desire to remain static – although there are numerous indigenous people for whom stasis is actually a virtue – but to be allowed to choose how to configure indigenous ways of life without incessant pressures, often of a violent nature, to abandon them. This is a primary goal of the international indigenous peoples' movement. It is reflected in culturally-based claims to rights as embodied in the UN Declaration on the Rights of Indigenous Peoples, virtually every article of which, through provisions for land, language and cultural rights, contains standards for states on the maintenance of indigenous cultural continuity.

To some anthropologists the indigenous peoples' movement and the scholars and NGOs that support it, signifies a return to the whole and bounded concept of culture, a form of essentialism that is politically dangerous. According to Adam Kuper (2003), whose article, 'The Return of the Native' was at the centre of an acrimonious and long-running exchange in the pages of *Contemporary Anthropology*, for example, the indigenous peoples' movement reflects a paternalistic attitude that regards indigenous peoples as primitives whose fragile, primordial and ancient way of life must be protected. In Kuper's view, this romantic 'noble savage' imagery falls back on a natural harmony thesis (Hugh Brody in particular is accused of this) and appeals to the blood-and-soil nationalism of the far right who believe that only the original inhabitants of a place have rights and that immigrants and settlers have none. It also, Kuper argues, arbitrarily designates particular peoples as indigenous, when in fact all groups are or were migrants at one time or another.

In his denunciations of the conceptual basis of indigenous peoples' rights, Kuper is silent on the colonial processes which have in many cases induced the kinds of changes which he believes make it absurd to promote specific indigenous rights. By ignoring the flagrantly racist policies of numerous countries with indigenous populations, Kuper is able to regard states as benign and to conceive of universalistic rights within them as the only valid basis for human rights. The observance of laws providing for special land and cultural rights for indigenous peoples such as those being advocated by Survival International for the San Bushmen in Botswana is equated with apartheid. Here, the San are morphed into some sort of equivalent of Cowan's Orangemen.

Underlying these critiques of cultural rights for indigenous peoples is an uneasiness with departures from the universalist or liberal tradition of human rights that the extension of collective rights in the UN Declaration represents. Liberal political and legal commentary is frequently assumed as correct in much contemporary anthropological discourse on the subject of indigenous peoples' rights. In turn, for liberal commentators, there is a tendency to reject the idea of collective rights since they are seen as detracting from the inalienable rights of the individual, which are the cornerstone of the European Enlightenment tradition. Individual rights are then naturalised and their origin with the growth of the liberal market economy is washed over by the assumed universalism and benevolence of liberalism. The *sociological* observation that individual rights are associated with the necessity of the individual becoming the fundamental unit of labour, consumption, and cultural production, and that individual economic gain must become a driving motivation and marker of value and success for liberal capitalism to function (see Polanyi 1944) is lost. Following this, one could argue that individual rights are in part a way in which the political order simply recognises the deeply individualistic social requirements of the economic system. Society becomes essentially a *market* society. This political order, of course, is simply one out of numerous possibilities open to humans. To use Bhikhu Parekh's (2006: 112) language, its absolutism renders liberalism a rather monocultural and essentialist vision of Western society, which constantly denies the validity of real cultural diversity.

What is equally threatening to liberals is that collective rights are conceived by indigenous activists as constituting much more than 'group rights' within a multicultural society (see Keal 2003: 178); they are conceived as parallel sover-eignties that allow the peoples themselves to determine their political status. Under self-proclaimed multicultural states such as Canada, the political status of indigenous groups has not been an open question. The only matter of limited and fairly one-sided political debate has been the terms of their incorporation into the state. Interestingly, this has not been the case for the French majority population of Quebec, who enjoy consociation, and are permitted periodic votes on secession from the state. On the whole, however, the British Diaspora states and the UK have been hostile to collective rights for indigenous non-European populations. Canada, the US, New Zealand, and Australia all voted against and have opposed their inclusion in the UN Declaration.

Such questions are highly pertinent to the debate on the human rights of indig-enous peoples, since what is at stake is the right to recognition as in some sense culturally whole and distinct. This recognition of cultural rights goes beyond 'strategic essentialism' (Cowan, Dembour and Wilson 2001: 10) and is for many groups inseparable with land rights. Yet this struggle for cultural integrity, apparent in indigenous projects to maintain connections with land, speak their languages and follow their religious observances as incarnated in the UN Declaration, runs up against a powerful view that these are naive and utopian longings. In this view, colonial history is seen not as an audacious exercise in social engineering, but a fact of human history that has created new realities. New sorts of rights redressing the manipulations of colonialism and contemporary states are headed off by howls of 'essentialism'. It is here that a breezy fatalism about the future of those wishing to preserve their uniqueness returns by the back door. This debate is by no means over, but in order to tackle the issues at stake seriously we cannot simply accept the way things are now as given. We must look at how certain unique features of indigenous peoples' way of life changed. This historical perspective is necessary to understand why many such peoples want to retain some of the special features of their way of life. Contemplating all this will help us consider how the liberal tradition of human rights as well as some anthropological discourse may become a cover for maintaining cultural domination.

Bibliography

Adelson, N. (2000) *'Being Alive Well': Health and the Politics of Cree Well-Being*, Toronto: University of Toronto Press.

Arnold, D. (1996) *The Problem of Nature: Environment, Culture and European Expansion*, Oxford: Blackwell.

Asch, M. (1992) 'Errors in *Delgamuukw*: An Anthropological Perspective', in Cassidy (ed.) *Aboriginal Title in British Columbia: Delgamuukw v. The Queen*, Vancouver: Oolichan Books.

Assembly of First Nations, (2003) Information Pack for National Chief Matthew Coon Come's Mission to Europe, Ottawa: Assembly of First Nations.

Baines, S. G. (1999) 'Waimiri-Atroari Resistance in the Presence of an Indigenist Policy of "Resistance"', in *Critique of Anthropology* 19(3): 211–16.

Berkhofer, R. (1978) *The White Man's Indian: Images of the American Indian from Columbus to the Present*, New York: Vintage.

Bidney, D. (1996) *Theoretical Anthropology*, 2nd edn, New Brunswick, NJ: Transaction Books.

Bonvillain, N. (2001) *Native Nations: Cultures and Histories of Native North America*, Upper Saddle River, NJ: Prentice-Hall.

Brody, H. (2001) *The Other Side of Eden: Hunter-Gatherers, Farmers and the Modern World*, London: Faber & Faber.

Burch, E. S. Jr. (2005) *Alliance and Conflict: The World System of the Iñupiaq Eskimos*, Lincoln: University of Nebraska Press.

Catlin, G. (1841, reprinted 1989) *North American Indians*, New York: Penguin.

Césaire, A. (1955) *Discourse on Colonialism*, trans. J. Pinkham, New York: Monthly Review Press.

Chagnon, N. (1992) *Yanomamö*, 4th edn, Orlando, FL: Harcourt Brace College Publishers.

Clifford, J. (1986) 'Introduction: Partial Truths,' in James Clifford and George Marcus (eds) *Writing Culture: The Poetics and Politics of Ethnography*, Berkeley: University of California Press, pp. 1–26.

—— (1988) *The Predicament of Culture: Twentieth Century Ethnography, Literature and Art*, Cambridge: Harvard University Press.

Colson, E. (1986) 'Obituary: Lucy Mair,' *Anthropology Today* 2(4): 22–4.

Cowan, J. (2006) 'Culture and Rights after *Culture and Rights*', *American Anthropologist* 108(1): 9–24.

Cowan, J., Dembour, M-B. and Wilson, R. (2001) 'Introduction', in Cowan, *et al.* (eds) *Culture and Rights: Anthropological Perspectives*, Cambridge: Cambridge University Press.

Darnell, F. and Hoem, A. (1996) *Taken to Extremes: Education in the Far North*, Oslo: Scandinavian University Press.

Dowd, G. E. (1992) *A Spirited Resistance: The North American Indian Struggle for Unity, 1745–1815*, Baltimore: Johns Hopkins University Press.

Elkins, C. (2005) *Britain's Gulag: The Brutal End of Empire in Kenya*, London: Jonathan Cape.

Fanon, F. (1965) *A Dying Colonialism*, New York: Grove Press.

Fleming, F. (2003) *The Cross and the Sword*, London: Granta Books.

Fontaine, P. (2007) 'Canada and First Nations at Crossroads: Confrontation or Negotiation', speech to Canadian Club of Ottawa, 15 May. Available online at http://www.canadianclubottawa.ca/en/events/archives/speeches/06/fontaine.html (accessed 19 August 2008).

Gall, S. (2002) *The Bushmen of Southern Africa: Slaughter of the Innocent*, London: Pimlico.

Gómez, V. (2003) 'The Inter-American System', *Human Rights Law Review* 3: 127–33.

Hedican, E. (1995) *Applied Anthropology in Canada: Understanding Aboriginal Issues*, Toronto: University of Toronto Press.

Honigmann, J. (1964) 'Indians of Nouveau Québec,' in Malaurie and Rousseau (eds) *Le Nouveau-Quebec Contribution a L'Etude de L'Occupation Humaine*, Paris: Mouton & Co.

Horsman, R. (1981) *Race and Manifest Destiny: The Origins of American Racial Anglo Saxonism*, Cambridge, MA: Harvard University Press.

Jahner, E. (1994) 'Transitional Narratives and Cultural Continuity', in Kroeber (ed.) *American Indian Persistence and Resurgence*, Durham, NC: Duke University Press.

Keal, P. (2003) *European Conquest and the Rights of Indigenous Peoples: The moral backwardness of international society*, Cambridge: Cambridge University Press.

Kuletz, V. (1998) *The Tainted Desert: Environmental and Social Ruin in the American West*, London: Routledge.

Kuper, A. (2003) 'The Return of the Native', *Current Anthropology* 44(3): 389–402.

Levi-Strauss, C. (1955, reprinted 1973) *Tristes Tropiques*, trans. J. and D. Weightman, Harmondsworth: Penguin.

Lewellen, T. (2002) *The Anthropology of Globalization: Cultural Anthropology Enters the 21st century*, Westport, CT: Bergin and Garvey.

Lindqvist, S. (2007) *Terra Nullius: A Journey Through No One's Land*, London: Granta.

Lips, J. (1947) 'Naskapi Law: (Lake St. John and Lake Mistassini Bands) Law and Order in a Hunting Society', *Transactions of the American Philosophical Society* 37(4): 379–490.

Malinowski, B. (1945) *The Dynamics of Culture Change: An Inquiry into Race Relations in Africa*, New Haven, CT: Yale University Press.

Miller, B. (2003) *Invisible Indigenes: The Politics of Nonrecognition*, Lincoln: University of Nebraska Press.

Momaday, N. S. (1976) *The Names: A Memoir*, Tucson: University of Arizona Press.

Niezen, R. (2003) *The Origins of Indigenism: Human Rights and the Politics of Identity*, Berkeley: University of California Press.

—— (2005) *A World Beyond Difference: Cultural Identity in the Age of Globalization*, Oxford: Blackwell.

Nisbet, R. (1969) *Social Change and History: Aspects of the Western Theory of Development*, New York: Oxford University Press.

Owusu, M. (1979) 'Colonial and Postcolonial Anthropology of Africa: Scholarship or Sentiment?', in Huizer and Mannheim (eds) *The Politics of Anthropology: From Colonialism and Sexism Toward a View from Below*, The Hague: Mouton.

Parekh, B. (2006) *Rethinking Multiculturalism: Cultural Diversity and Political Theory*, London: Palgrave Macmillan.

Philpott, D., Cahill, M., Nesbit, W. and Jeffrey, G. (2004) 'An Educational Profile of the Learning Needs of Innu Youth', St. Johns: Memorial University of Newfoundland.

Polanyi, K. (1944) *The Great Transformation: The Political and Economic Origins of Our Time*, Boston: Beacon Books.

Rabben, L. (1998) *Unnatural Selection: The Yanomami, the Kayapó and the Onslaught of Civilisation*, Seattle: University of Washington Press.

Sale, K. (1991) *The Conquest of Paradise: Christopher Columbus and the Columbian Legacy*, New York: Plume.

Samson, C. (1999) 'The Dispossession of the Innu and the Colonial Magic of Canadian Liberalism', *Citizenship Studies* 3(1): 5–26.

—— (2001) 'Sameness as a Requirement for the Recognition of the Rights of the Innu of Canada: the Colonial Context', in J. Cowan, M.-B. Dembour and R. Wilson (eds) *Culture and Rights: Anthropological Perspectives*, Cambridge: Cambridge University Press.

—— (2003) *A Way of Life That Does Not Exist: Canada and the Extinguishment of the Innu*, London: Verso Press.

Samson, C. and Pretty, J. (2006) 'Environmental and Health Benefits of Hunting Lifestyles and Diets for the Innu of Labrador', *Food Policy* 31(6): 528–3.

Shelley, T. (2003) *Endgame in the Western Sahara: What Future for Africa's Last Colony?*, London: Zed Books.

Speck, F. (1935, reprinted 1977) *Naskapi: The Savage Hunters of the Labrador Peninsula*, Norman, OK: University of Oklahoma Press.

Stocking, G. (1968) *Race, Culture and Evolution: Essays in the History of Anthropology*, Chicago: University of Chicago Press.

Strong, P. T. (2004) 'Representational Practices', in Thomas Biolsi (ed.) *A Companion to the Anthropology of American Indians*, Oxford: Blackwell, pp. 341–59.

Survival International (2000) *Disinherited: Indians of Brazil*, London: Survival International.

Tanner, V. (1947) *Outlines of the Geography, Life & Customs of Newfoundland-Labrador (The Eastern Part of the Labrador Peninsula)*, two volumes, Cambridge: Cambridge University Press.

Turner, F. J. (1961) *Frontier and Section: Selected Essays of Frederick Jackson Turner*, Englewood Cliffs, New Jersey: Prentice-Hall.

United Nations (1994) Draft United Nations Declaration on the Rights of Indigenous Peoples as Agreed upon by Members of the Working Group on Indigenous Populations at its Eleventh Session. Adopted by the Sub commission on Prevention of Discrimination and protection of Minorities by its resolution 1994/45, 26 August 1994.

Wilson, R. (2000) 'The Right to Difference is a Fundamental Human Right: Against the Motion', contribution to Group for Debates in Anthropological Theory Debate No. 10, Department of Social Anthropology, University of Manchester.

Zimmerly, D. W. (1975) *Cain's Land Revisited: Culture Change in Central Labrador, 1775–1972*, St. John's: Institute of Social and Economic Research Press.

Zimmerman, L. (1997) 'Anthropologists and Responses to the Reburial Issue', in T. Biolsi and L. Zimmerman (eds) *Indians and Anthropologists: Vine Deloria Jr. and the Critique of Anthropology*, Tucson: University of Arizona Press.

5 Democratic human rights

Kate Nash

Human rights are globalising. In one sense, of course, human rights are inherently global. As they were developed after World War II, with the horrors of genocide in mind, they are not just universal in form; at least in terms of the intentions of those who drafted the Universal Declaration of Human Rights (UDHR), and in contrast to the great eighteenth-century declarations of the 'rights of man', which were very clear that 'man' was a citizen, they were really meant to abolish state persecution of *all* human beings regardless of whether they were citizens or not. As Article 2 of the UDHR has it:

> Everyone is entitled to all the rights and freedoms set forth in this Declaration, without distinction of any kind, such as race, colour, sex, language, religion, political or other opinion, national or social origin, property, birth or other status.

In addition, human rights are also now globalising in that they are becoming institutionalised globally: the vast majority of states have committed themselves to precise and detailed international human rights agreements; and, human rights activists try to deepen and extend that commitment through interpretations which include even those states that have not formally bound themselves to such agreements.

The globalisation of human rights is the result, then, of the efforts of those Arendt called 'well-meaning idealists who stubbornly insist on regarding as 'inalienable' those human rights ... which are enjoyed only by citizens of the most prosperous and civilized countries' (Arendt 1968: 279). Looking back to the chaos and catastrophe that resulted from the disintegration of empires with World War I, Arendt was highly critical of human rights developments of the 1940s because she saw them as based on the abstraction of humanity rather than on any possibility of participation, whether democratic or revolutionary, in a concrete political community. Reflecting on the fate of the huge numbers of refugees who had been made stateless during this period she noted that:

> The conception of human rights, based upon the assumed existence of a human being as such, broke down at the very moment when those who professed to believe in it were for the first time confronted with people who had indeed lost

all other qualities and specific relationships – except they were still human. The world found nothing sacred in the abstract nakedness of being human.

(Arendt 1968: 299)

Over half a century later, living as we are through the globalisation of human rights that was inaugurated with the Universal Declaration of Human Rights, we are now in a position to assess her scepticism. Is it still the case at the beginning of the twenty-first century that, although there is a good deal of talk about the value of human rights, the world still finds nothing sacred in the bare fact of 'being human'?

There is no doubt that the globalising institutionalisation of human rights has complicated the fundamental distinction between citizens and non-citizens on which modern states were founded. Yasemin Soysal's comparative work on post-national citizenship in Europe has effectively shown how denizens – long-term residents of European states who are not citizens – have won social entitlements by appealing to international human rights agreements (Soysal 1994). David Jacobson has made a similar analysis of post-national citizenship in the US in relation to illegal migrants (Jacobson 1996). Achieving post-national citizenship status for themselves and their families, denizens blur the sharp legal distinction between citizens and non-citizens within states along some dimensions – notably access to education, healthcare and employment. The status of refugees and asylum-seekers who have rights in the societies in which they are resident *only* as a result of the international human rights agreements is another example of a shift towards post-national citizenship. Interestingly, however, considering Arendt's suspicions of human rights, non-citizens virtually never have political rights to vote or to stand in elections in states in which they are long-term residents.

How secure are the rights of these quasi-citizens? As Soysal herself argues, as it is states historically constituted on an absolute distinction between national citizens and non-citizens which administer international human rights agreements, progress towards a more flexible citizenship is complex and highly uncertain (Soysal 1994: 156–62; Soysal 2001). There have been changes in the practices of human rights since Arendt wrote, but these changes are partial, paradoxical, and in principle, and sometimes in practice, reversible (Castles and Davidson 2001).

A good example of the complexities of the relationship between citizenship and non-citizenship status with respect to human rights is that of the 'Belmarsh detainees' in the UK. Following 9/11, the UK government passed the Anti-Terrorism, Crime and Security Act (ATCSA) enabling the detention without charge and without access to lawyers of *non-citizens* only who were suspected of terrorism. The details of who was held under this Act are secret but it seems that most could not simply be deported because, whether or not they had successfully secured political asylum legally in Britain, they could show that they had a well-founded fear of persecution in the states of which they were nationals. According to European human rights legislation, individuals may not be deported to countries where they are likely to be persecuted (*Chahal* v. *UK* 1996). What this case demonstrates is the paradoxes and complexities of human rights today: safeguarding the human rights of non-citizens (protecting them from persecution by other states), the UK state then subjected the same non-citizens to arbitrary detention (in violation of fundamental human rights) (see Nash 2009a).

As a result of the globalisation of human rights, then, the fundamental distinction between citizens and non-citizens has been significantly altered, but Arendt's scepticism concerning human rights is nevertheless confirmed. Non-citizens may enjoy *some* human rights, but they remain vulnerable to state persecution when tensions arise within states, especially between minorities and the majority population. What then of Arendt's view that it is particularly through political participation that citizens safeguard their privileged position against non-citizens?

Certainly there is a popular view that human rights as such are anti-democratic, that they are in tension with the rights of citizens to define their own political community. This view is to be found in the writings of social scientists as well as in politicians' speeches and the media. Ulrich Beck, for example, argues that the human rights regime is self-legitimating: based not on popular consent but on the exercise of reason; human rights do not therefore need democratic deliberation and decision-making (Beck 2006: 297). This view overlaps with an assumption that is especially well entrenched in the political culture of the US – that international human rights undermine democratic sovereignty and that whilst the US leads the world in terms of promoting human rights abroad, international human rights law is developed by officials from many states and should not be imposed in the US, where law must originate from elected representatives of the people (Ignatieff 2005). Perhaps most disturbingly, given the history of persecution of minorities within states against which human rights have been developed, the position of denizens may even be seen as embodying the opposition between democracy and human rights and therefore as dangerous for democracy itself. For example, David Jacobson and Gayla Ruffer argue that not only do international human rights undermine democratic sovereignty but, because denizens organise transnationally to put pressure on states using international law, they are introducing modes of social action into the political community which bypass traditional, democratic forms of political mobilisation (Jacobson and Ruffer 2003). Arendt's republican view that participation is what makes for membership of the political community and therefore for relative security of rights is here turned on its head: it is because those resident in the political community are not permitted to participate in it, because their political rights are explicitly limited by the states under whose jurisdiction they live, that they are seen as threatening the democratic community itself.

In this chapter I will argue that opposing human rights to democracy is not only potentially dangerous for those who, as 'bare humans' must rely on human rights, but it is also misguided. It is, however, understandable that human rights should have come to be seen as undemocratic because of the focus of human rights activism on developing human rights at the international level which are then used by non-governmental organisations (NGOs) to put pressure on states from above and below (Keck and Sikkink 1998; Risse, *et al.* 1999). Similarly, the academic study of human rights is also overwhelmingly concerned with the legalisation of human rights in international law (Meckled-Garcia and Cali 2006). Here I will argue that a shift in focus to how human rights have been designed to be democratically institutionalised at the national level gives quite a different perspective on the relationship between human rights and democracy. From this perspective it is better to see human rights as universal moral principles that usefully guide the structuring of political communities in our globalising times, as the national state is transforming from within and without. Understanding human rights in this way need not challenge their universalism; it should rather legitimate it democratically from *within* states.

How are human rights democratic?

In this section I address how human rights are designed to be democratic, at least in principle. Human rights do not, as is commonly argued, work against state sovereignty and therefore against the will of the people as expressed through their democratically elected representatives. On the contrary, to a large extent human rights have been designed – very problematically for their enforcement – to bolster state sovereignty. Nor do human rights impose international norms on the democratic political community. They have rather been designed to be implemented through democratic public policy.

In the first place, let us look at the popular view that human rights are eroding state sovereignty and therefore democratic accountability. For example, David Forsythe has said that human rights law is 'revolutionary because it contradicts the notion of national sovereignty – that is, that a state can do as it pleases in its own jurisdiction' (quoted in Krasner 1999: 105). Similarly, David Hirsh says that 'human rights are instruments that seek to limit the scope of state sovereignty' (quoted in Sznaider and Levy 2006: 659). This view is not quite accurate. Because sovereignty is socially constructed, historically specific and mutable (see Biersteker and Weber 1996), it is better understood as *transformed* rather than eroded or contradicted by human rights. It is transformed insofar as the moral language of universal norms of human rights is one that the leaders of states find it increasingly difficult to ignore in justifying sovereign acts that may contravene international human rights agreements. The *legitimacy* of state sovereignty is increasingly called into question when human rights are violated. However, with the partial exception of the International Criminal Court which we will discuss briefly below (and regardless of arguments concerning whether or not state sovereignty *should* trump human rights or not), human rights have been constructed precisely in order *not* to impact on the legal doctrine of state sovereignty.

State sovereignty is obviously not the same as democracy. They are related, however, insofar as universal suffrage depends upon effective mechanisms by which law can be enacted. Popular sovereignty no less than state sovereignty requires 'monopoly over the means of violence', as Weber has it, to administer justice, manage the economy, make social policy and so on (Benhabib 2007: 21). In very stark terms sovereignty is what authorises the state to have the 'last word' (Montgomery 2002: 5). Sovereignty is the ultimate authority: there is no authority over the sovereign which it must obey. On the contrary, sovereignty is obeyed *because* it is sovereign.

At the international level sovereignty is supported and even bolstered in the United Nations (UN) system of human rights – no doubt to allay the fears of the leaders of the most powerful states at the end of World War II that it would give them nothing to fear in restricting their domestic decision-making capacities. In the UN system human rights are monitored and state breaches of human rights are deplored, but there are no mechanisms for their enforcement. Indeed, sovereignty is explicitly safeguarded in the system by which international human rights agreements are drawn up in the first place: not only are they the product of long-negotiated consensus amongst state and NGO delegates, but before they are finally accepted states have the option of making reservations against those articles with which they are not completely in agreement. A notorious example is the reservation the US put on the International Covenant on Civil and Political Rights (ICCPR) which allowed capital punishment, even for juveniles, though 'right to life' is the key provision of the Convention, and Article 6 (5) prohibits the imposition of the death penalty 'for crimes committed by persons below eighteen years of age' (Roth 2000). Whilst this reservation may be against the spirit of the ICCPR, leaving the US open to moral condemnation, the UN system of human rights is constructed precisely in order to enable the safeguarding of state sovereignty it exemplifies.

In recent times the most serious threat to state sovereignty in the name of human rights appears to many to be the possibility of 'humanitarian intervention' by military means. However, the idea that powerful states are able to use the UN system to invade and overthrow the leaders of a sovereign state in the name of human rights is simplistic. The question of humanitarian intervention is extremely complex, and there is no room here to go into the debates over whether it should be allowed or not (see Chandler 2006; Cushman 2005). It is sufficient to note , however, that the only military intervention that appears not to have been strongly motivated by geo-political strategy or conflict over economic resources, the NATO intervention in Kosovo, not only had no mandate from the UN but was actually justified in terms of the 'vital interest' of a functioning liberal-democracy on Europe's borders. The invasions of Afghanistan and Iraq, which were certainly accompanied by the rhetoric of enforcing respect for human rights and even regime change, were actually carried out in the name of national security: the human rights atrocities that had undoubtedly been committed against the people of these countries were not the motivation, nor the primary justification for the invasions. It is true that throughout the 1990s and into the twenty-first century the UN Security Council increasingly used the language of human rights in relation to the issues of peace and war with which it has traditionally been concerned, but its actions in this respect have been a good deal more limited than the rhetoric would suggest.

Indeed, not even in the European system of human rights, generally agreed to be the most rigorous in the world, are there any external powers which can strike down the legislation of a sovereign state or interfere with its foreign policy decisions. When the European Court of Human Rights finds a state in breach of its human rights commitments under the European Convention on Human Rights (ECHR) it has powers only to require its government to consider relevant legislation: there are no mechanisms for enforcing the Court's judgement, and indeed, states frequently disregard it or take many years to introduce new legislation to deal with the issues. Even where violations of human rights are egregious, concerning torture for example, the Court's decision does no more than add to the moral pressure which is exerted on such states by parliamentarians, activist lawyers, NGOs, journalists and so on.

Sovereignty is also bolstered by human rights insofar as the traditional state prerogative to suspend law in times of emergency is explicitly enabled in international human rights law. Both the ECHR and the ICCPR permit derogation from (opting out of) certain fundamental human rights provided that the actions taken subsequently are consistent with other obligations in international law and do not discriminate against particular groups of persons on the basis of race, ethnicity, nationality etc. One such right is that specified in Article 5 of the ECHR to personal freedom: a sovereign declaration of a state of emergency enables a state to detain any individual without requiring that proper procedures of law should be followed, including telling them the reasons for their detention, charging them and bringing them 'speedily' before a judge. Such powers are hugely problematic from the point of view of safeguarding individuals from arbitrary detention and the practices of torture that often accompany it as they suspend fundamental individual rights just at the point at which they are most needed, when minorities are likely to be the victims of a majority fearful for its safety. The point here, however, is that the ultimate sovereign decision to detain those who appear to threaten the state is not prevented by international human rights agreements. Even in the European system international human rights agreements do no more than establish the political and legal context within which derogation from fundamental human rights may be judged.

The only legal system that comes close to enforcing human rights and therefore impacting on state sovereignty is the International Criminal Court (ICC), which may override national law or domestic political settlements (such as an amnesty) in order to subject state leaders to criminal trial for gross violations of human rights committed during war time. This is undoubtedly a new development in international law, representing, as we shall discuss further below, an example of cosmopolitan law in practice. It has been possible since the Nuremberg Trials immediately after World War II, but it is only now being fully realised with the International Tribunals for the former Yugoslavia and Rwanda, and since 2002 in the ICC. However, with regard to the implications for state sovereignty, even where the ICC is concerned, it is important to be clear about their limitations. Firstly, the ICC will only apply to those states that have agreed to come under its jurisdiction (not including, notoriously, the US) and only to crimes after the date at which they do so: in this respect it is, like other supra-national organisations such as the European Union, exemplary of states agreeing to *share* sovereignty rather than having it forcibly infringed. Secondly, the Rome Statute which sets up the terms under which the ICC operates, explicitly states that it is only after domestic remedies are exhausted or it is clear that they will not be possible for political reasons that the Court may choose to take up a case. The Court is intended to supplement rather than to replace national courts. Thirdly, the Court will hear accusations of human rights violations only in the context of war and only after the event: it has no means to demand interference directly in state affairs in order to prevent such violations.

Far more important than these high-level, dramatic and comparatively rare cases of international judgements concerning the legitimacy of the actions of state leaders or of state sovereignty is the way in which human rights have been designed to allow for flexibility in their domestic institutionalisation. Far from being self-legitimating and anti-democratic, human rights are actually *designed for* democracy.

There are very few international human rights that are absolute, though it is these that most readily capture the imagination of human rights activists. They are supposed to provide the conditions for democracy itself; they are fundamental to any form of democracy as popular rule. In the UDHR, for example, which is the basis of all international human rights law, there are very few Articles which take the absolute form 'No one shall …'. What is absolutely prohibited is enslavement; torture; and cruel, inhuman or degrading treatment or punishment. Arbitrary arrest, detention or exile and arbitrary interference with privacy are also absolutely prohibited except where there is a sovereign declaration of a state of emergency facing the nation. These rights are the foundation of democratic participation as such; they are fundamental to individuals' capacities to express opinions and organise against the re-election of a government they oppose.

However, although these absolute human rights are not explicitly designed to be adapted to particular circumstances but rather to be respected without question, they necessarily leave scope for interpretation: what counts as torture, as arbitrary arrest, as cruel, inhuman or degrading punishment? Although there are strong precedents to establish the limits of interpretation of these norms in international law, their meanings cannot ultimately be fixed in abstraction; they must, of necessity, be defined in concrete regulations and practices. Who decides how they are to be defined for a particular political community depends on how states organise their procedures for law-making, administration and the juridical interpretation of human rights.

Most Articles of the UDHR, however, are more 'relative'. They take the form 'Everyone has the right to …' and they have been developed precisely to enable the tailoring of standards to particular social and political circumstances whilst retaining their core conception of the value of the human person as an individual (Merry 2006: 8). Examples include the right to 'life, liberty and security of person' (Article 3), 'recognition everywhere as a person before the law' (Article 4), and so on. Human rights specified in this form, which is not that of absolute prohibition, are much more open than those which take the form 'No one shall …'. The ECHR makes this understanding of human rights explicit, with many of its Articles stating that individual rights must be balanced by consideration of the interests and values of the political community. Article 10, which concerns the freedom of expression, is typical. Stating '(1) 'Everyone has the right to freedom of expression …' it then goes on to specify that:

(2) The exercise of these freedoms, since it carries with it duties and responsibilities, may be subject to such formalities, conditions, restrictions or
penalties as are prescribed by law and are necessary in a democratic society,
in the interests of national security, territorial integrity or public safety, for the
prevention of disorder or crime, for the protection of health or morals, for the
protection of the reputation or rights of others, for preventing the disclosure
of information received in confidence, or for maintaining the authority and
impartiality of the judiciary.

Human rights are not opposed, then, to democracy. On the contrary, the fact that
international systems of human rights bolster and safeguard state sovereignty
and that so few absolute rights are stipulated within states may rather be seen as
problematic from the point of the view of guaranteeing fundamental individual
rights. It is, however, in keeping with the fact that human rights are designed to
enable the conditions for democracy, in the case of absolute rights to personal
freedom, and to be interpreted flexibly relative to the interpretations of particular
political communities in the case of the great majority of human rights. Human
rights are designed to be administered democratically, by officials elected within
political communities. Nevertheless, the chief focus of human rights activism
has been on making and enforcing international human rights law by influencing
lawyers and judges.

Nationalising human rights

International law has been the focus of human rights activism since the beginning
of the globalisation of human rights. Human rights activism has, however, become
a good deal more energetic in this respect since the end of the Cold War, when we
see the beginning of what is sometimes called 'cosmopolitan law'. It is cosmopolitan law which, the more clearly it becomes established as far as lawyers and human
rights activists are concerned, is increasingly controversial in democratic terms for
those opposed to human rights. However, the introduction of cosmopolitan law
through courts rather than through legislatures is not a necessary structural feature
of human rights as such. It is rather that historically this is how human rights have
generally been introduced into domestic polities.

Traditionally international law concerned only relations between sovereign
states. After World War II, liberal internationalism began more systematically to
challenge the distinction between citizens and non-citizens on which state sovereignty was based. These changes to international law are sometimes known as the
'Nuremberg principles' because they were initially developed in the Nuremberg
trials that followed World War II. Two major changes in international law came
together in the legal aftermath of this war. Firstly, individuals became criminally
accountable for violations of the laws of war ('just obeying orders' was no longer a
legitimate legal defence, however lowly a position the accused held in the military
or state hierarchy). Secondly, principles of human rights began to be developed,
which prescribed limits to a government's conduct towards its own citizens, to

apply in times of peace *and* war (Ratner and Abrams 2001: 4; see also Held 1995: 101–2). This second principle was carried forward and extended with the UDHR, beginning international human rights law in the UN human rights system.

With the partial exception of the European system of human rights, however, the balance of power until the end of the Cold War meant that international law effectively maintained classic state sovereignty, being overwhelmingly concerned with keeping the peace between states (Held 2002). Since the Cold War we are now seeing the beginning of cosmopolitan law. In contrast to international law, and building on the 'Nuremberg principles', cosmopolitan law reaches inside states, to enforce claims against human rights violators (see Held 2002; Hirsh 2003). The most interesting example of cosmopolitan law from the point of view of the supposed opposition between democracy and human rights is customary international law, defined as established state practice, which states understand to be followed 'from a sense of legal obligation' (Steiner and Alston 2000: 70). Customary international law is not made exclusively by treaty or convention and state officials need not have explicitly agreed its terms and scope as they do in conventional human rights agreements like the ICCPR or the ECHR. The sources used to establish customary international law include such a diverse array as 'newspaper reports of actions taken by states ... statements made by government spokesmen [sic] to Parliament, to the press, at international conferences ... a state's laws and judicial decisions' and multilateral treaties (Steiner and Alston 2000: 73). They also include judicial decisions and the teachings of highly qualified legal experts, and the resolutions and declarations of international governmental organisations like the General Assembly of the UN (Charlesworth and Chinkin 2000).

Customary international law is increasingly drawn upon in national as well as international courts. Celebrated examples of the use of customary international law in national courts include the extradition case against General Pinochet, former President of Chile, in the UK and cases using the Alien Tort Claims Act (ATCA) in the US. In the Pinochet case, a sovereign head of state was (almost) held accountable for crimes against humanity committed during peace time for the first time. There is no room to go into the complexities of the case here, which as an extradition case involved, not prosecution as such, but the decision that prosecution should proceed (see Davis 2003). The first judgement of the Law Lords that Pinochet should be extradited to Spain to be tried for genocide, torture and crimes against humanity drew on customary international law. Lawyers in the case successfully argued that the arbitrary detention, torture and murder of political opponents which occurred while Pinochet was President of Chile are absolutely forbidden, such that *any state* may exercise jurisdiction to try *any individual* with a case to answer for such crimes. They are acts which are committed against humankind itself, and in the name of universal human rights they are proscribed whether or not they are formally codified as law within a particular state.

Similarly, in the US, cases that use the ATCA to sue foreign agents for human rights violations committed against non-American citizens also draw on customary international law. ATCA has been successfully used by activists and lawyers in the US since *Filartiga* v. *Pena-Irala* in 1980 in which the family of a victim killed by state-sponsored torture in Paraguay was permitted to sue the perpetrator in the US. ATCA means that US courts may judge whether or not an individual has been subjected to torture, slavery, unlawful killing or other crimes deemed to be absolutely forbidden by the international community, whether or not the perpetrator or the crime explicitly and formally falls within US jurisdiction (Stephens and Ratner 1996; Steinhardt and D'Amato 1999).

Despite these clear confirmations of a core of acts as contravening cosmopolitan law through the due process of national courts, cosmopolitan law remains extremely controversial *as law*. Its opponents argue that it is judge-made law, especially when, as it does when customary international law is drawn on from across a wide-range of sources, it relies on unratified treaties and other documents which are not formally legally binding on states. It is argued that it therefore allows judicial imperialism over the branches of the state which are legitimately concerned with making and executing law in the name of the sovereign people: the elected representatives who make law in the legislature; and the executive who administer it, especially in relation to foreign policy. Moreover, because it is so politically contentious, it is actually very hard for cosmopolitan law to function *as law*. It lacks the predictability and uniformity that is supposed to characterise law. Although the Pinochet case and ATCA cases are celebrated by human rights activists, the controversial nature of the arguments that have been made in such cases have actually limited the effectiveness of cosmopolitan law as such.

This is evident from the Pinochet case. In fact, the Law Lords met three times to consider this case on appeal from the Divisional Court which initially found that Pinochet was entitled to diplomatic immunity as a former head of state. In the first judgement (Pinochet 1) the majority of the Lords found that Pinochet should be extradited to face criminal charges in Spain because customary international law, which would otherwise have prevented prosecution of a head of state for acts whilst committed in office, could not be understood to sanction crimes against humanity. This judgement was then set aside for reasons of alleged bias on the part of one of the judges (Pinochet 2), an unprecedented decision that could have triggered a constitutional crisis on the eve of reform of the House of Lords (Woodhouse 2003). Finally, the Lords decided that Pinochet should be extradited (Pinochet 3), on much narrower technical grounds than Pinochet 1. In the end it is unclear precisely what legal precedent it set, as eventually, in Pinochet 3, the decision was made on a completely different legal basis from that of customary international law, and one, indeed, which was at odds with it (Bianchi 1999). In fact, the judgement in Pinochet 3 was made on the basis of national law, which had in 1988 incorporated the Torture Convention into English law in the Criminal Justice Act. The Law Lords granted extradition on narrow technical grounds, allowing only those charges of crimes to stand which were committed *after* the Criminal Justice Act was passed. In this respect the decision was at odds with judges' interpretation in Pinochet 1 that some acts, including torture and hostage-taking, are crimes in international law, wherever and whenever they are committed. In this way the Law Lords also avoided the logical conclusion of their finding in Pinochet 1, that as *any state* was obliged under customary international law to try Pinochet, and as he was actually imprisoned in the UK, there was no good reason not to try him in British courts. Finally, indeed, Pinochet was never extradited for trial in Spain, as the British Home Secretary decided he was too ill to defend himself in a long court case, a decision that was widely understood as diplomatic given the international politics of the case.

ATCA cases appear to be more straightforward than the Pinochet case, and yet, if to a lesser degree, they are similarly highly politicised: the cases are often not allowed, for a variety of legal reasons, and they are extremely slow and subject to ambiguous and contradictory legal judgements and reversals when they do proceed (Stephens 2004). Indeed, human rights activists themselves allow that what is more important than winning these cases is the publicity they generate which may persuade others, especially corporations with products to sell, to think twice before getting involved in human rights abuses.

Given the general prejudice of the US system against implementing international human rights in the national political system, however, it is surprising that ATCA is in operation at all. In fact, it has even been confirmed as US law in recent years. In this respect ATCA is actually exemplary of a very different way of realising cosmopolitan norms in national polities – through national legislatures. Although it may seem more obvious to look to international law for the development of cosmopolitan law, cosmopolitan law may certainly be made by national legislatures. The origins of ATCA itself are obscure. The phrase which has been used to prosecute human rights abusers since 1980 appears in the Judiciary Act of 1789 and states only that 'The district courts shall have original jurisdiction of any civil action by an alien for a tort only, committed in violation of the law of nations of a treaty of the United States' (The Alien Tort Statute, 28 U.S.C. 1350). ATCA was, however, confirmed in the Torture Victim Prevention Act (TVPA) of 1992, which was widely seen as ratifying the *Filartiga* decision. As a result, when the Bush administration asked the Supreme Court to rule ATCA as unconstitutional because the way in which the judiciary had interpreted it trespassed on the powers of the executive over foreign policy, one of the most important considerations of the Court was the fact that Congress had passed the TVPA, clearly holding the firm view that such cases should be allowed in the US courts (*Sosa* v. *Alvarez-Machain*). In passing the TVPA the democratically elected legislature clearly instructed the judiciary to take customary international law upholding universal human rights into account in tort cases brought by non-citizens against individuals and corporations accused of human rights violations in US courts.

Legislatures not only *can*, then, pass cosmopolitan law upholding universal human rights for citizens and non-citizens alike, they actually *do* pass such law on occasion. Indeed, it is quite common for European states to pass law explicitly designed to conform to the ECHR. The UK Human Rights Act (HRA) 1998, which effectively made the ECHR into national law to be observed by parliament and upheld by domestic courts wherever relevant, would be a good example. The fact that in passing the TVPA the US Congress has done so even in a political system which is otherwise so hostile to the implementation of international human rights norms at home is perhaps even more significant. No doubt, however, the fact that

ATCA was already part of US law, even if its origins are obscure, was important to this legislation. In this sense it is highly unusual in the US context.

Moreover, recent legislation on anti-terrorism measures give us grounds for far greater caution before reaching an optimistic conclusion concerning the willingness of national legislatures to democratically enact cosmopolitan norms of universal human rights. In both the US and UK, legislatures have been faced with legal judgements by their highest courts that anti-terrorism measures adopted after 9/11 have been in contravention of very well-established principles that forbid arbitrary detention. In response, far from adjusting the law to take universal human rights into account, they have made legislation that contravenes the spirit if not (possibly, in the case of the UK) the letter of human rights law.

For example, following protracted litigation by human rights organisations in the US, the Supreme Court eventually found that it did have jurisdiction over the detainees in Guantanamo Bay, contrary to the arguments of the Bush administration, and despite the Presidential Military Order 2001 which had enabled them to be tried by military tribunals with greatly reduced standards of due process (including reliance on evidence that might have been gathered by torture, and which the defendant would have no right to see) (*Hamdan* v. *Rumsfeld* 2006). The Court found that the military tribunals satisfied neither US nor international military standards of due process. The legislation that Congress passed in response to this ruling, however, was just as dubious in terms of fundamental human rights as the Military Order it replaced. The Military Commissions Act 2006 explicitly stated that detainees deemed to be 'unlawful enemy combatants', which is not a term that is recognised in international law, should *not* be permitted to challenge their detention in US courts, but must go through Military Commission Trials which, similarly to the courts the Supreme Court ruled as unacceptable, have been widely criticised as allowing evidence (including from torture), procedures and definitions that would not be permitted in any normal court of law, military or civilian. Clearly in contravention of any understanding of fundamental human rights to personal freedom from arbitrary detention and to due process of the law, in 2008 the Supreme Court finally again ruled that these trials were inadequate and unconstitutional (*Boumediene* v. *Bush* 2008).

Similarly, in the UK, in response to a ruling by the Law Lords in 2004 that the imprisonment of non-citizen terrorist suspects, the'Belmarsh detainees', who had been detained for up to four years without being charged was unlawful, parliament also responded by passing legislation that was not in keeping with fundamental human rights norms to personal freedom and due process of law. The Prevention of Terrorism Act (PTA) 2005 granted the executive the power to keep suspected terrorists under 'control orders' based on 'reasonable suspicion' founded on secret evidence. The legislation permits electronic surveillance, curfews, and restrictions on communication for citizens and non-citizens alike. Whilst the government has explicitly declared its belief that the PTA is within the letter of the ECHR, imposing such severe restrictions on an individual's personal freedom without due process of law certainly contravenes the spirit of human rights norms.

If national legislatures can in principle, and sometimes actually do make law in conformity with cosmopolitan norms of human rights, why are they so reluctant to do so on other occasions? In the case of anti-terrorist legislation in the US and UK, the courts have repeatedly found laws designed to permit arbitrary detention unlawful, but legislatures still seem unwilling to respect very well-established international human rights norms. No doubt as elected representatives of the sovereign people, legislatures fear the consequences of appearing to be weak on those who threaten its safety. They would rather compromise on respect for individual human rights than face the prospect of being voted out of office for being weak on terrorism. One reason, then, for the lack of institutional support for cosmopolitan norms of human rights is that, at least in certain situations, and especially where minorities are concerned, human rights simply are not popular.

Popularising human rights

This brings us back to Arendt's argument that human rights, especially for non-citizens, are irrelevant where it is membership in a political community and the possibility of active political participation that generate what she calls 'the right to rights' (Arendt 1968: 296). Given, however, as we have seen, there have been some changes in uses of human rights, especially the granting of quasi-citizenship rights to non-citizens and the use of international human rights law in national courts, are we now in a position where a cosmopolitan political community might be possible? And is this what is needed to institutionalise genuine respect for human rights?

In the first place we must note that *membership* of a political community is clearly not sufficient to ensure that the fundamental rights of individuals are respected. It is quite possible that membership of existing political communities organised in relation to states could now be widened to become more cosmopolitan. The granting of political rights to vote could be made quicker and easier than the naturalisation as a citizen that is currently required. Dora Kostakopoulou suggests, for example, that those who are able to demonstrate their commitment to a country through domicile and other criteria should be granted rights to vote through a civic registration scheme (Kostakopoulou 2008). However, it is clear from the example of German Jews, amongst others, whose citizenship was withdrawn before they were deported and killed by the Nazis, that even those who enjoy full citizenship rights may not escape persecution. What is needed is more than just membership, it is *solidarity*: members of a political community who are able to influence state institutions must protect the 'right to have rights' that is shared by all.

Seyla Benhabib has argued that we see such forms of cosmopolitan solidarity developing in Europe as a result of what she calls 'democratic iterations' of universal human rights. Democratic iterations involve:

> complex processes of public argument, deliberation, and exchange through which universalist rights claims and principles are contested and contextualized, invoked and revoked, posited and positioned throughout legal and political institutions, as well as in the associations of civil society. Democratic iterations can take place in the 'strong' public bodies of legislatives, the

judiciary and the executive, as well as in the informal and 'weak' publics of civil society associations and the media.

(Benhabib 2007: 31)

Granted that, as we have seen in the brief account outlined in this chapter, universalist human rights principles *are* being repeated and at the same time modified as they circulate through 'strong' and 'weak' publics according to Benhabib, they are thus producing the effect of creating a cosmopolitan political community, one which finds itself to be 'not only the *subject* but also the *author of the laws*' and which includes both citizens and non-citizens (Benhabib 2007: 32). In my view, however, whilst iterations of universal human rights may well have the effect of creating a *human rights movement* comprising local and global activists, human rights innovators who act from within the state and their supporters in civil society, there is little evidence that cosmopolitan norms are becoming popular more widely.

Let us return to the example of the Pinochet case and consider how it was covered in the media. Extraordinarily widely publicised, the case was a massive, and unprecedented, media event. The Law Lords' decisions in the case were broadcast live on TV, the story of Lord Hoffman's association with Amnesty that led to Pinochet 2 broke on a news programme on the BBC, and there was blanket media coverage of the story, at the beginning and at peak moments throughout the course of events. The dominant media discussion of the case was, however, couched strongly in nationalist rather than cosmopolitan terms.

The nationalist terms of the debate over Pinochet were, unsurprisingly, most evident in conservative perspectives that opposed his extradition and trial. These represented the case primarily in terms of 'national interests', in maintaining loyalty to an ally and good friend of the UK, rather than in upholding international human rights. There were, of course, liberal voices sympathetic to cosmopolitan norms, which did not just demand Pinochet's extradition but which explicitly and actively constructed a *global* community covered by and supportive of human rights as realised in cosmopolitan law. These perspectives were very important insofar as they introduced cosmopolitan ideals into a political community that was otherwise coded as national. It was these advocates of global citizenship – activists, international lawyers and some liberal journalists – who were responsible for the 'democratic iterations' of cosmopolitan norms in the mediated public around the Pinochet case. The limits of cosmopolitanism are clear, however, in that even the majority of *supporters* of Pinochet's prosecution framed it in nationalist terms: his extradition was supported because 'we' take pride in 'our' state insofar as, and only where it is prudent for national interests, it upholds universal human rights that are applicable across the world (see Nash 2007 for more details).

There is, then, little evidence to suggest that, even in this, the most celebrated of human rights cases, iterations of universal human rights significantly dislodged the nationalist terms within which existing political communities, 'ours' and 'others', continued to be framed. Benhabib is correct, in my view, that what is needed to forge cosmopolitan solidarity is a cultural politics of human rights within political communities: the regular contestation of the frames within which politics takes place to open up the means by which fundamental human rights might be democratically secured for *everyone*, citizens and non-citizens alike. But it is very far from obvious how that aim might be achieved. Human rights activists and legal innovators are effecting changes in law, especially international law. However, as international law becomes increasingly cosmopolitan, reaching inside states to enforce claims against human rights violators, so law itself risks losing its prestige, coming under suspicion as anti-democratic. Remedying the democratic deficit of cosmopolitan law by legislating for universal human rights in assemblies elected to represent the people is far from impossible, but without a significant change in the public orientation towards universal human rights it can not be relied upon. Cosmopolitan law is least likely to be made, or enforced, precisely when it is most needed, during times of crisis when the majority of the population feels itself to be at threat from members of minority groups. What is left, then, is the long, slow process of bringing about a cultural transformation in orientations towards what it means to be a member of a political community and a forging of solidarity across racial, ethnic and national boundaries so that all individuals are valued as equally due respectful treatment in terms of human rights principles. Whilst our vantage point in history does not warrant quite as pessimistic a conclusion as Arendt's about the possibility of forging such a solidarity – there have been some successes in institutionalising human rights – it is not possible to be optimistic about the prospect that human rights might protect people in times of crisis and conflict in the future.

Bibliography

Arendt, H. (1968) *The Origins of Totalitarianism*, San Diego: Harvest Books.

Beck, U. (2006) *Power in the Global Age*, Cambridge: Polity.

Benhabib, S. (2007) 'Twilight of Sovereignty or the Emergence of Cosmopolitan Norms? Rethinking Citizenship in Volatile Times', *Citizenship Studies* 11(1):19–36.

Bianchi, A. (1999) 'Immunity versus Human Rights: The Pinochet Case', *European Journal of International Law* 10(2): 237–77.

Bickerton, C., Cunliffe, P. and Gourevitch, A. (2007) *Politics without Sovereignty: A Critique of Contemporary International Relations*, London: University College Press.

Biersteker, T. and Weber, C. (eds) (1996) *State Sovereignty as Social Construct*, Cambridge: Cambridge University Press.

Castles, S. and Davidson, A. (2001) *Citizenship and Migration*, Basingstoke, Hampshire: Macmillan.

Chandler, D. (2006) *From Kosovo to Kabul and Beyond: Human Rights and International Intervention*, 2nd edn, London: Pluto.

Charlesworth, H. and Chinkin, C. (2000) *The Boundaries of International Law: a Feminist Analysis*, Manchester: Manchester University Press.

Cushman, T. (2005) 'The Human Rights Case for the War in Iraq: a Consequentialist View', in Wilson (ed.) *Human Rights in the 'War on Terror'*, Cambridge: Cambridge University Press.

102   *K. Nash*

Davis, M. (2003) 'Introduction: Law and Pin the Pinochet case' in Davis (ed.) *The Pinochet Case: Origins, Progress, Limitations*, London: The Institute of Latin American Studies.

Forsythe, D. (2000) *Human Rights in International Relations*, Cambridge: Cambridge University Press.

Held, D. (1995) *Democracy and the Global Order: from the Modern State to Cosmopolitan Governance*, Cambridge: Polity Press.

—— (2002) 'Law of States, Law of Peoples: Three Models of Sovereignty', *Legal Theory* 8(1): 1–44.

Hirsh, D. (2003) *Law against Genocide: Cosmopolitan Trials*, London: Glasshouse Press.

Ignatieff, M. (ed.) (2005) *American Exceptionalism and Human Rights*, Princeton: Princeton University Press.

Jacobson, D. (1996) *Rights Across Borders: Immigration and the Decline of Citizenship*, Baltimore: John Hopkins University.

Jacobson, D. and Ruffer, G. (2003) 'Courts Across Borders: the Implications of Judicial Agency for Human Rights and Democracy', *Human Rights Quarterly* 25(1): 74–92.

Keck, M. and Sikkink, K. (1998) *Activists beyond Borders: Advocacy Networks in International Politics*, Ithaca, New York: Cornell University Press.

Kostakopoulou, D. (2008) *The Future Governance of Citizenship*, Cambridge: Cambridge University Press.

Krasner, S. (1999) *Sovereignty: Organized Hypocrisy*, Princeton: Princeton University Press.

Montgomery, J. (2002) 'Sovereignty in Transition' in Montgomery and Glazer (eds) *Sovereignty Under Challenge*, New Brunswick, Transaction.

Meckled-Garcia, S. and Cali, B. (2006) *The Legalization of Human Rights: Multidisciplinary Perspectives on Human Rights and Human Rights Law*, Routledge: London.

Nash, K. (2007) 'The Pinochet Case: Cosmopolitanism and Intermestic Human Rights', *The British Journal of Sociology* 58(3): 417–35.

—— (2009a) 'Dangerous Rights: Of Citizens and Humans', *Sociology*, forthcoming.

—— (2009b) *The Cultural Politics of Human Rights: Comparing the US and UK*, Cambridge: Cambridge University Press, forthcoming.

Ratner, S. and Abrams, J. (2001) *Accountability for Human Rights Atrocities in International Law: Beyond the Nuremberg Legacy*, Oxford: Oxford University Press.

Risse, T., Ropp, S. and Sikkink, K. (1999) *The Power of Human Rights: Institutional Norms and Domestic Change*, Cambridge: Cambridge University Press.

Roth, K. (2000) 'The Charade of US Ratification of International Human Rights Treaties', *Chicago Journal of International Law* 1(2): 347–54.

Soysal, Y. (1994) *Limits of Citizenship: Migrants and Postnational Membership in Europe*, Chicago: Chicago University Press.

—— (2001) 'Postnational Citizenship: Reconfiguring the Familiar Terrain', in Nash and Scott (eds) *The Blackwell Companion to Political Sociology*, Oxford: Blackwell.

Steiner, H. and Alston, P. (eds) (2000), *International Human Rights in Context: Law, Politics, Morals*, 2nd edn, Oxford: Oxford University Press.

Steinhardt, R. and D'Amato, A. (1999) (eds) *The Alien Tort Claims Act: An Analytical Anthology*, Ardsley, New York: Transnatioanal Publishers.

Stephens, B. (2004) 'Upsetting Checks and Balances: The Bush Administration's Efforts To Limit Human Rights Litigation', *Harvard Human Rights Journal* 17(Spring): 169–205.

Stephens, B. and Ratner, M. (1996) *International Human Rights Litigation in the US Courts*, New York: Transnational Publishers.

Sznaider, N. and Levy, D. (2006) 'Sovereignty Transformed: A Sociology of Human Rights', *The British Journal of Sociology* 57(4): 657–76.

Woodhouse, D. (2003) 'The Progress of Pinochet through the UK Extradition Procedure; An Analysis of the Legal Challenges and Judicial Decisions', in Davis (ed.) *The Pinochet Case: Origins, Progress, Limitations*, London: The Institute of Latin American Studies.

Legal references

Boumediene v. *Bush* 553 U.S. (2008).

Chahal v. *United Kingdom* (Application 22414/93) ECHR 54 (1996).

Filartiga v. *Pena-Irala*, 630 F.2d 876 (2nd Cir. 1980).

Hamdan v. *Rumsfeld* (126 S.Ct. 2749 2006).

Sosa v. *Alvarez-Machain* (124 S.Ct. 2739 2004).

6 Taking the sociology of human rights seriously

Anthony Woodiwiss

In the West, on the assumption that the individual is ontologically prior to the social or the collective, there appears to be a consensus amongst both advocates and critics that in the end taking human rights seriously can only mean one thing: the selective privileging of the value of the individual over the social or the collective, especially where the latter takes the form of the state. This privileging has had the tragic policy consequence that taking human rights seriously is often of little practical consequence as a mode of social amelioration. Indeed, as Upendra Baxi (2002) has argued, the ultimate effect of taking human rights seriously can all too often be to the detriment of those whom one might otherwise have thought were their intended beneficiaries. This is because many politicians and policy-makers today are strongly committed to the view that, for the sake of protecting human rights, collective or state intervention in, and management of, economic and social life should be kept to a minimum. Nothing could be further from the truth as, if a nepotistic reference may be forgiven, my brother Michael Woodiwiss has demonstrated in his recent book *Gangster Capitalism* (2005). The book is a comprehensive account of the corporate abuse of human rights in the US that results from weak or absent state regulation. The abuses he discusses include a startling array of frauds on the sick; food poisoning (a quarter of the American population experiences food poisoning every year); industrial injuries; and the massive and racially biased over-imprisonment of the poor. It is not my intention to repeat or add to this catalogue of horrors. Rather, what I wish to do is say something about the genesis of the consensus that these horrors call into question since this process involved the exclusion, albeit unknowingly, of sociology from the debate over human rights. I will then go on to present a sociological challenge to the assumption upon which the reigning consensus was constructed before ending by illustrating what it means to take the sociology of human rights seriously today.

Taking rights seriously?

In the US and Britain the intellectually most significant text in the making of the consensus that I wish to challenge was that whose title mine intentionally echoes, namely Ronald Dworkin's *Taking Rights Seriously* (1977). In the 1970s, prior to the appearance of Dworkin's book, the most influential theory of law was the restatement of what is known as Legal Positivism set out in Herbert Hart's *The Concept of Law* (1961). According to the Legal Positivists, who, to avoid confusion, it should be said are by no means necessarily also epistemological positivists, individuals only have rights insofar as they have been created by positive (that is, explicit) legal or political actions. Any suggestion that there might be rights that are naturally or morally inherent in human beings is, in words taken from Jeremy Bentham's *Anarchical Fallacies*, 'nonsense upon stilts'. This is the view that, as his title suggests, Dworkin challenged. His counter argument was that, in one way or another, and so far from promoting anarchy, those rights that are termed 'natural' and the morality they consequently carry into legal reasoning impart not just ethical significance but also an essential intellectual coherence to legal systems and indeed societies. According to Dworkin the unlegislated moral principle that provides this coherence is the idea that society owes all its members a certain 'equality of concern and respect'. However, for Hart the separation of law from morality was important not only because it made it easier to demarcate the basic lineaments of the legal, but also precisely because it preserved the idea that morality 'is something *outside* the official system, by reference to which in the last resort the individual must solve his problems of obedience' (ibid.: 206, emphasis added). By keeping law and morality separate from one another, Hart sought to preserve an autonomy for the moral sphere that would allow both the distinguishing of certain legal rights as natural rights and the possibility of criticising both this idea and the content of any particular effort to specify the rights that should be afforded this status.

In contrast, what Dworkin meant by 'taking rights seriously', given that his principle of 'equality of concern and respect' was derived from his reflections on the 'original position' set out in John Rawls's *Theory of Justice* (1972), was that liberalism was a universal ethical necessity in the sphere of governance and one moreover that legitimated many of the less capital-threatening aspects of the socialist approach to social development (for a highly influential example of the role of the work of Rawls and Dworkin in the making of the liberal consensus, see Donnelly 2003: 43ff.). Also, because his text revived philosophical interest in rights by presenting itself as a critique of Hart, Dworkin's intervention greatly reduced the likelihood that much interest might be shown in developing the approach to the study of legal phenomena such as rights that Hart had pointed towards when he wrote in the preface to *The Concept of Law*, that it could be read as 'an essay in descriptive sociology'. From my particular sociological viewpoint this was especially regrettable since, despite his unpromising formal commitment to Peter Winch's (1958) far from epistemologically positivist variant of social constructionism, Hart's sociology was far from simply descriptive, animated as it was by the following 'sobering truth':

> The step from the simple form of society, where primary rules of obligation are the only means of social control, into the legal world with its centrally organised legislature, courts, officials, and sanctions brings its solid gains at a certain cost. The gains are those of adaptability to change, certainty, and efficiency,

and these are immense; *the cost is the risk that the centrally organised power may well be used for the oppression of numbers of those with whose support it can dispense*, in a way that the simpler regime of primary rules could not.

(Hart 1961:197–8, emphasis added)

In other words, whereas Dworkin assumes that rights are the inherent property of human beings and unproblematically serve to protect them against the abuse of power, Hart acknowledges that the law and therefore rights too exist in a world where power is unequally distributed and he therefore allows the possibility that rights might embody and so be complicit with this inequality to the degree that some individuals may have no rights at all. By developing his Legal Positivist concept of law, then, Hart appears to have hoped to separate the law from liberal morality in particular and so to preserve not only the possibility of other moralities but also the law itself and therefore the concept of rights too for articulation with such other and arguably preferable moralities. In Hart's own case his preferred morality was markedly socialistic in character.

In sum, Dworkin's critique of Hart was mightily effective in reducing the likelihood that a sociology of human rights could be taken seriously: there was no need to enquire seriously into the historical genealogy or policy significance of rights thinking since philosophical speculation about some imagined 'original position' was regarded as sufficient to satisfy all but the most extreme political desires. Indeed so effective was Dworkin's text in this regard that even Hart himself in the end came to doubt the wisdom of his sociological aspirations, as Nicola Lacey (2005) has shown in her recent insightful and moving biography – of course, it should also be said that Hart was not helped by the fact that at the time sociologists had little or no interest in rights and were consequently unable to take advantage of the opportunity he had offered them. Finally, the ease with which Dworkin was able to remobilise the concept of rights on behalf of the liberal cause confirmed the immobilising belief on the part of the sociological and other rights sceptics that the category of rights was intrinsically subversive of any efforts to transcend liberal society or indeed to avoid the establishment of such a society.

All of this has proved to be particularly damaging to the causes of those who hope that history has not ended, whether because they consider liberalism to be ethically impoverished or because the insufficiently individuated character of the societies in which they live renders liberalism ineffective as a discourse of empowerment, as in the case of what might be termed the 'familialistic' societies of Asia. This has been especially so since the collapse of communism, from which moment the consequent delegitimisation of almost any kind of communitarian discourse of rule, as well as an intensified global interconnectedness, has meant that human rights discourse is now the only available, globally legitimate and secular political language that might be used to further such causes. One sign of quite how intellectually and politically disturbing the situation has become is that even sociologists, who are otherwise almost congenitally rights-sceptical, have belatedly bestirred themselves and felt obliged to begin taking rights seriously. Here I am thinking, in particular, of the work of Bryan S. Turner (1993), Johan Galtung (1994), Fred Twine (1994), and Boaventura de Sousa Santos (1995). Fortunately, and in my view at least, these sociological efforts represent clear confirmation of the old saw 'better late than never' in that the answers they have provided have made it possible once again to see that because, whilst they may be analytically separable, the individual and the social or collective are in fact mutually constitutive of one another and that rights discourse in fact remains susceptible to social-democratic and other non-liberal or communitarian as well as liberal and libertarian readings.

The two sides of human rights

What does one discover about the origins of the assumption as to the individual being ontologically prior to the social upon which the current consensus rests when one takes the sociology of human rights seriously? Reading the conventional histories as a sociologist, the first thing one is struck by is their teleological character (see Kersch 2004). This is because, and on this point I have to acknowledge that philosophers like Dworkin and indeed Donnelly are rather more sophisticated, the conventional histories present the social process involved as centring on an idea, supposedly long present in the human mind, namely freedom or liberty, that gradually gained self-conscious expression as the clouds of ignorance were burnt off by the steadily intensifying light of modernisation. By contrast, according to the classical sociological theorists, the story of rights as individual entitlements begins not in prehistory nor even with Magna Carta but with the social dislocation caused and represented by the emergence of a new form of economic organisation, namely capitalism. More specifically, and as all the classical social theorists also agree, the story begins with the need on the part of the avatars of the new economic system to find a way to establish and protect individual ownership in the course of the ever lengthening circuits of capital – from the site of production, to the market, to the bank, and back again to the site of production. As Marx says in *Capital I* (1964: 84), 'commodities cannot take themselves to market … we must therefore have recourse to their guardians': and as the great communist jurist Evgeny Pashukanis (1978: 112) commented '[t]he guardians must therefore recognize each other as owners of private property' – in other words, they must have rights.

Thus, as Hart was later to echo in the passage quoted earlier, although what was gained with the arrival of capitalism and rights were certain freedoms such as to own property in the means of production, to work, and to make contracts, what was lost as a result was any control by the propertyless over the use of their labour power and therefore any sense of control over, or security as to, their economic fate. In sum, when looked at sociologically, what the conventional story presents as a cumulative and progressive process in which one development more or less automatically led to another may be more accurately regarded as a product of an ideological hindsight that resulted in the concealment of the negative side of rights discourse.

For such key influences on the conventional histories as John Locke and all those who have followed him, liberty or freedom was an aspect of the god-given, natural condition of humanity before the existence of states, an aspect that had to be rediscovered, institutionalised and protected by the formulation of the social contract. By contrast, and as but one example, for Durkheim liberty was a very late development in human history that was the more or less accidental creation of states as they gained knowledge of their populations and tried to work out how to govern them:

> [The political economists] have, however, been mistaken as to the nature of this liberty. Since they see it as a constitutive attribute of man, since they logically deduce it from the concept of the individual in itself, it seems to them to be entirely a state of nature, leaving aside all of society. Social action, according to them, has nothing to add to it; all that it can and must do is to regulate the external functioning in such a way that the competing liberties do not harm one another. And, if it is not strictly confined within these limits, it encroaches on the legitimate domain of the individual and diminishes it. But, *besides the fact that it is false to believe that all regulation is the product of constraint, it happens that liberty itself is the product of regulation. Far from being antagonistic to social action, it results from social action.* It is far from being an inherent property of the state of nature. On the contrary, it is a conquest of society over nature.
>
> (Durkheim 1893: 386–7; see also Michel Foucault's discussions of what he terms 'governmentality' in Burchell and Gordon, 1991 (emphasis added))

All this was secured by the state's gradual confirmation and autonomisation of a more and more complex system of rights and modes of reasoning in terms of these rights which allowed individuals to protect their stakes in the emerging order; that is, by the establishment of the rule of law.

In the context of the present argument it is important to understand, in addition, that social contract theorists like Locke, against whom Durkheim was ultimately reacting, developed their ideas in opposition not only to those of feudal privilege but also in opposition to the 'communism' of radical, seventeenth-century English groups such as the Ranters and Diggers (Hill 1971) who had fashioned a very different concept of liberty. It is this fact, plus the reaction of later radicals to Locke's ideas, that converted the double-sidedness of rights discourse into a potential polyvalence. For what may be termed the 'major tradition' within rights discourse, the rights related to property and contract, represented, in the literal sense of pictured, the means (that is, owning things and making agreements) by which the essential elements of humanity's supposed primordial liberty could be preserved despite the recognition of the need for social order. By contrast, for the 'minor tradition' that was initiated by the articulation of the thought of Locke with that of the Ranters and Diggers, and was first exemplified by the Levellers, humanity's original position was governed by the principle of reciprocity rather than that of liberty. The result was that the establishment of the same rights of property and contract as were celebrated by the major tradition was represented by the minor tradition as a severe challenge to freedom in the form of the danger that reciprocity might be replaced by selfishness as the core social value. During the nineteenth century, in legal fact, if not in wider rhetorical terms, and as the minor tradition had feared, the major tradition indeed became narrowly focused on the defence and extension of property rights as the core of what became aptly known as the '*rule* of law.' Nowhere is the narrowness of this focus more clearly apparent than in the work of the originator of the concept of the 'rule of law', Alfred Venn Dicey, whose textbook, *Introduction to the Study of the Law of the Constitution*, was first published in 1885:

> The rule of law, as described in this treatise, remains to this day a distinctive characteristic of the English constitution. In England no man can be made to suffer punishment or to pay damages for any conduct not definitely forbidden by law; every man's legal rights or liabilities are almost invariably determined by the ordinary Courts of the realm, and *each man's individual rights are far less the result of our constitution than the basis on which that constitution is founded* .... It means, again, equality before the law, or the equal subjection of all classes to the ordinary law of the land administered by the ordinary Law Courts; the "rule of law" in this sense excludes the idea of any exemption of officials or others from the duty of obedience to the law which governs other citizens or from the jurisdiction of the ordinary tribunals. (From the preface (emphasis added))

The narrowness arose because the 'rights ... on which that constitution is founded' were rigorously limited to the supposedly ancient ones to 'personal freedom; the right to freedom of discussion; the right of public meeting', whose principal purpose, as Dicey subsequently insisted more and more strongly as his book went through successive editions, was keeping 'secure or sacred' a deeper layer of rights, namely 'private rights' or 'the important rights of individuals ... [that is,] property or ... the contracts of private persons'. Thus Dicey was untroubled by the fact that many laws severely limited the 'ancient rights' of the propertyless (Ewing and Gearty 2000: Chapter 1). In other words, for Dicey as for Marx, the law's constraining of the possibilities for social development arose because an economic system based on the supposedly still more ancient 'private rights' of property and contract, capitalism, rather than the individual person, had always been the sacred grounding of the law:

> The principles that guide us, in public and in private, as they are not of our devising, but moulded into the nature and the essence of things, will endure with the sun and moon—long, very long after Whig and Tory, Stuart and Brunswick [suffragist/suffragette, and anti-suffragist], and all such miserable bubbles and playthings of the hour, are vanished from existence and memory. (From the preface)

Moreover, Dicey was nothing if not consistent in that he frankly acknowledged that following such principles meant accepting all other inequalities. Hence his bitter opposition to trade union use of the freedoms of speech and association – 'the triumph of legalised wrongdoing' – as well as to the idea of enfranchising women, which he argued should be rejected because:

> it treats as insignificant for most purposes that difference of sex which, after all, disguise the matter as you will, is one of the most fundamental and far-reaching differences which can distinguish one body of human beings from another. (From the preface)

Thus, from the moment the rule of law was 'discovered', any effort to assert any rights other than those considered ancient and/or private or extend them to ordinary men and women, had to overcome an enormous disadvantage in that it appeared to challenge the rule of law and also therefore not only the god-given laws of nature and the authority of science but also and therefore, allegedly, the very idea of a just community.

Democratising rights discourse

The restoration of reciprocity to a central position alongside liberty in rights discourse did eventually occur, and therefore so did the democratisation of the rule of law. This was not, however, because of developments that originated within rights discourse and represented the working out of some immanent logic, but thanks instead to the further changes in the social and political formations of which the discourse was a part, as summarised by the emergence of trade unions, socialist parties, and social movements such as the suffragettes, all of whom may be located within the minor tradition (Mann 1993; Rueschemeyer, *et al.* 1992; Stephens 1972). As Max Weber put it:

> Rigorously formalistic and dependent on what is tangibly perceivable as far as it is *required for security to do business*, the law has at the same time become informal for the sake of business goodwill where this is required ... [and] interpreted as some '*ethical minimum*'.
>
> The law is drawn into anti-formal directions, moreover, by all those powers which demand that it be more than a mere means of pacifying conflicts of interest. These forces include *the demand for substantive justice by certain social class interests and ideologies; they also include the tendencies inherent in certain forms of political authority of either democratic or authoritarian character concerning the ends of law* ... finally, ... anti-formal tendencies are being promoted by the ideologically rooted power aspirations of the legal profession itself .... [Nevertheless] the notion must expand that the law is a rational technical apparatus, which is continually transformable in the light of expediental considerations and devoid of all sacredness of content .... All of the modern sociological and philosophical analyses ... can only contribute to strengthen this impression.
>
> (Weber 1922: 894–5 (emphasis added))

In other words, Weber, on the one hand, confirmed Marx's judgement that in the end rights exist in order to provide the 'security to do business' and, on the other hand, acknowledged that rights may also provide a means of securing what he terms an 'ethical minimum' in the conduct of such business, and as defined by the clash of class and political forces.

In this way, then, and reinforced by the general horror at the crimes of the Nazis, rights had regained at least some of their eighteenth-century popular allure by the time the US decided to join the war against fascism in 1941. Rights discourse was therefore available to provide the surprisingly inclusive language, for a mainstream American politician, that President Roosevelt used to outline the war aims of the US in his *Four Freedoms* speech of that year. This inclusive language was especially apparent when Roosevelt spoke, in the manner of the minor tradition, of freedom from want, which, to quote him, 'translated into world terms, means economic understandings which will secure to every nation a healthy peacetime life for its inhabitants – everywhere in the world'. This was also the speech in which, borrowing what was apparently an established Latin-American usage (Glendon 2003), the term 'human rights' was first used in the West as an alternative to the 'rights of man', thereby initiating international human rights discourse.

Thus, to summarise the sociological argument and contra Locke and the liberal tradition more generally, there was no original position in which it makes sense to imagine that either certain rights or indeed what we regard as freedom existed prior to power and therefore deserve any sort of privileged status. Rather, both were constituted by, and constitutive of, a new mode of social life – capitalism. However, the ideas of freedom and rights not only contributed through the major tradition to the production of the social divisions and corporate identities that we call the class system but also through the minor tradition provided much of the language that enabled these divisions and identities to be discussed and contested. This is also how rights came to be seen by the propertyless, much to Marx's annoyance (as he explained in his *Critique of the Gotha Programme*), not just as means of exercising power but also as prizes or objects of desire, so to speak: valuable prizes in that they were thought capable of enlarging the sphere of freedom and bringing the power of the state on to the winner's side; but limited prizes in that neither the value of liberty nor even that of reciprocity is necessarily antithetical to the continuing legitimacy of the inequality that is a necessary prerequisite for, as well as consequence of, the existence of capitalism (for an elaboration of this idea, see Woodiwiss 2005: Chapter 1).

The sociology of human rights

More positively, this alternative history not only challenges the key assumption upon which the reigning consensus rests by historicising and provincialising human rights but in so doing also creates the possibility of moving beyond the by now very tired and tiring debate between universalism and relativism and towards the practical realisation of what might be termed a real cosmopolitanism. For sociologists, human rights are understood to be simply means to an end and a melancholy end at that: the protection of human beings from abuses of power. Human rights, therefore, represent the tip of a social iceberg; that is, to repeat, contrary to what is argued by the natural law tradition, rights are not immanent within humanity and therefore are neither self-generating nor self-enforcing, but are instead consciously produced discursive constructs that are strongly marked by the wider sets of social relations within which they were produced and continue to be reproduced. The rights now identified as human rights were initially produced within particular national and geopolitical sets of social relations, specifically those of Western Europe, the US, and the world circa 1948, as means of reinforcing new modes of social discipline nationally and internationally. Minimally, therefore, taking the sociology of human rights seriously both allows the possibility that there may be many and varied means to achieve the same ethical end, and requires that one neither forgets the local sources and circumstances of international human rights discourse nor neglects to investigate the values and social circumstances of any new locality within which one hopes human rights may be made protectively effective.

Human rights, therefore, are nothing special but simply a subset of the much larger set of social relations that produce and enforce behavioural expectations, a subset distinguished by their legal form and their focus on the limitation of abuses of power. That is, just as there is far more in rights than law alone, so for rights to work far more than law alone is required. Thus human rights as such, and like the law in general, do not carry the whole or even much of the weight, so to speak, of ensuring that the desired social expectations are met, but simply reinforce other means of preventing and punishing abuse by making the provision of certain specific civil, political, economic, social and cultural entitlements legally enforceable. Indeed the presence of rights is therefore often a mark of some kind of social change, whether welcome or not, in that it indicates either that social expectations have changed or that pre-existing or other methods of ensuring the meeting of such expectations are no longer, or not yet, working effectively. By the same token, the absence of rights does not necessarily indicate that rights are needed since there may be no such change, and even if there is, it may not be of a kind that can be fixed by either legal innovation or the legal reinforcement of existing sets of social relations – if, for example, there is no or very little 'liberty' in everyday life, no amount of legislated liberties will magic it into existence, with the result that other means (for example, various alternative legal and institutional innovations) of achieving the desired protections and/or delivering any designated entitlements would have to be sought. For example, in societies, and there are many of them, where victims do not, as a matter of course, demand redress, those who both know that abuse has occurred and have the power to do something about it could have a duty laid upon them to both provide redress and take measures to prevent any recurrence (Kuper 2006).

Towards a more cosmopolitan future for human rights

To sociologise our understanding of human rights in this way in no way diminishes the discourse's significance. On the contrary, it reveals the discourse to be potentially much richer, more open-ended and more suggestive as to the nature of the effective localisation strategies that could make it a truly cosmopolitan discourse than is commonly recognised. In his recent and excellent study of the process whereby international human rights discourse was introduced in Malawi and of the consequences of this introduction, the anthropologist Harri Englund (2006) argues that the words used to translate human rights texts into the local language played a significant role in ensuring that the discourse would bring few benefits to the poor. Specifically, he stresses the significance of the fact that the local words used in these translations so strongly identified human rights with freedom or liberty and indeed national independence that any notion that the poor may possess certain economic, social or cultural entitlements vis-à-vis the state was excluded from the local version of the discourse. Englund's point is well made and indeed, given my ignorance of Malawi, compelling in the particular circumstances he describes. However, I fear that Englund may have missed something by giving so much significance to individual words when the discourses of which these words are a part would have been the proper object of study. This is because the meanings of individual words are often transformed when they are used in different discursive contexts. Consequently, what he may have missed is the possibility that the 'moral panics' he describes may be read as prefiguring a distinctively local form of human rights discourse rather than simply underlining the need to ensure that economic and social rights are given the same attention as civil and political rights.

The point about discourses as a whole rather than individual words being the proper object of study derives from my own experience of, and difficulties with, trying to understand the wider social significance of local translations of rights texts originally written in English. I will now briefly describe this experience by telling a story against myself before outlining some of the more general conclusions I drew from it. What initially seduced me into undertaking a prolonged study of Japanese labour rights was the fact that, although the texts in which they are specified are pretty literal translations of American statutes, because of the very different discursive and social contexts to be found in Japan the result of putting them into practice was the creation of a system of industrial justice that was entirely different from the American original. For example, the same provisions concerning 'unfair labour practices' that have never, or not until very recently, provided any protection to American employees against unfair dismissals not only rather rapidly came to provide such protection in Japan but were also developed by the Japanese Supreme Court to provide a presumptive right to lifetime employment. In 1992, I published a book entitled *Law, Labour and Society in Japan: From Repression to Reluctant Recognition.* In it I argued that what was distinctive about Japanese society in general and its labour law system in particular was the fact that both the society and the labour law system were ordered and legitimated by a 'phoney, patriarchalist communitarianism' that I termed *Kigyoshugi* or '*Enterprisism*'.

Today, I would stick by *Kigyoshugi* and 'patriarchalist communitarianism' but drop '*phoney*'. And the reason I would drop 'phoney' is because of an article written by two area studies specialists, one a specialist in Japan and the other a specialist in Germany (Kettler and Tickney 1996). Sensitised by their knowledge of Weimer labour law and its academic influence in early postwar Japan, what they discovered was something that I, and indeed everyone else working in the Japanese industrial relations area, had missed. This was that the central and most profoundly communitarian component of what is known as the *Japanese Employment System*, namely lifetime employment, was not a product of bargaining between unions and companies, as had been hitherto assumed, but had in fact been fashioned by the Japanese Supreme Court as it wrestled with the problem of 'unfair dismissal' during the 1950s: employee loyalty requires that the company reciprocate by doing its very best to avoid laying people off. Why had I not seen this, even though I had been very keen to discover instances of judicial autonomy in doctrinal matters? Well, simply because I did not have the local knowledges, chiefly linguistic and historical, of Kettler and Tickney. More specifically, lacking *Nihongo*, I depended on translations of cases selected and made by others in order to go beyond the secondary literature in my knowledge of Japanese labour law. More specifically still, I depended on a very large collection of translations kindly given to me by a leading American legal academic, William Gould, who went on to be the chair of the National Labor Relations Board in President Clinton's first term: a very distinguished labour lawyer then, but in a jurisdiction, the US, where at the federal level at least there is no such thing as 'unfair dismissal', which explains why he had had no pertinent Japanese cases translated. Chief amongst the general conclusions I drew from this experience was the conviction that, in the human rights sphere as in any other, a close understanding of localities – in the case just discussed of Germany, Japan and the US – is essential if one wishes to understand the global.

What, several years later, finally enabled me to 'cash in', so to speak, my hard-won knowledge of the local in the global and argue that the Japanese system of industrial justice was part of a distinctive human rights regime (Woodiwiss 1998), was the realisation that the anti-naturalistic and pluralistic conception of juridical or legal relations set out in Wesley Hohfeld's classic text, *Fundamental Legal Conceptions* (1919), could be used sociologically to distinguish and therefore, by implication, to design human rights discourses that could achieve the same protective aims in the diverse ways appropriate to different social contexts. According to Hohfeld, and I have changed his nomenclature slightly, rights may be understood as discursively defined clusters of: 'liberties' to perform certain actions; 'claims' or expectations vis-à-vis specified others; 'powers' that allow legal subjects to assume certain specified roles and change certain social relations; and 'immunities' against prosecution and/or civil suit when pursuing ends that are otherwise defined as illegal.

What this suggested to me was that, provided democracy and the rule of law are present (for an explanation of this requirement, see Woodiwiss 2003), human rights may be effective policy instruments despite, or indeed because of, their uneven development along one or more of these dimensions. That is, given the mutually implicatory character of the different dimensions of rights and the similarity of the protective outcomes that can be achieved, and although liberties etc. are ultimately irreducible to one another, the more, so to speak, there is of one, the less need there is for the others. To elaborate, if liberties are clearly and broadly defined, there is less need for their implications in terms of claims or whatever to be spelt out, since the existence of the latter are juridically and socially implied, albeit as a last resort in order to enable people to exercise their liberties. Thus even the ultraliberal US has some sort of social safety net. Likewise, if claims, for example, are clearly and broadly defined, there is less need for their implications in terms of liberties or whatever to be spelt out, since acceptance of the existence of claims against another juridically and socially implies acceptance of one's liberty to require their satisfaction from that other, albeit again as a last resort as seems to be the case in Japan. Neither the institutions through which claims are delivered nor the social behaviours directly protected as claims are the same as those that deliver, and are protected as, liberties but a similar protective effect is achieved – for example, in the case of the Japanese as opposed to the American industrial relations system, enterprise rather than craft or industrial unions represent employees and conflicts are more often resolved by mediation or conciliation than by strikes or lockouts. The similarity of protective effects occurs because, whereas liberties allow one to try to force a limitation on the freedom of the more powerful, claims achieve the same limitation on the powerful by imposing a prior duty or obligation on them. Given the particular cultural and social-structural circumstances obtaining in Japan, notably the continuing importance of the hierarchical principle, the latter mode of limitation is one that is much more widely supported, and indeed more safely insisted upon, than might be the case if employees had only their liberties to rely on.

It is, then, because of the realisation of the sociological pertinence of this system of differences in how rights may be written and the equivalencies in the outcomes that have nevertheless been achieved that I regard international human rights discourse as in fact far richer and more open-ended than is conventionally supposed. That is, what the equivalencies with regard to protective outcomes allow are translations between differently configured and institutionalised discourses of rights. More specifically still what, in turn, these equivalencies allow today, provided again that democracy and the rule of law are present, is that a discourse that was originally configured in terms of the liberties that have proved to be reasonably effective in protecting Americans in a society where individualism dominates the value system and there is ready access to the court system, may be translated into discourses configured in terms that stress claims, powers or immunities where other values are dominant and non-legal institutions are more salient in terms of providing means of enforcement.

I will now briefly outline some of the legal/social ideal types revealed or made thinkable by comparative historical sociology and which are what make such translations possible (Woodiwiss 2003: Chapters 3 and 4). Systems configured in terms that stress claims appear to be particularly appropriate, albeit for rather different reasons and consequently in rather different ways, not only in developed hierarchical societies such as Japan where the dominant value is familialism and the company is the key social institution, as we have seen, but also in Western European social democracies where the dominant value is social partnership and there is a solidaristic welfare state. Systems configured in terms that stress immunities appear to be particularly appropriate in societies where particular social groups are otherwise totally dominant as in Britain in the late nineteenth century where these dominant values were nevertheless contested and the legislature consequently became the critical social institution. And finally, systems configured in terms that stress powers may in time prove to be particularly appropriate in states, as in much of Sub-Saharan Africa, where collectivist values and kinship relations retain their importance. In sum, the differences between different rights regimes are neither accurately nor most usefully thought of in terms of the relative importance of different kinds of rights (that is, civil and political or economic and social) but instead are best understood in terms of different forms of discourse and their modes of institutionalisation.

The polyvalence of human rights discourse that has resulted from the reactions to their double-edged character, plus the prizes the discourse promises mean that there remains something to fight over and for in the sphere of human rights. Indeed, the discourse's referential ambiguity – does it refer to the major tradition's liberty or to the minor tradition's combination of liberty and reciprocity? – has anyway made it a veritable engine of challenges not only to economic and political power but also to the human rights status quo itself. That is, disagreements over the meaning of the central human rights texts have regularly led to subaltern groups finding something to fight for as they have attempted, to use Galtung's (1994) formulation, to arraign various structural relationships before the court of public opinion. Thus, in the 1960s, non-white peoples, including many from newly independent countries, asked themselves if the discourse applied equally to them and, on finding that it did not do so explicitly enough, set about ensuring that it would do so in the future by successfully campaigning for the International Convention on the Elimination of All Forms of Racial Discrimination (ICEARD). Moreover, asking the same question initiated the most often rather less successful campaigns for recognition on behalf of women, children, sexual minorities, the informationally excluded, developing countries, and non-Western cultures more generally.

In my view, and despite the failures just mentioned, the case for the continuation of a rights-based and indeed legally focused strategy for social amelioration inspired by the minor tradition still remains compelling because the most important source of the social dislocations/failures that are the primary causes of abusive behaviour today is the globalisation of the same disruptive capitalism that spawned rights discourse in the first place. However, to say that capitalism is globalising means that even the supposedly already universalistic discourse of human rights is now being expected to work in very different social circumstances from those in which it originated. Putting aside the critical and indeed criticisable aspects of their position, the proponents of Asian Values have pointed to social order, hierarchy, benevolence, duty, and loyalty – a value complex I have termed patriarchalism or familialism – as additional or alternative sources of virtue, and therefore of rights and wrongs. In my view (Woodiwiss 1998, 2003), if not always that of the original proponents, such values ought to be incorporated into international human rights discourse if it is to be regarded as more truly cosmopolitan and therefore to work for the global majority.

Some of these virtues, notably those validating social order and hierarchy, already inform international human rights discourse. Thus it is well established that rights should not endanger social order and, as I indicated earlier, the very idea of rights assumes, and to that degree validates, the existence of hierarchies that may result in abuse, most obviously those hierarchies intrinsic to capitalism (see also Woodiwiss 2005: Chapter 1) – after all, why else would protection be necessary? However, thanks to the anti-familialist stance of the early social contract theorists, to colonialism and to the pernicious concept of tradition ('pernicious' because it automatically represents non-Western societies as in some sense backward or inferior when compared to 'modern' Western societies), the other and more positive non-Western values related to the principle of reciprocity still have no place in international human rights discourse. As a result no protection is available when states or superiors more generally in familialist societies fail to do their duty, act benevolently, or reward loyalty, since they may justify their failures on the basis that any such actions on their part are discretionary. Nevertheless, the fact remains that the majority of the world's population, and not simply people living in Asia, still depends for protection, not on the law but upon the consistent enactment of such benevolence etc. and therefore on the underlying vivacity of the values that inform them (cf. Asad 1997: 285). This suggests two things. First, that economic and social institutions as well as civil, political and legal institutions (that is, through innovations in the economic and social spheres as well as the establishment of democracy and the rule of law) should be developed to promote and *enforce* benevolence and dutiful behaviour on the part of the powerful in Asia and elsewhere. And second, that to exclude these values from international human rights discourse is both to diminish the local effectiveness of so-called 'traditional' modes of governance and to deny to the global majority what little protection global human rights institutions can provide.

Before concluding, I would like to anticipate and respond to two possible objections to this part of my argument. The first objection is that familialist values, for example, are inherently antithetical to those articulated as human rights. Here I simply wish to point out that this objection appears to have been effectively countered by the arguments associated with the 'responsibilities approach' (Kuper 2005; O'Neill 1996). The latter stresses the duties of the state and the powerful more generally, on the grounds that, as again Hohfeld explained, every right, including those that take the form of liberties, implies a duty on the part of those who are in a position to do something to support its realisation. The second objection is that these values are inherently antithetical to the commitment to gender equality that is part of the human rights canon. Here my response is to agree with Carol Gould (2004) when she points out that the feminist notion of an ethics and politics of care (Robinson 1999) also has its roots in the originally patriarchalist values of benevolence and reciprocity. More specifically, Gould has derived from these values a non-gendered ethic of 'receptivity' which 'refers to responsiveness to others in terms of their individual differences and needs' (Gould 2004: 101) that is to me richly suggestive as regards how familialist and feminist values might be reconciled with one another.

Conclusion

According to this sociologist at least, the normative choice one is confronted with when considering how to go about localising human rights is not that between two kinds of rights but rather between different ways of writing and institutionalising both kinds of rights. The challenge, then, is to discover or invent ways in which rights originally written and institutionally delivered as liberties may be rewritten and institutionally delivered as claims or whatever. Fortunately, human social inventiveness is such that we already have available a huge inventory, drawn from the past as well as the present, of statutory forms and institutional modalities to refer to in search of inspiration (for samples from this inventory see Coomans 2007).

My argument has been that, by following Dworkin in fusing the law and morality, the reigning consensus has both obscured the role of non-liberal intellectual traditions and social movements in the making of human rights discourse and, perhaps unintentionally, attempted to exclude such traditions and movements from contributing to its future development. What I hope I have shown in my work as a whole and at least suggested in this paper is that when one takes the sociology of human rights seriously, it is possible to see that ever since the seventeenth century, and thanks to social groups integral to capitalist societies such as the small farmers who produced the Levellers of the English Civil War period, the political reformers and trades unionists of the nineteenth and twentieth centuries, and today's myriad social movements, there has always been and remains a polyvalence to rights discourse. That is, there has always been and remains far more to human rights today than civil and political freedoms, unquestionably valuable though such freedoms are, and this more includes economic, social and cultural entitlements that impose duties and responsibilities on the powerful and into whose terms, moreover, civil and political freedoms can be translated (Woodiwiss 2003). Indeed it may even be said that, on occasion, achieving respect for individual human rights may require and therefore mean the selective privileging of the collective over the individual.

Where Dworkin found moral consensus, a source of coherence, and acceptance of the capitalist ordering of social relations within past and present rights discourse, I have found moral division, ambiguity and a desire for social transformation. Thus it should not be necessary to provide justifications for the existence of economic, social and cultural rights and still less for their indivisibility from civil and political rights, intellectually impressive and convincing though many of these may be (see for example, Shue 1996 and Gould 2004), since the legitimacy of their inclusion in the human rights canon is simply a matter of descriptive sociological fact. In other words, whatever the Bush administration may have said to the contrary (Whelan 2005), because what one might term the ownership of rights discourse has long since passed from the US to the global community and from individuals to collectivities, the ultimate consequences of taking the sociology of human rights seriously would be very radical indeed. Quite how radical may be illustrated by the conclusion drawn, in terms that echo those of President Roosevelt in 1941, by George Kent in his recent study of the right to adequate food: 'you do not solve the hunger problem by feeding people – that only perpetuates it. The problems of hunger and malnutrition can only be solved by ensuring that people can live in dignity by having decent opportunities to provide for themselves' (Kent 2005: 4; see also Thomas Pogge 2002). It is therefore difficult to avoid the conclusion that solving the world's hunger problem would imply redistributing the world's wealth and facilitating the free movement of labour. Although the necessity of such measures does not necessarily imply the ending of capitalism, it does indicate that thinking in terms of human rights could yet have far more radical consequences than are imagined or indeed allowed by the liberal consensus, but only because the moral autonomy Hart so valued has been preserved. How, then, could it ever have been even implied that Hart did not take rights seriously?

Bibliography

Asad, T. (1996) 'On Torture, or Cruel, Inhuman, and Degrading Treatment', *Social Research*, 63(14): 1081–1109.

Beckmann, G. (1957) *The Making of the Meiji Constitution*, Lawrence: University of Kansas.

Burchell, G. and Gordon, C. (eds) (1991) *The Foucault Effect: Studies in Governmentality*, London: Harvester Wheatsheaf.

Coomans, F. (2006) *Justiciability of Economic and Social Rights: Experiences from Domestic Systems*, Intersentia, Antwerp.

Dicey, A. V. (1885) *Introduction to the Law of the Constitution*, London: Palgrave-MacMillan.

Donnelly, J. (2003) *Universal Human Rights in Theory and Practice*, 2nd edn, Ithaca: Cornell University Press.

Dworkin, R. (1977) *Taking Rights Seriously*, London: Duckworth.

Englund, H. (2006) *Prisoners of Freedom: Human Rights and the African Poor*, University of California Press, Berkeley.

Felice, W. (2004) *The Global New Deal: Economic and Social Human Rights in World Politics*, Lanham: Rowman and Littlefield.

Galtung, J. (1994) *Human Rights in Another Key*, Cambridge: Polity Press.

Glendon, M. A. (2003) 'The Forgotten Crucible: the Latin American Influence on the Universal Human Rights Idea', *Harvard Human Rights Journal*, 17: 27–40.

Gould, C. (2004) *Globalizing Democracy and Human Rights*, Cambridge: Cambridge University Press.

Hart, H. L. A. (1961) *The Concept of Law*, Oxford: Oxford University Press.

Hill, C. (1971) *World Turned Upside Down*, Harmondsworth: Penguin.

Hohfeld, W. (1919) *Fundamental Legal Conceptions as Applied in Judicial Reasoning*, New Haven, CT: Yale University Press.

Kennedy, D. (2004) *The Dark Sides of Virtue: Reassessing International Humanitarianism*, Princeton: Princeton University Press.

Kent, G. (2005) *Freedom from Want: The Human Right to Adequate Food*, Washington DC: Georgetown University Press.

Kersch, K. (2004) *Constructing Civil Liberties: Discontinuities in the Development of American Constitutional Law*, Cambridge: Cambridge University Press.

Kuper, A. (ed.) (2005) *Global Responsibilities: Who Must Deliver on Human Rights?*, Abingdon: Routledge.

Lacey, N. (2005) *A Life of H. L. A. Hart: The Nightmare and the Noble Dream*, Oxford: Oxford University Press.

Mann, M. (1993) *The Sources of Social Power, vol.2, the Rise of Classes and Nation-States, 1760–1914*, Cambridge: Cambridge University Press.

Marx, Karl (1964) *Capital*, Volume 1, London: Lawrence and Wishart.

—— (1977 [1875]) *Critique of the Gotha Programme*, Delhi: Progress Publishers.

Neary, I. (2002) *Human Rights in Japan, South Korea and Taiwan*, Abingdon: Routledge.

O'Neill, O. (1996) *Towards Justice and Virtue*, Cambridge: Cambridge University Press.

Pashukanis, E. B. (1978) *Law and Marxism*, London: Ink Links.

Pogge, T. (2002) *World Poverty and Human Rights*, Cambridge: Polity.

Rawls, J (1972) *A Theory of Justice*, Oxford: Clarendon Press.

Robinson, F. (1999) *Globalizing Care*, Boulder: Westview Press.

Rose, N. (1999) *Powers of Freedom*, Cambridge: Cambridge University Press.

Rueschemeyer, D., Stephens, E., and Stephens, J. (1992) *Capitalist Development and Democracy*, Cambridge: Polity Press.

Santos, B. de S (1995) *Toward a New Commonsense: Law, Politics and Science in a Paradigmatic Transition*, New York: Routledge.

Shue, H. (1996) *Basic Rights: Subsistence, Affluence and U.S. Foreign Policy*, Princeton: Princeton University Press.

Stephens, J. (1979) *The Transition from Capitalism to Socialism*, London: Macmillan.

Turner, B. S. (1993) 'Outline of a Theory of Human Rights', *Sociology*, 27(3): 489–512.

Twine, F. (1994) *Citizenship and Social Rights*, London: Sage.

Whelan, D. (2005) 'The United States and Economic and Social Rights: Past, Present and Future', Human Rights and Human Welfare, Working Paper 26.

Woodiwiss, A. (1990) *Rights v. Conspiracy: A Sociological Essay on the History of Labour Law in the United States*, Oxford: Berg.

—— (1992) *Law, Labour and Society in Japan*, Abingdon: Routledge.

—— (1998) *Globalisation, Human Rights and Labour Law in Pacific Asia*, Cambridge: Cambridge University Press.

—— (2003) *Making Human Rights Work Globally*, London: Routledge-Cavendish.

—— (2005) *Human Rights*, Abingdon: Routledge.

Woodiwiss, M. (2005) *Gangster Capitalism*, London: Constable.

7 Forging indigenous rights at the United Nations

A social constructionist account

Rhiannon Morgan

Overview

In September 2007, following nearly three decades of intensive negotiations between independent human rights experts, Member States of the United Nations (UN), and indigenous peoples' representatives, the UN General Assembly adopted the UN Declaration on the Rights of Indigenous Peoples. The declaration contains a right of indigenous peoples to self-determination, and substantially reflects the aspirations of indigenous lawyers, leaders, and community representatives participating in its production, who constitute members of a global indigenous movement. Focusing in particular on a strategy of legal or normative mobilisation, this chapter explores the role of the global indigenous movement in shaping the form and content of the declaration, and particularly in persuading a majority of Member States to accept the inclusion in the declaration of Article 3 on the right to self-determination. It therefore contributes to an understanding of the social construction of human rights, by which human rights come into being following negotiations and contest between assorted social and political actors with diverse and conflicting interests and means of asserting power or influence. This case highlights not only the important role of social movements in the contemporary construction of human rights, but also the potential strategic value of already existing institutional logics and norms for social movements seeking to influence the emergence of new specifications of human rights.

Introduction

In the last 50 years or so, the human rights doctrine has emerged as an organising principle of truly global relevance. In this period, and both reflecting and promoted by diverse processes of globalisation, we have witnessed the combined expansion of a global legal framework for promoting and protecting human rights and the global diffusion of a human rights culture, as human rights have become the pre-eminent discourse of normative evaluation, political mobilisation, and social justice in the contemporary world (Soysal 1994), as well as a principal discourse of governance (Baxi 2002; Ignatieff 2001). The expansion of the international human rights regime has been dramatic to say the least, and has even engendered discussion regarding the possible 'overproduction' of human rights (e.g. Baxi 2001, 2002; Landman 2006). It has taken place in part as transnational social movement organisations (TSMOs) and non-governmental organisations (NGOs) mobilising in and around supra-national institutions have sought to create new categories of rights and to attach rights to new subjects and objects, contributing to the evolution of what is a changing, flexible, and responsive system that develops over time (Messer 1997). One vivid illustration of the changing nature and evolution of this system is the recent development of a global legal repertoire addressing indigenous peoples' rights, which finds its most concrete form in the International Labour Organization Convention (ILO) No. 169 on Indigenous and Tribal Peoples in Independent Countries (ILO 1989) and the UN Declaration on the Rights of Indigenous Peoples (United Nations 2007). Indigenous rights are attached to collectives rather than individuals, and represent a dramatic example of the way in which contestations over rights call into question long established understandings of the nature of rights.

The process of production of the UN Declaration on the Rights of Indigenous Peoples has evolved over a protracted period, and in three main institutional stages. The first was between 1985 and 1993, when the UN Working Group on Indigenous Populations (UN WGIP), a group of independent human rights experts, formulated the Draft UN Declaration on the Rights of Indigenous Peoples of 1994 (United Nations 1994). The second, from 1996 to 2006, saw a change in institutional context as the Draft Declaration was diverted into an inter-sessional working group of the Commission on Human Rights (UN WGDD) for further review. Comprised of the representatives of 53 Member States, the UN WGDD held its last session from 30 January to 3 February 2006, following which the newly constituted UN Human Rights Council adopted by Resolution 2006/2 the UN Declaration on the Rights of Indigenous Peoples and recommended its adoption by the General Assembly (United Nations 2006a). After some delay, the Declaration was finally adopted by the General Assembly on 13 September 2007. The text of the declaration recognises the right of indigenous peoples to self-determination (United Nations 2007: Article 3), which is the 'central tenet and main symbol of the indigenous movement' (Daes 2000: 303).

The case of the development of a global framework addressing indigenous peoples' rights presents a compelling illustration of the dynamism and inherently flexible character of rights. It also dramatically exemplifies the connection between human rights and human rights movements, which Baxi (2002) argues is a particular feature of 'contemporary' human rights, the authorship of which is increasingly inclusive and marked by the participation of non-state actors in negotiations with constellations of states. The UN in particular has since the 1970s progressively deepened the extent of NGO participation in its policy and law-making processes,[1] though to a lesser or greater extent the majority of supra-national institutions now grant access to NGOs representing the socially disadvantaged. The production of indigenous peoples' rights within the UN system has been characterised by unprecedented levels of participation by the representatives of indigenous peoples' organisations, who have engaged in extensive 'human rights work' (Plummer 2006) to construct rights appropriate to their specific circumstances and forms of suffering. This chapter explores a central feature of that human rights work, namely a strategy based on evoking the existing normative context, and its role in the emergence of a comprehensive set of standards addressing indigenous peoples' rights.

Social constructionism and foundationalism

To say that human rights are socially constructed is to recognise that ideas and institutions of human rights are produced following a competitive process between social and political actors located in different times and places. It is to conceive of specifications of human rights as socially and historically bound products of struggle and interaction between human actors with conflicting interests in particular socio-historical settings characterised by specific social conditions and thought. Put succinctly by Stammers (1995: 488), it is to say that 'ideas and practices concerning human rights are created by people in particular historical, social, and economic circumstances'. Such a claim is relatively uncontroversial amongst social scientists, who have tended to view human rights as social inventions attached to individuals by external forces. In much of mainstream praxis, however, and particularly amongst human rights lawyers, NGO activists, and other proponents of human rights, there is a tendency to talk about human rights in terms not dissimilar to those used by historical theorists of natural rights, that is, as natural, inalienable, and inviolable, and existing in all persons whether or not they are formally recognised or enjoyed. From a social constructionist perspective, the idea that human rights are natural phenomena existing external to political engagements is itself a social and political construction, with roots stretching back to the late seventeenth century and the natural law theories of John Locke, which found a metaphysical basis for rights in 'God' and 'nature'.

In spite of a preference amongst social scientists of various disciplines to talk about human rights as socially constructed institutions, theoretically and empirically the study of human rights as a social and political project has been relatively neglected. The closest we have to an attempt to theorise the social construction of human rights is offered by Waters (1996), who identifies the critical role of political interests in their formation. He argues that the core assumption of a social constructionist theory of human rights must be that 'the institutionalisation of rights is a product of the balance of power between political interests' (ibid.: 595). Focusing on the construction of the Universal Declaration of Human Rights (UDHR) of 1948, he explains its human rights specifications by reference to four sets of interests: the interests of the Allies in stigmatising and penalising the defeated Axis powers following their victory in World War II; the interests of Cold Warriors in seeking to undermine each other's legitimacy; the interests of superpowers in justifying intervention in the internal affairs of other states; and the interests of disadvantaged groups in claiming protection from the abusive actions of states (ibid.: 597). An important contribution, Waters' account of the historical origins of the UDHR nevertheless suffers from being both state-centric and realist in that it places states and their 'egoistic' interests (Donnelly 1998: 9) at the centre of the construction of human rights. It also privileges powerful states over small or traditionally less powerful states, therefore overlooking the important contributions of less visible but nevertheless influential actors in the construction of the UDHR, including Muslim states (Waltz 2001, 2004) and Third World states (Rajagopal 2003). Further, it is reductivist regarding the influence that the recent memory of the Holocaust played in the creation of what has become the cornerstone document of international human rights theory and practice, and the need for the Allies to somehow morally respond through the articulation of strong human rights principles to what is described in the preamble to the UDHR as the 'outraged conscience of mankind' (Levy and Sznaider 2004). In this respect, then, Waters fails to do justice to the normative dimensions of its construction. Finally, Waters underestimates the role of ordinary individuals and social movements representing the socially disadvantaged in the construction of the UDHR, whose interests and influence he mentions but radically underplays (see e.g. Korey 1998).

This article makes no attempt to offer a social constructionist model of human rights. It does, however, draw attention to the role of social movements as agents in respect of human rights, and suggests an account of their present-day construction that involves a diversity of protagonists, or what Landman (2006: 19) terms 'human rights organizational fields' beyond elite entities such as nation-state governments and their respective inter-governmental assemblages and institutions. Exactly *who* is included in the authorship of human rights is critical to understanding the form in which they emerge, and their relationship to extant relations and structures of power (Stammers 1999). This article also suggests an account of the construction of conceptions of human rights that, alongside interests, emphasises the role of norms in the emergence of new specifications of human rights, and that particularly highlights their usefulness in supporting and legitimising the claims of social movement organisations (SMOs) and NGOs seeking to reshape the contours of human rights. As I will demonstrate in this article, the representatives of indigenous peoples have evoked the memory of colonial genocide and the ongoing reality of ethnocide and discrimination experienced by indigenous peoples as 'a frame of reference justifying action' (Levy and Sznaider 2004: 1), but they have also been empowered in their campaign to persuade states and inter-governmental organisations to write new norms into international law by already existing human rights logics and principles. These inhere in international law and institutions, and have a significant impact upon processes of construction of human rights because they inform expectations of state behaviour and constitute standards that Member States are concerned to uphold.

Though my preference in this article is to explain the social construction of a particular set of human rights in a particular time and place, the adoption of a social constructionist perspective is not to deny the possibility or value of finding a foundationalist ontology for human rights, meaning some shared or universal characteristic(s) of humankind that might serve to justify the existence of human rights. Whereas there is evidently a problem connecting accounts of the social construction of human rights with an understanding of human rights that views them as metaphysical abstractions existing entirely independently of any social or political context, there is, in my view, no necessary incompatibility between recognising that ideas and practices of human rights are socially constructed while at the same time committing to the search for their justification. Foundationalist and social constructionist approaches are, however, frequently considered to be in opposition (e.g. Waters 1996), a consequence of the fact that, certainly in political theory and philosophy, foundationalist arguments are often based upon forms of metaphysical abstraction and *do* in fact constitute a form of reification, by which I refer to the mistaken collapse of the social into the natural (Lukacs 1971). A justification for human rights, however, need neither reify human rights nor romanticise either the reasons why we need them or the human beings that hold them. Turner (1993, 1997, 2006; Turner and Rojek 2001), for example, argues that universal foundations for human rights can be found in the universal condition of human vulnerability as derived from our bodily frailty and the social precarious-ness of institutions.

Foundationalist and social constructionist approaches to human rights comple-ment each other in important ways. Social constructionist approaches benefit from the ability to describe the origins and development of human rights institutions in both their local and global manifestations, to relate them to social forces in the form of social movements, NGOs, or other social change vehicles, and to explain historical and cultural variations in conceptions of human rights. They also benefit from being able to reveal the configurations of interests and power relations that lie behind human rights institutions, thereby exposing the potentially 'sustaining' dimensions of human rights in respect of relations and structures of power (Stammers 1999; see also Baxi 2002; Woodiwiss 2005). Foundationalist approaches, on the other hand, provide social scientists with the means to go beyond descriptive accounts of the practices around human rights and to engage in normative evaluation of human rights abuses. They also enable us to defend human rights via appeal to moral discourse. This is particularly important to the extent that human rights appear to be open to continual contestation and dismantling, as we have seen, for example, in the recent erosion of basic civil and political rights in the US, Australia, and the UK in the context of the so-called 'War on Terror.' As Bobbio (1996: xi) has put it, 'human rights are established gradually, not all at the same time, *and not for ever*' (my emphasis). My focus here on social constructionism should not therefore be read as implying that foundationalist accounts are not also important.

The emergence of the global indigenous movement, globalisations, and human rights

The historical roots of indigenous rights stretch back to the era of European expan-sion in the sixteenth to eighteenth centuries, which for the majority of indigenous peoples marked the beginning of a long history of genocide, ethnocide, and imposed policies of assimilation resulting in cultural erosion, but it is not until the early 1970s that we can trace the emergence of a global indigenous movement articulating a set of claims in terms of human rights. This was a decade in which indigenous communities, both on their own account and on the instigation of North American and European advocacy organisations, came increasingly to foster relationships and networks with each other and to organise into national and international political organisations with an international strategy. Its emergence at this time can be understood in relation to a number of new political and legal opportunities (Tarrow 1994), but what we also see from early campaign materials is that the 1970s was a period of renewed incentive and urgency for indigenous peoples facing what Maybury-Lewis (1984) has called 'the second conquest', that is, increasing penetration of the forces of predatory globalisation and global capitalism into indigenous lands and territories (Brysk 2000; Mander and Tauli-Corpuz 2006; Rodriquez-Garavito and Arenas 2005; Santos 2002). A process well documented elsewhere (e.g. Howitt, *et al.* 1996), 'globalisation as commodification' (Brysk 2002) has seen even the most remote indigenous territories opened to development and extractive projects, seriously threatening the continued existence of indigenous ways of life and cultures and instilling even greater urgency into collective efforts to protect them. At the same time, such efforts have been supported by those more benign or empowering dimensions of globalisation, notably the rise of global media and the diffusion of global telecommunications and computer networking technology enabling the exchange of information, passage of norms, and formation of new identities amongst even geographically dispersed populations (Bob 2002; Brysk 2002; Weyker 2002). In this way, exploration of the global indigenous movement illustrates the threats and opportunities generated by the process of globalisation, and the confrontation between forms of so-called hegemonic and counter-hegemonic globalisation (Santos and Rodriquez-Garavito 2005).

Focusing on the internationalisation of indigenous politics and its orientation towards the UN and international law also highlights the difference between citizenship rights and human rights. While human rights are generally or often enacted within the context of nation-states and in the form of citizenship rights, they are in fact extra-governmental or supra-societal in that they are products of international normative consensus, gain their legitimacy beyond the state (Turner 1993), and in theory if not always in practice are constraining on the actions of nation-states, making them less sovereign or autonomous in matters concerning violations of human rights. They therefore provide an indispensable resource for those groups like indigenous peoples whose treatment at the hands of states is such that it necessitates appealing to supra-national norms and authorities as a means to counter repressive state actions defined in terms of national interests. Human rights are also universal, whereas citizenship rights can function as a tool of exclusion or social closure for those defined by the state as non-citizens (Brubaker 1992), a category that has historically included women, slaves, Jews, blacks, indigenous peoples, and which increasingly today consists of migrants, asylum seekers, and refugees. Inclusion into formal or undifferentiated citizenship regimes, moreover, may be harmful for certain groups, indigenous peoples being a prime example. The extension of equal rights of citizenship to indigenous individuals without a corollary policy of accommodating indigenous peoples' collective and community-based demands for local autonomy, including over their lands and territories, has been shown to be particularly damaging for indigenous peoples, leading to demands for a redefinition of citizenship (e.g. Yashar 2005) in part via an appeal to a reformed discourse of human rights capable of dealing with the claims of indigenous peoples.

For some writers on international law, human rights discourse offers limited promise for aspirations framed in terms other than those based on a liberal conception of politics. Rajagopol (2003), for example, argues that human rights discourse is incapable of understanding or acknowledging certain violations, for example those caused by the market as opposed to the state. The liberal paradigm, according to which rights are of course held by individuals, has been central to states' resistance to indigenous rights, but with time the indigenous movement has effectively articulated an alternative conception of rights based on a collective understanding of entitlements and identity. The indigenous case therefore illustrates the flexibility of the international human rights system, if also the glacial progress of negotiations involving states in a reconceptualisation of rights that collide with the liberal paradigm. Another related concern with legal- or rights-based strategies, expressed by both sociolegal scholars and sociologists writing on social movements, is that they present a co-optive trap for social movements and a turn away from anti-systemic discourse (e.g. Costain 1992; Walby 2002). Again, however, what is suggested by the indigenous case is that claims developed in close relation to institutional discourses and declarations can be anti-systemic where they seek a reapplication of already existing rights to new subjects. The movement's central claim for the right to self-determination is drawn from the UN's own legal arsenal, but it is also one that has been perceived as implicating a variety of state interests when applied to indigenous peoples. What this case also reveals is that far from constraining movements, rights strategies that start from the existing legal canon but that expose its vulnerable points and take advantage of its normative content can prove highly effectual in struggles for social change. In what immediately follows, I discuss states' interests in relation to the legal and political claims of indigenous peoples, focusing particularly on self-determination, before exploring strategies based on manipulating the normative context.

Claims and interests: self-determination versus state sovereignty

The text of the UN Declaration on the Rights of Indigenous Peoples contains 46 Articles recognising a wide range of collective rights including protections from genocide and forced assimilation, rights of indigenous peoples to their lands and territories, rights to cultural integrity, and rights to establish their own political, social, economic, and legal institutions (United Nations 2007: e.g. Articles 7, 8, 25, 26, 27, 28, 29, 30, 34, 4, 12, 13, 14), but for indigenous political activists congregating in and around the UN the most important right therein is Article 3 containing self-determination. An acclaimed UN rule, self-determination is broadly speaking a principle concerned with human freedom, and grounded in the idea that peoples should be free to control their own destinies without undue interference.

In the context of indigenous peoples, it includes interrelated political, economic, social, and cultural elements and has been identified as a 'prerequisite for the enjoyment of all other rights and freedoms' (Moses 2000: 156) and as the means by which indigenous peoples may determine the nature and extent of their relationship with the state and maintain control over their institutions, territories, and resources without undue interference (Berman 1993). Its appeal, therefore, is as a 'universe of human rights precepts' (Anaya 1996: 81), that is, as a right that contains or enables other rights. Self-determination is also a territorialised right as implied in international law, which recognises in common Article 1 (2) of the International Human Rights Covenants that 'in no case may a people be deprived of its means of subsistence' (United Nations 1966a, 1966b). A conceptualisation of self-determination as a territorialised right is of paramount importance to indigenous peoples, whose interests in a secure land base are economic, political, social, and cultural. It is a widely accepted tenet of international concern for indigenous peoples that the relationship of indigenous peoples with their lands and territories has a profound cultural or spiritual aspect (Anaya 1996), a quality that is recognised in Article 25 of the text of the UN Declaration (United Nations 2007).

Given prominence in the UN Charter of 1945 as a principle *desiderata* of the UN (United Nations 1945: Art. 55), self-determination has a significant place in international legal consciousness. Following World War II, it was the guiding principle of decolonisation, and granted colonised peoples their independence as directed by the UN Declaration on the Granting of Independence to Colonial Countries of 1960 (UN Declaration on Colonial Countries) (United Nations 1960a). In 1966, the adoption of the International Human Rights Covenants saw the right of self-determination seemingly attain the status of a 'super rule', that is, a rule that 'stands apart from the normal discourse of rights and directly affects political power and organisation within and among states' (Steiner and Alston 2000: 1248). These recognise in Common Article 1 that:

> All peoples have the right to self-determination. By virtue of that right they freely determine their political status and freely pursue their economic, social, and cultural development.
>
> (United Nations 1966a, 1966b: Article 1)

As a claim voiced by indigenous political activists, however, aspirations for self-determination have been regarded with acute distrust (Anaya 1996; Lam 2000; MacKay 2002). Objections during the drafting process took many forms, but principal among them was the expressed anxiety that the recognition of self-determination in the context of indigenous peoples would lead to secession and the creation of breakaway indigenous states. An assumption traceable to the fact that the vast majority of Third World peoples availing themselves of the right to self-determination after World War II opted for full political independence, it does not, however, follow from international law, which stipulates that the establishment of a sovereign state, free association with an independent state, and integration with an independent state are *all* ways of exercising a people's right to self-determination

(United Nations 1960b: Article 29; United Nations 1970: Article 1). For their part, moreover, the nature of self-determination that indigenous peoples seek is one that casts them in continuing association with their encompassing states but that enables them through various forms of autonomous arrangements to develop their institutions on their own territories and determine their own development in accordance with their own values (Coulter 1995; Whall 2002). In this respect, indigenism is distinct from ethno-nationalism (Niezen 2003).

For most indigenous peoples, separation is just not practical. As Inuit lawyer Dalee Sambo (2002: 47) has pointed out, 'the political, demographic and economic realities don't point to political independence as a viable option for the vast majority of indigenous peoples'. In this context, it could be argued that the vigorous efforts of certain Member States to deny the right of self-determination on the basis of threats to their territorial integrity seem like manifestations of bad faith. The reality is, however, that even without the likelihood of secession, the meaningful recognition of the right to self-determination for indigenous peoples necessarily entails the establishment of spheres of territorial autonomy where indigenous political, legal, social, economic, and cultural jurisdiction can flourish, and so inherently involves the state in a loss of some of its territorial sovereignty (*not* integrity). This is a primary concern for modern states, territory being 'the literal and figurative foundation of the state' (Hannum 1990: 463) and indeed part of what defines a state in international law, as per the 1933 Montevideo Convention on the Rights and Duties of States (Barker 2000: 38–9). The conveying of territorial sovereignty also immediately implicates the issue of resource sovereignty, which for many authors writing on the challenge of indigenous movements for states (e.g. Howitt, *et al.* 1996; Perry 1996) is at the core of tensions between indigenous peoples and modern states, as indigenous claims to self-determination are judged against the prerogatives of capital and development as defined by the sovereign state. State fears of a loss of sovereignty have also extended to the political and legal field, where claims to indigenous jurisdiction over 'doing politics and applying justice' (Assies, *et al.* 1999) appear to generate internal legal and political competition, and sit uncomfortably with the sovereign prerogatives of states.

Sovereignty at this point should be defined in its simplest sense as the right to exercise supreme authority. It is a defining characteristic of modern states (Sassen 1995), which are organised around the holding and exercise of authority that is *prima facie* not shared or subservient to any other authority (Scott 2001: 33). There are two recognised aspects to sovereignty – external and internal. The former is concerned with relationships between international personalities and the latter with 'the formal organisation of political authority within the state and the ability of public authorities to exercise effective control within the borders of their own polity' (Krasner 1999: 9). International human rights are instruments that seek to limit the scope of state sovereignty by placing restrictions on the ways in which states can treat citizens and non-citizens within their borders, and imply a loss of sovereignty to an external community of norms. Like all international human rights, indigenous rights take the way in which states treat indigenous peoples within their borders outside the exclusive domestic jurisdiction of the state and thus entail a loss of sovereign authority in the external (Westphalian) sense described above, but they also oblige the state to share or transfer sovereignty in the domestic context, therefore also placing limits on state sovereignty in an internal sense. Claims to indigenous jurisdiction over spheres of legal, political, territorial, economic, and cultural autonomy therefore challenge state sovereignty above and beyond other human rights.

Human rights work: turning the bureaucracy to account

Given the fundamental concerns the issue of indigenous rights has raised among Member States of the UN, the adoption of the UN Declaration on the Rights of Indigenous Peoples represents a substantial achievement. Though not supported by all Member States – there were four votes against and 11 abstentions – the declaration received a clear majority of 144 votes in favour. Moreover, when viewed against the strength of opposition that existed just over ten years ago, when state and indigenous delegations congregating at the first meeting of the UN WGDD in 1995 were apparently intractably polarised over the right to self-determination (Barsh 1996), the adoption of the Declaration represents an extraordinary achievement. Indeed, the sensitivity of states at that point in time was such that the name of the drafting group as it originally appeared on the draft agenda – 'the working group on the draft United Nations Declaration on the Rights of Indigenous Peoples' – had to be altered to the much more oblique title of 'working group established in accordance with Commission on Human Rights resolution 1995/32 of 3 March 1995', thus avoiding an impasse over the use of the term 'peoples' with all its implications in international law.

Indigenous representatives have employed diverse tactics intended to lessen Member States' resistance based on perceived or real threats to their manifold interests, but perhaps the most effective has been to engage in what might be described as a 'war of position' (Gramsci 1991) that has involved justifying claims in relation to norms, judgements, and statements drawn from the existing international legal context. Amounting to a strategy of legal mobilisation, by which, following Zemans (1983), I refer not simply to litigation but to a wider process of 'invoking legal norms', legal mobilisation tactics have generally been overlooked by social movement scholars, who have until more recently been inclined to define their interests in terms of those forms of political behaviour that are the resort of political outsiders and to overlook strategies directed into formal institutional channels (Burnstein 1991; Rubin 2001). The campaign of the global indigenous movement to reform the international human rights regime, however, is insufficiently understood without an analysis of legal tactics. To take advantage of inconsistencies and contradictions, to turn the rules against the rulers, to turn the bureaucracy to account – these methods have provided the movement with the required legitimation for their claims.

It is useful at this point to cite Hunt (1990) on the role of rights-based strategies in struggles for social change. Hunt dismisses the criticism levelled at rights strategies that they require social movements to accommodate themselves to the discourses of the powerful and advances an 'unambiguously positive case' (ibid.: 310) in favour of rights strategies. Drawing on Gramsci's treatment of hegemony, Hunt argues that counter-hegemonic politics 'is not some purely oppositional project conceived of as if it were constructed elsewhere .... [It] has to start from that which exists, which involves starting from "where people are at"' (1990: 313). More specifically, he argues, 'it involves the "reworking", that is, doing "new work" on old materials; here it may appeal to elements already present in popular discourses: democracy, freedom, equality, liberty (and a few other key symbols) ... what is decisive is the way in which concrete political discourses mobilize re-combinations of well-tried elements' (ibid.: 324). What we see in the case of the global indigenous movement is an acclaimed UN principle – self-determination – becoming a source of resistance for indigenous peoples via both its attachment to concrete statements of international law and its re-combination with fundamental normative principles that in many cases are encoded in the legal canon but no longer require supporting citation due to their peremptory character in law and politics.

Indigenous advocates have found a number of vulnerable points in the existing international law of self-determination from which to justify its application to indigenous peoples. The most obvious weak point, and indeed one that contributed towards the emergence in the 1970s of the global indigenous peoples' movement (Sanders 1980), lies in the original framing of the right to self-determination as a universal right of peoples. As stated above, both the UN Declaration on Colonial Countries and the International Human Rights Covenants state that 'all peoples have the right to self-determination' (United Nations 1960a: Article 2; United Nations 1966a, 1966b: Article 1), thus enabling if not inviting indigenous representatives to argue that international law currently provides for a right of self-determination for indigenous peoples *if the current rules are applied*. The following statement is illustrative:

> The International Covenants state that 'all peoples' have the right of self-determination. These International Covenants were drafted to protect peoples, all peoples, without exception. There is no provision whereby these protections may be applied selectively to certain peoples and denied to other peoples. The Covenants are explicit: they apply to 'all peoples'. The Universal Declaration is also explicit: international human rights protections are to apply universally and indivisibly.
>
> (Ted Moses, North American Indigenous Caucus, Statement to the 11th Session of the UN WGIP, 1993, on file with author)

International legal experts have pointed out that statements couched in terms of application of existing international law do not reflect the intention to confine the right of self-determination to non-self-governing territories defined according to colonial geography, that is, to those peoples colonised by overseas colonial powers (e.g. Daes 1993). This can be gleaned from the *travaux preparatoires* of the International Covenants, but a limit is also explicitly written into international law in a companion resolution to the UN Declaration on Colonial Countries. Known as the 'saltwater' thesis, this states that the principles of decolonisation should apply to any territory 'geographically separate and distinct ethnically or culturally from the country administering it' (United Nations 1960b). A more forceful line of argument, however, has anyway focused on *what the law should be and why*. This has hinged on the norm of non-discrimination, which is less a statement of international law than an example of a peremptory norm of international customary law, meaning a rule of customary law so fundamental that it cannot be departed from or set aside by treaty (Brownlie 1998: 515). Indigenous advocates have argued that the denial or qualification of self-determination for indigenous peoples would create a double standard in international law on the basis of their indigenousness and thereby implicate the norm of non-discrimination. The following intervention is illustrative of hundreds reflecting this argument:

> As virtually all participants in this working group acknowledge, the affirmation of the right to self-determination of indigenous peoples is a core element of the draft declaration and essential to its integrity. As provided in the international human rights Covenants, this right applies to 'all peoples'. Consequently, it would violate the peremptory norm prohibiting racial discrimination to create a different and lesser standard for the world's indigenous peoples concerning this crucial human right.
>
> (Tonya Fischer, American Indian Law Alliance, Statement to the 8th Session of the UN WGDD, 2002, on file with author)

Currently, the dominant and indeed most developed theoretical framework for understanding the influence of social movement campaigns framed in terms of principled norms is to be found in the field of international relations (IR), but more particularly that field of IR known as constructivism (see e.g. Klotz 1995; Risse, *et al.* 1999; Khagram, *et al.* 2002). Constructivists argue that the international system is a social system and that within that system states have interests not only in power and authority but also in particular identities. They argue, moreover, that norms are constitutive of identities and that states conform to principled norms otherwise at odds with their material or other interests because to do so is appropriate for a given identity, for example, that of liberal or 'modern and civilised statehood' (Risse, *et al.* 1999: 234). This framework not only views instrumental or material interests as interacting with interests in acting appropriately for a given identity, but also the range of a state's interests as defined in the first place *through* identity.

The discrimination 'frame' (Snow and Benford 1988) has depended on embarrassing member states concerned with upholding standards considered appropriate for civilised members of the international community, and is a good example of what Crenshaw describes as a 'demand for change that reflects the institutional logic' (1988: 1367). It has been supported by a more reassuring discourse aimed at tackling secession anxiety, which has also relied upon statements and norms inhering in the UN's own legal arsenal. Indigenous representatives have argued that international law already provides safeguards against secession, for example in the form of the 1970 UN Declaration on Friendly Relations, which only authorises secession in cases where the national political system is so exclusive and undemocratic that it fails to represent the whole of the population, states that:

> By virtue of the principle of equal rights and self-determination of peoples enshrined in the Charter, all peoples have the right to freely determine, without external interference, their political status and to pursue their economic, social and cultural development, and every State has the duty to respect this right in accordance with the provisions of the Charter .... Nothing in the foregoing paragraphs shall be construed as authorising or encouraging any action which would dismember or impair, totally or in part, the territorial integrity or political unity of sovereign and independent States *conducting themselves in compliance with the principle of equal rights and self-determination of peoples* as described above and thus possessed of a government representing the whole people belonging to the territory without distinction as to race, creed, and colour.
>
> (United Nations 1970: Article 1, my emphasis)

Ironically for a statement intended to place limitations on the exercise of what had already apparently been recognised as a universal right, this statement has provided an important resource for indigenous advocates. It stipulates that the self-determination of peoples and the territorial integrity of states are not necessarily in conflict where states are 'conducting themselves in compliance with the principle of equal rights and self-determination of peoples', and can also be interpreted as tempering the principle of territorial integrity by making it conditional on a state respecting the human rights and self-determination of all the people or constituent peoples within its borders. It therefore defuses state objections based on secession by imposing a requirement of legitimacy on states invoking the principle of territorial integrity against a self-determination claim. Indigenous representatives have made this point in numerous interventions to international forums. The following statements are illustrative:

> The right of secession is a dormant right that may only be triggered by extremes of political disenfranchisement, ruthless exploitation, or material dispossession. On the other hand the right may be neutralised by access to meaningful political participation. States 'conducting themselves in compliance with the principles of equal rights and self-determination of peoples' keep secession at bay. It makes no sense for the US to raise this obscure, well nigh irrelevant issue of secession and use it to erect a barrier to indigenous peoples' right to determine their own futures.
>
> (National Congress of American Indians and Native American Rights Fund, Joint Statement to the 8th Session of the UN WGDD, 2002, on file with author)

We have to question the concern of some governments over territorial integrity. If their claim to land, their claim to exist as sovereign nations is well founded, why are they so threatened by international human rights law? It leads me to believe, as a Lakota person, that these governments know their existence and title is questionable, its integrity in the eyes of justice not without reproach. Perhaps the US government fears that its own human rights record is founded more on might than right and close examination could threaten its own territorial integrity.

(Kent Lebsock, Teton Sioux Nation Treaty Council, Statement to the 8th Session of the UN WGDD, 2002, on file with author)

A final source of legitimacy has come from interpretations of human rights law made by the so-called UN treaty bodies. The UN is an expansive bureaucracy comprising two kinds of bodies, namely those that derive their authority from the UN Charter and those originating from the eight major human rights treaties.[2] The treaty bodies were established in the 1970s to monitor states' compliance with their treaty obligations, and they tend to exist in tension with the Charter-based bodies, which are states-composed organs responsible for creating international law. The tension arises predominantly from their different handling of human rights issues, for where Charter-based bodies handle human rights in a political rather than legal way, the treaty bodies are comprised of independent human rights experts who are relatively insulated from political pressure. Their chief purpose is to monitor state compliance through a reporting system, under which state parties are required to submit periodic reports for review and comment.[3] In theory, a state should implement a Committee's 'concluding observations', but there is no requirement to change domestic legislation; the committees are not courts and have no punitive powers (Coliver and Miller 1999: 180). Nevertheless, the constitution of the treaty bodies by experts with 'high moral character' and 'recognised competence' in the field of human rights means that they carry authority in the UN system, and in this regard they play an important role in what Baehr (1999) terms the 'politics of shame'.

Indigenous delegates have drawn attention to a number of judgements in their advocacy, but particularly to the now seemingly established pattern of application of common Article 1 of the International Covenants to indigenous peoples shown by the Human Rights Committee (HRC) and the Economic, Social, and Cultural Committee (ESC Committee). In 1999, the HRC twice applied the right of self-determination to indigenous peoples in the cases of Canada and Norway (United Nations 1999a, United Nations 1999b), whilst in 2000 the ESC Committee requested state responses from Australia on the rights of indigenous Australians to self-determination (United Nations 2000: Para. 3). More recently, the HRC confirmed its approach in the case of the US, which it has called upon to 'take further steps in order to secure the rights of all indigenous peoples under articles 1 and 27 of the Covenant' (United Nations 2006b: Para. 37).

Conclusion

This chapter has explored the important role of the global indigenous peoples' movement in the process of social construction of a UN Declaration on the Rights of Indigenous Peoples. It therefore contributes to a research agenda concerned with the genealogy of human rights institutions, and more particularly the role of social movements in the construction of human rights (e.g. Stammers 1999). Taking place in the context of the human rights law-making bodies of the UN, the process of production of a UN declaration on indigenous rights has involved independent human rights experts, member states, and representatives of indigenous peoples and their organisations in protracted negotiations over the content of indigenous peoples' rights. The adoption of the UN Declaration in September 2007 must be tied to a multiplicity of factors and conditions, but it is above all testament to the human rights work of the global indigenous movement.

In linking the activities of the global indigenous movement to a radical transformation in the international law of indigenous rights, this chapter has focused particularly on a strategy based on evoking the normative context. This is not a strategy commonly associated with social movements, but one appropriate for institutional settings like the UN characterised by an institutional logic and rules of appropriate state behaviour. Nor is it the singular strategy employed by the indigenous movement (see e.g. Morgan 2004, 2007; Niezen 2003). It remains to be seen to what extent the declaration will be adhered to by Member States of the UN. It is lamentable that four states with particularly large indigenous populations – the US, Canada, New Zealand, and Australia – oppose the Declaration.

Notes

1 NGO access within the UN system is limited to the Economic and Social Council (ECOSOC), a nevertheless important structure within the UN system with remit in relation to the environment, the economic and social field, and human rights.

2 The eight human rights treaties are the International Covenant on Civil and Political Rights (ICCPR); the International Covenant on Economic, Social and Cultural Rights (ICESCR); the International Convention on the Elimination of All Forms of Racial Discrimination (CERD); the International Convention on the Elimination of All Forms of Discrimination Against Women (CEDAW); the Convention Against Torture and Other Cruel, Inhuman, or Degrading Treatment (CAT); the Convention on the Rights of the Child (CRC); the Convention on the Protection of the Rights of All Migrant Workers and Members of their Family (CMW); and the Convention on the Rights of People with Disabilities (CRPD). The treaty bodies are, respectively, the Human Rights Committee (HRC); the Committee on Economic, Social and Cultural Rights (ESC Committee); the Committee on the Elimination of Racial Discrimination (CERD); the Committee on the Elimination of Discrimination Against Women (CEDAW); the Committee Against Torture (CAT); the Committee on the Rights of the Child (CRC); the Committee on Migrant Workers (CMW); and the Committee on the Rights of People with Disabilities (CRPD).

3 The HRC also supervises implementation of the ICCPR pursuant to a complaints procedure. Complaints can be from individuals or other states, but only where a signatory state has agreed to be subject to the Individual Communications Procedure (the so-called Optional Protocol) or the Inter-State Communications Procedure respectively (Alston

1992: 370). The Inter-State Communications Procedure is barely used, whereas the Optional Protocol has served as an important vehicle for focusing on rights violations, including indigenous rights. However, the Committee's practice of receiving only highly individualised complaints has proved limiting for indigenous peoples seeking to claim violations of collective rights, including self-determination. For example, in 1990, Chief Ominayak on behalf of the Lubicon Lake Band in Canada brought a complaint under the Optional Protocol that Canada had violated the Lubicon Lake Band's right of self-determination. The Band claimed that in allowing the provincial government of Alberta to expropriate the Band's territory, Canada violated their right to freely determine its political status and pursue its economic, social, and cultural development, as well as its right to freely dispose of its natural wealth and resources, as established in Article 1 and 1(2). What was an opportunity for the Committee to issue an interpretation on whether or not indigenous peoples constituted peoples with the right to self-determination under the Covenant was, however, missed, as the HRC declined to entertain complaints of violations of Article 1 under the individual complaints procedure, stipulating instead that complaints under the Optional Protocol must relate to violations of Articles 6–27. Ultimately, however, the Committee did find a violation of Article 27 (Pritchard 1998: 197).

Bibliography

Alston, P. (1992) *The United Nations: A Critical Appraisal*, Oxford: Clarendon Press.

Anaya, J. (1996) *Indigenous Peoples in International Law*, Cambridge: Cambridge University Press.

Assies, W., van der Haar, G., and Hoekema, A. J. (1999) 'Diversity as a Challenge: a Note on the Dilemmas of Diversity', in Assies, *et al.* (eds) *The Challenge of Diversity: Indigenous Peoples and Reform of the State in Latin America*, Amsterdam: Thela Thesis.

Baehr, P. (1999) *Human Rights: Universality in Practice*, Basingstoke: Macmillan.

Barker, C. (2000) *International Law and International Relations*, London: Continuum.

Barsh, R. (1996) 'Indigenous Peoples and the UN Commission on Human Rights: A Case of the Immoveable Object and the Irresistible Force', *Human Rights Quarterly* 18: 783–813.

Baxi, U. (2001) 'Too Many, or Too Few, Human Rights?', *Human Rights Law Review* 1(1): 1–11.

—— (2002) *The Future of Human Rights*, New Delhi: Oxford University Press.

Berman, H. (1993) 'The Development of International Recognition of the Rights of Indigenous Peoples', *Indigenous Affairs* 4(1).

Bob, C. (2002) 'Globalisation and the Social Construction of Human Rights Campaigns', in Brysk (ed.) *Globalisation and Human Rights*, Berkeley: University of California Press.

Bobbio, N. (1996) *The Age of Rights*, Cambridge: Polity Press.

Brownlie, I. (1998) *Principles of Public International Law*, Oxford: Clarendon Press.

Brubaker, R. (1992) *Citizenship and Nationhood in France and Germany*, Cambridge, Mass.: Harvard University Press.

Brysk, A. (2000) *From Tribal Village to Global Village: Indian Rights and International Relations in Latin America*, Stanford: Stanford University Press.

—— (2002). 'Introduction: Transnational Threats and Opportunities', in Brysk (ed.) *Globalisation and Human Rights*, Berkeley: University of California Press.

Burnstein, P. (1991) 'Legal Mobilisation as a Social Movement Tactic: The Struggle for Equal Employment Opportunity', *American Journal of Sociology* 96(5): 1201–25.

Coliver, S. and Miller, A. (1999) 'International Reporting Procedures', in Hannum (ed.) *International Human Rights in Practice*, 3rd edn, Ardsley, NY: Transnational Publishers.

Costain, A. (1992) *Inviting Women's Rebellion: A Political Process Interpretation of the Women's Movement*, Baltimore: John Hopkins University Press.

Coulter, R. (1995) 'The Draft Declaration on the Rights of Indigenous Peoples: What is it? What Does it Mean?', *Netherlands Quarterly of Human Rights* 13: 123–38.

Crenshaw, K. (1988) 'Race, Reform, and Retrenchment: Transformation and Legitimation in Anti-Discrimination Law', *Harvard Law Review* 101(7): 1331–87.

Daes, E.I. (1993) 'Some Considerations on the Right of Indigenous Peoples to Self-Determination', *Transnational Law and Contemporary Problems* 3(1): 367–77.

—— (2000) 'Protection of the World's Indigenous Peoples and Human Rights', in Sambo

Dorough, D. (ed) (2002) 'Indigenous Peoples and the Right to Self-Determination: The Need for Equality – An Indigenous Perspective', *Collected Papers and Proceedings: Seminar on the Right to Self-Determination of Indigenous Peoples, New York, May 18 2002*. Montreal: Rights and Democracy.

Donnelly, J. (1998) *Realism and International Relations*, Cambridge: Cambridge University Press.

Gramsci, A. (1991) *Selections from the Prison Notebooks*, London: Lawrence and Wishart.

Hannum, H. (1990) *Autonomy, Sovereignty, and Self-Determination: The Accommodation of Conflicting Rights*, Philadelphia: University of Pennsylvania Press.

Howitt, R., Connel, J., and Hirsh, P. (eds) (1996) *Resources, Nations, and Indigenous Peoples: Case Studies from Australia, Melanesia, and Southeast Asia*, Melbourne: Oxford University Press.

Hunt, A. (1990) 'Rights and Social Movements: Counter Hegemonic Strategies', *Journal of Law and Society* 17(3): 309–28.

Ignatieff, M. (2001) *Human Rights as Politics and Idolatry*, Princeton: Princeton University Press.

Khagram, S., Riker, J., and Sikkink, K. (eds) (2002) *Restructuring World Politics: Transnational Social Movements, Networks, and Norms*, Minneapolis: University of Minnesota Press.

Klotz, A. (1995) *Norms in International Relations: The Struggle Against Apartheid*, Itacha: Cornell University Press.

Korey, W. (1998) *NGOs and the Universal Declaration of Human Rights: 'A Curious Grapevine'*, Basingstoke: Macmillan.

Krasner, S. (1999) *Sovereignty: Organised Hypocrisy*, Princeton, NJ: Princeton University Press.

Lam, M.-C. (2000) *At the Edge of the State: Indigenous Peoples and Self-Determination*, Ardsley, NY: Transnational Publishers.

Landman, T. (2006) *Studying Human Rights*, Abingdon, Oxon.: Routledge.

Levy, D. and Sznaider, N. (2004) 'The Institutionalization of Cosmopolitan Morality: The Holocaust and Human Rights', *Journal of Human Rights* 3(2): 143–57.

Lukacs, G. (1971) *History and Class Consciousness*, Cambridge: MIT Press.

Mackay, F. (2002) 'The Rights of Indigenous Peoples in International Law', in Zarsky (ed.) *Human Rights and the Environment: Conflicts and Norms in a Globalising World*, London: Earthscan Publications.

Maher, K. H. (2002). 'Who has a Right to Rights? Citizenship's Exclusions in an Age of Migration', in Brysk (ed.) *Globalisation and Human Rights*, Berkeley: University of California Press.

Mander, J. and Tauli-Corpuz, V. (eds) (2006) *Paradigm Wars: Indigenous Peoples' Resistance to Globalisation*, Berkeley: University of California Press.

Maybury-Lewis, D. (1984) 'Demystifying the Second Conquest', in Schmink and Wood (eds) *Frontier Expansion in the Amazon*, Gainesville: University of Florida Press.

Messer, E. (1997) 'Pluralist Approaches to Human Rights', *Journal of Anthropological Research* 53: 293–317.

Morgan, R. (2004) 'Advancing Indigenous Rights at the United Nations: Strategic Framing and its Impact on the Normative Development of International Law', *Social and Legal Studies* 13(4): 481–500.

—— (2007) 'On Political Institutions and Social Movement Dynamics: The Case of the United Nations and the Global Indigenous Movement', *International Political Science Review* 28(3): 273–92.

Moses, T. (2000) 'The Right to Self-Determination and its Significance to the Survival of Indigenous Peoples', in Aikio and Scheini (eds) *Operationalizing the Rights of Indigenous Peoples to Self-Determination*, Turku/Abo: Abo Akademi University.

Niezen, R. (2003) *The Origins of Indigenism: Human Rights and the Politics of Identity*, Berkeley: University of California Press.

Perry, R. (1996) *From Time Immemorial: Indigenous Peoples and State Systems*, Austin: University of Texas Press.

Plummer, K. (2006) 'Rights Work: Constructing Lesbian, Gay and Sexual Rights in Late Modern Times', in Morris (ed.) *Rights: Sociological Perspectives*, London: Routledge.

Pritchard, S. (1998) *Indigenous Peoples, the United Nations, and Human Rights*, London: Zed Books.

Rajagopal, B. (2003) *International Law from Below: Development, Social Movements and Third World Resistance*, Cambridge: Cambridge University Press.

Risse, T., Ropp, S., and Sikkink, K. (eds) (1999) *The Power of Human Rights: International Norms and Domestic Change*, Cambridge: Cambridge University Press.

Rodriquez-Garavito, C. and Arenas, L. C. (2005) 'Indigenous Rights, Transnational Activism, and Legal Mobilisation: The Struggle of the U'wa people in Colombia', in Santos and Rodriquez-Garavito (eds) *Law and Globalisation from Below: Towards a Cosmopolitan Legality*, Cambridge: Cambridge University Press.

Rubin, E. (2001) 'Passing through the Door: Social Movement Literature and Legal Scholarship', *University of Pennsylvania Law Review* 150(1): 1–84.

Sanders, D. (1980) 'Background Information on the WCIP: The Formation of the WCIP', Olympia, W.A: Fourth World Documentation Project, Centre for World Indigenous Studies.

Santos, B. de S. (2002) *Toward a New Legal Common Sense: Law, Globalisation, and Emancipation*, London: LexisNexis Butterworths.

Santos, B. de S. and Rodriquez-Garavito, C. (eds) (2005) *Law and Globalisation from Below: Towards a Cosmopolitan Legality*, Cambridge: Cambridge University Press.

Sassen, S. (1995) *Losing Control: Sovereignty in an Age of Globalisation*, New York: Colombia University Press.

Scott, J. (2001) *Power*, Cambridge: Polity Press.

Snow, D. and Benford, R. (1988) 'Ideology, Frame Resonance, and Participant Mobilisation', in Klandermans, *et al.* (eds) *From Structure to Action: Comparing Social Movement Research Across Cultures*, Greenwich, CT: JAI Press.

Soysal, Y. (1994) *Limits of Citizenship: Migrants and Postnational Membership in Europe*, Chicago: Chicago University Press.

Stammers, N. (1995) 'A Critique of Social Approaches to Human Rights', *Human Rights Quarterly* 17: 488–508.

—— (1999) 'Social Movements and the Social Construction of Human Rights', *Human Rights Quarterly* 21: 980–1008.

Steiner, H. and Alston, P. (2000) *International Human Rights in Context: Law, Politics, Morals – Texts and Materials*, 2nd edn, Oxford: Oxford University Press.

Symonides, J (ed.) (2000) *Human Rights: Concept and Standard*, Paris: UNESCO Publishing.

Tarrow, S. (1994) *Power in Movement*, Cambridge: Cambridge University Press.

Turner, B. S. (1993) 'Outline of a Theory of Human Rights', *Sociology* 27(3): 489–512.

—— (1997) 'A Neo-Hobbesian Theory of Human Rights: A Reply to Malcolm Waters', *Sociology* 31(3): 565–71.

—— (2006) *Vulnerability and Human Rights*, University Park, PA: Penn State University Press.

Turner, B. S. and Rojek, C. (2001) *Society and Culture: Principles of Scarcity and Solidarity*, London: Sage.

United Nations (1960a) *Declaration on the Granting of Independence to Colonial Countries and Peoples*, G.A. Res. 1514 [XV].

—— (1960b) *Principles Which Should Guide Members in Determining Whether or Not an Obligation Exists to Transmit the Information Called for in Article 73(e) of the Charter of the United Nations*, G.A. Res. 1541 [XV].

—— (1966a) *International Covenant on Civil and Political Rights, G.A. Res. 2200A (XXI)*, UN Doc. A/6316 (1966).

—— (1966b) *International Covenant on Economic, Social, and Cultural Rights, G.A. Res. 2200A (XXI)*, UN Doc. A/6316 (1966).

—— (1970) *Declaration on Principles of International law Concerning Friendly Relations and Co-operation among States in Accordance with the Charter of the United Nations*, G.A. Res. 2625 [XXV].

—— (1994) *Draft United Nations Declaration on the Rights of Indigenous Peoples*, UN Doc. E/CN.4/Sub.2/1994/56 (1994).

—— (1999a) *Consideration of Reports Submitted By State Parties Under Article 40 of the Covenant, Concluding Observations of the Human Rights Committee, Canada*, UN Doc. CCPR/C/79/Add.105, 7 April 1999.

—— (1999b) *Consideration of Reports Submitted By State Parties Under Article 40 of the Covenant, Concluding Observations of the Human Rights Committee: Norway*, UN Doc. CCPR/C/79/Add.112, 1 November 1999.

—— (2000) *UN Doc. E/C.12/Q/AUSTRAL/1, 23 May 2000.*

—— (2006a) *Human Rights Council Resolution 2006/2. Working Group of the Commission on Human Rights to elaborate a draft declaration in accordance with paragraph 5 of the General Assembly resolution 49/214 of 23 December 1994.*

—— (2006b) *Consideration of Reports Submitted By State Parties Under Article 40 of the Covenant, Concluding Observations of the Human Rights Committee, United States of America*, UN Doc. CCPR/C/USA/CO/3, 15 September 2006.

—— (2007) *Resolution adopted by the General Assembly 61/295, United Nations Declaration on the Rights of Indigenous Peoples*, UN Doc. A/RES/61/295, 2 October 2007.

Walby, S. (2002) 'Feminism in a Global Era', *Economy and Society* 31(4): 533–7.

Waltz, S. (2001) 'Universalizing Human Rights: The Role of Small States in the Construction of the Universal Declaration of Human Rights', *Human Rights Quarterly* 23: 44–72.

—— (2004) 'Universal Human Rights: the Contribution of Muslim States', *Human Rights Quarterly* 26: 799–844.

Waters, M. (1996) 'Human Rights and the Universalisation of Interests: Towards a Social Constructionist Approach', *Sociology* 30(3): 593–600.

Weyker, S. (2002) 'The Ironies of Information Technology', in Brysk (ed.) *Globalisation and Human Rights*, Berkeley: University of California Press.

Whall, H. (2002) *Indigenous Self-Determination in the Commonwealth of Nations*, London: Institute of Commonwealth Studies.

Woodiwiss, A. (2005) *Human Rights*, Abingdon, Routledge.

Yashar, D. (2005) *Contesting Citizenship in Latin America: The Rise of Indigenous Movements and the Postliberal Challenge*, Cambridge: Cambridge University Press.

Zemans, F. (1983) 'Legal Mobilisation: the Neglected Role of the Law in the Political System', *American Political Science Review* 77(3): 690–703.

8 The new humanism

Beyond modernity and postmodernity

Judith Blau and Alberto Moncada

We begin this essay with an account of a research paradigm that was dominant in American sociology in the decades after the end of World War II and one that captured the prevailing American Zeitgeist. To be more precise, we would put it in brackets, between the publication of Blau and Duncan's *The American Occupational Structure* (1967) and the English-language publication of Bourdieu's *Distinction* (1984). At least as far as domestic issues were concerned, this was a period of great optimism in America, with a growing economy, and the expansion of Civil Rights and Great Society programs. Sociologists confirmed that opportunities were expanding for white, working- and middle-class Americans, and were hopeful for African Americans. David L. Featherman and Robert M. Hauser wrote:

> Americans assent to the awarding of widely different prizes to persons depending on their performance in the economic 'race.' But we [that is, we Americans] insist that all run the race under the same set of rules so that ability and talent show themselves in a fair way …. Our social programs to increase equality of economic opportunity – to overcome the 'handicaps' of social background – issue from this logic.
>
> (Featherman and Hauser 1978: 1)

Within this framework, it was recognized that the rules were not yet fair for American blacks, but given a broad egalitarian ethos in America (Gans 1968: xi), many assumed, as Featherman and Hauser stated, that social programs would increase economic opportunity for everyone. They were bound to. They had to. Thus, in general, the prevailing assumption among American sociologists was that progress was an operable concept and that American society was moving in the direction of greater fairness, more equality, and expanding opportunities. Because these are not testable assumptions, but rather sensitizing and orienting ones, we can refer to them as comprising the *opportunities paradigm*, at least one that was meaningful within US empirical sociology. Its counterpart in economics was development economics, particularly expressed in the work of Nobel Prize winning Simon Kuznets (1966), who contended that over the long run, inequalities would decline with economic growth. Thus, many empirical sociologists shared with some economists a great optimism in 'progress,' and the belief that growth and development would bring about economic and social equality.

To be sure, there was not unanimous agreement among sociologists that Western societies were moving in the direction of greater fairness, more equality, and expanding opportunities. Such optimism was not shared by Marxist sociologists who framed their research in terms of enduring class differences. For example, John Goldthorpe (1974) and Eric Olin Wright (1979) concluded that class divisions were tenacious. Instead of being the beneficiaries of evolutionary and progressive social and economic change, people, according to Marxist social scientists, would have to disrupt oppressive cycles and structures. To a certain degree, both Marxist sociologists and those we have described as embracing the *opportunities paradigm* understood the human actor as being the object of economic and social forces – malevolent in the case of the former, and benevolent in the case of the latter.

Sociology: from optimism to pessimism

Without debate and, perhaps, even little notice, the term, 'opportunities,' had by about the mid-1980s disappeared from the lexicon of Western sociology. Instead, the term, 'inequalities' has taken its place, more in line with Goldthorpe's and Wright's earlier writings than those of stratification researchers. The dominant view now is that opportunities are highly unequal, as are people's life chances (Blalock 1991; Gans 1995). Institutional economists asserted that labor markets are segmented with rigid barriers to entry (Gordon, Edwards and Reich 1982). Bourdieu (1984) argued that dominant classes ensure their reproduction and control of the social field through symbols, education, and language. For Tilly (1998), inequalities operate through enduring social categories, such as black and white, female and male, non-native and native, gays and straights. Others have examined how inequalities are established and maintained by power (Mann 1986; Epstein 2007), micro-cultural processes (Lamont and Fournier 1992), social networks (Lin 1999), and, in America, by the dynamics that perpetuate a black underclass (Oliver and Grant 2000), exclude Hispanics (Moncada and Olivas 2003), and marginalize indigenous Americans (Smith 2007).

Opportunities, as a research paradigm in the Kuhnian sense (Kuhn 1962), has run its full course, and virtually the only mention of the term these days is in the pejorative sense – of people 'hoarding opportunities' (Morris 2000). There is no more optimism in economic progress. And, there is no expectation that the tides of progressive social change will raise all boats. What is more surprising is that Marxism is also losing some of its relevance. This has happened for a variety of reasons: because of the realization that half the world's dispossessed are peasant-farmers, not proletariats; because Marx and Engels failed to theorize the exploitation of women and people of color; because the rules of capital accumulation are so fundamentally different now compared with the era of classical capitalism; and because capital lacks spatial fixity, which greatly disadvantages labor.

It is foolish to propose that the *opportunities paradigm* and Marxism are comparable as intellectual frameworks. The former was short-lived and grew out of a circumscribed, empirical tradition within mainly Anglo sociology while the latter was a worldview, shared by billions of people around the world, and powerful enough to fuel revolutions and shape governments and empires. Yet at another level they are entirely comparable. Each drew from a conviction of justice, a desire for a equality, a longing for fairness. We will make a case that the emerging world view of *human rights* will be ever as much the global worldview that Marxism was, perhaps even more so because the world is far more connected now than at any other time in history. This worldview is powerful precisely because it draws from universal conceptions of justice, equality, and human dignity and besides has the backing of the United Nations (UN), the International Labour Organization (ILO), and international non-governmental organizations (NGOs), such as Human Rights Watch. It also affirms universal rights, such as the rights to security, as well as particular rights, such as the rights to culture, language, and traditions.

It is evident, moreover, that the human rights paradigm allows social scientists to be intellectually honest. We do not have to conceal that we support justice, equality, equity, and fairness. Works in this field amply demonstrate the forthright embrace of such values as these, e.g. Donnelly (1989), Turner (1993, 2006a, 2006b); Falk (2000); Orend (2002); Blau and Moncada (2005); Woodiwiss (2005); and Brysk (2005). Below we will see how this new-found intellectual honesty is becoming evident at least in the journal culture.

The abandoned modernist project

It could be said that the *opportunities paradigm* was part of the much larger modernity project, which embraced reason, rationality, the idea of progress, and which was interrupted towards the end of the twentieth century by the postmodern project. Were we to put a precise date on the year that postmodernism stepped onto the world stage as a sensibility and as an aesthetic, it would be 1973 when Charles Jencks popularized the term in his *Postmodern Architecture* (Jencks 1973; see Blau 1984). In the more general sense, postmodernism swept away grand narratives, rationality, reason, optimism, legitimacy, originality, and progress. In Lyotard's (1992:18) words, postmodernity 'liquidated modernity' (also see Touraine 1995: 187). Postmodern theory failed to have much of a direct influence on empirical sociology in the US – mostly because postmodernists are unsympathetic to empirical claims – but empiricists shared with postmodernists a growing disillusionment with progress. Among empiricists this was evident in a growing pessimism about solving the perplexing racial divide. Whereas sociologists in the 1960s through the mid-1980s were confident that American blacks would achieve equality with whites, the mood after 1985 was grim and pessimistic (Wilson 1987; Massey and Denton 1993). (Relatively ignored were other trends that were more encouraging, including declines in the crime rates (Blumstein and Wallman 2000) and declines in the divorce rates (Goldstein 1999).) American sociologists were not in the mood for good news.

Rather important changes have occurred in mainstream American sociology journals, but have received little comment. First, whereas ethnographic studies were relatively rare even a decade ago, they have become quite common now in mainstream journals. The assumption here is that human experiences are plural and each person's experiences are unique, authentic and special, and it is important for the social scientist to capture the depth and range of personal experiences (see, for example, Duneier 1999).[1] This signals to us an emerging humanistic orientation in sociology. Second, critical race theory (e.g. Bonilla-Silva 2001) and feminism (e.g. Harding 2003), which have uncompromising points of view have become, if not mainstream, generally acceptable. More generally, espousing values in journal articles was an anathema a decade ago, and now is considered quite appropriate. Two hypothetical illustrations are helpful. A contemporary article may begin, 'It is urgent to understand the dramatic increase in childhood poverty, which puts children at risk of illness, impairs their learning ...', whereas an article published a decade ago was more likely to begin something like, 'This paper investigates the increase in childhood poverty and how it relates to variation in health and learning ...'. Or to give another example, a contemporary article may begin, 'The denial to workers of their benefits threatens their well-being ...', compared with the likely opening of an earlier article, 'There exists variation among workers with regard to benefit coverage ...'. In other words, there is a fundamental shift taking place within American sociology, as is evident in contemporary sociology journal culture.

Intellectual currents are not completely divorced from one another. Postmodernism had little direct impact on empirical sociology and vice versa, but the pessimism that swept through sociology also swept through the humanities. Writing about postmodernism in 1991, Frederic Jameson describes the 'inverted millenarianism in which premonitions of the future, catastrophic or redemptive, have been replaced by senses of the end of this or that (the end of ideology, art, or social class; the 'crisis' of Leninism, social democracy, or the welfare state, etc., etc.); taken together, all of these perhaps constitute what is increasingly called postmodernism' (Jameson 1991: 1). Jameson captures much better than we possibly can the sense of loss, collective ennui, and intellectual collapse that overtook the Western academy after around 1980. Jameson, however, was not completely pessimistic. He hints at the possibilities that class distinctions will collapse, or that a new international proletariat will emerge (158), that a 'lapse back into humanism' (138) will occur, or even an 'enlargement of the peopled universe' (139). There is the suggestion here of a transition, from postmodernism to a new utopianism.

If contemporary humanists, of whom Jameson is arguably one, are pursuing a new utopianism, we also believe that many US sociologists are newly embracing a version of humanism, advocating for the rights of vulnerable and powerless people, speaking truth to power, and no longer embracing the detachment and neutrality they would have a decade or so ago. This is accompanied by an eagerness to understand the 'whole person,' rather than the person as a composite of variables, to do research that is relevant, and not to have to hide behind scientism. Of course this is somewhat speculative, but we base these speculations on the ways that sociologists have lately defined their roles as liaisons with NGOs in New Orleans and elsewhere, in the anti-war movement, in the US Social Forum, and, especially, the World Social Forum, at which intellectuals, generally, play important roles.

Globalization

No one would disagree that economic globalization is a dominant force in the world today, but when did globalization begin? We propose that what triggered the explosive acceleration of corporate transnationalism was the commercial development of the Internet, beginning in around 1985, and what triggered the development of the contemporary world's financial infrastructure was the abandonment of the gold standard in 1972–3 in favor of fluctuating rates of currency exchange. Together, these provided the wherewithal for a transnational economy and a transnational capitalist class (Robinson 2004), global financial speculation, and worldwide flexible production. Transnationals could seek the world over for the cheapest labor, the laxest environmental standards, the lowest taxes, and the most favorable trade laws. World financial speculative transactions are currently about US$2 trillion per day! Tax loopholes are provided by tax havens, with combined assets estimated at US$9.3 trillion! (Hahnel 1999).

Cutting to the chase, the global economy has generated economic inequalities on a scale never seen before in all of human history. The most comprehensive study of personal wealth ever undertaken was carried out by the World Institute for Development Economics Research (2006), which found that the richest 2 percent of adults in the world own more than half of global household wealth; that the richest 1 percent of adults own 40 percent of the global wealth, and that the richest 10 percent of adults own 85 percent of global wealth.

We might now be nostalgic for the decentered angst and haunting subjectivities of postmodernism. The realities of globalization press hard on the collective conscience. People in Western countries no longer have job security; plant closings and downsizing are routine; local markets have collapsed; and, in the US, many lack health care insurance and pensions for their old age. Peasants in poor countries are losing their lands to agribusiness, drought, desertification, and cannot compete against subsidized imported agricultural products. They migrate in huge numbers to urban slums where the chances of survival in informal economies are better than in rural areas. Contrary to earlier predictions, poverty is increasing in the Third World (International Labour Organization 2004; United Nations 2006; Woodward and Simms 2006), and economic inequalities are increasing in rich countries (Jackson 2004; Brady 2005; Alderson, Beckfield and Nielsen 2005).

Global capitalism, owing to the practices allowed transnationals by electronic technologies and to the instruments allowed financial speculators, does not face the spatial and temporal constraints that capitalism did a few short decades ago, which has allowed a particularly virulent form of capitalism to sweep the globe. Often termed 'neoliberalism' (see Harvey 2005) or the Washington Consensus (Stiglitz 2003), global capitalism is coercively and fiercely individualistic and competitive, and opposes any obstruction, including trade unions, managerial hierarchies, social institutions, political structures, environmental regulations, and even majority rule. Because neoliberalism is hostile to any impediments to capital investments and capital flow, it 'trumps any social democratic concern for equality, democracy, and social solidarities' (Harvey 2005:176).

The major institutions responsible for neoliberal policies – the International Monetary Fund (IMF), the World Trade Organization (WTO), and the World Bank (WB) – now all face growing opposition from the global justice movement (as we will discuss), but also from some UN agencies, most especially the United Nations Development Program (UNDP), the Food and Agricultural Organization (FAO), the United Nations Conference on Trade and Development (UNCTAD), and the ILO (see Blau and Moncada 2007). Some, including Walden Bello (2004), contend that no economy will be fair and equitable until countries stand up in opposition to global capitalists and accept responsibilities for land redistribution and reform, promote new production capacities and build new community economies. The monolithic, global economy, in Bello's view, must be replaced by pluralistic systems of decentralized markets and production economies. He shares the opinion with a growing number of economists that the IMF, the WTO and the WB must be completely reformed so that they operate transparently and are internally democratic. Most of all, their policies must advance the needs of human populations, not those of wealthy elites.

Global justice movements

As we will describe, the global justice movements spawned since 1999 exhibit a curious mixture of, on the one hand, resistance and revolutionary zeal, and, on the other hand, deep humanistic compassion. In the remainder of this chapter we will try to make sense of that. First, it is important to stress that there is widespread solidarity throughout the Third World because, with the possible exception of some Asian countries, free trade has not brought Third World peoples the benefits heralded by neoliberal reformers. People who struggle to get by on US$2, or even US$1 a day have little use for the commodities that free trade brings to a country – automobiles, toasters, refrigerators, and hair dryers.

Besides, free trade has had devastating effects on the agriculture in poor countries because rich countries protect their own farmers by dumping subsidized crops on Third World markets, forcing peasant farmers off the land. Intellectual property rights that protect (especially) pharmaceutical and seed companies, harm people in poor countries. Multinational companies such as Coca-Cola have poisoned ground water and streams, and others, such as Nike and Wal-Mart, have brutally exploited labor.[2] We could elaborate the grievances, but the point we wish to make is that peasants, the landless, the urban poor, and indigenous peoples are now seeking alliances to protest their oppression, and, increasingly, posing alternatives in the pursuit of a better, more equitable world.

Resistance to liberalization

Popular resistance to liberalization dates from the Seattle 1999 WTO Ministerial Meetings, and there have been demonstrations at all subsequent WTO Ministerial Meetings, in Mexico at the 2002 Conference on Financing for Development, and at the annual IMF/WB meetings, drawing each time between 10,000 and 20,000 protestors. Since the beginning, in 1999, the movement has included labor groups, environmentalists, women's groups, and farmers, and has increasingly won over academics, politicians, and progressive NGOs. Since 1999 it has become increasingly evident to others outside the movement that neoliberalism was set on a destructive path, bringing harms to societies and human populations. In 2006 a coalition of think tanks, including the US Institute for Policy Studies, launched an international campaign, 'The IMF: Shrink It or Sink It.'[3] There is also evidence of growing divisions within WTO itself (Strickner 2006).

Popular movements in poor countries are growing and are most often aimed at local economic elites, but sometimes at international ones as well, and include the Shaming Campaign aimed at foreign investors in Malawi, the Indigenous Network in southern Mexico, the Argentinean recovered factory movement, Burmese mobilization against a World Bank-funded dam, the Landless Movement in Brazil, the Indian farmers movement (Bija Yatra) opposing GM seeds, India's National Campaign Committee for Rural Workers, the Zapatistas opposition to the North American Free Trade Agreement (NAFTA), the Shack Peoples movement in various African countries, the Philippine Maquila Solidarity Network's campaign against Wal-Mart, the Liberian campaign against Firestone, and so on.

NGOs

Both remedy and opposition are reflected in the explosive growth of both local and international NGOs, sometimes termed movement organizations or advocacy organizations, and sometimes termed, especially by the UN, civil society organizations. A UN estimate in 1999 of the number of international NGOs was put at 29,000 (see Paul 2000). The number of local NGOs is much more difficult to estimate owing to nonstandard registration, but Paul's estimate, which includes Community Based Organizations (CBOs), is two million.[4] That seems very high, but for anyone who has traveled in the Third World, it probably does not seem unrealistic. NGOs serve every conceivable purpose, from advocacy to provision of services, and they work in every conceivable area – housing, health care, education, the advance of women's rights, the rights of Dalits, children's rights, refugees, and so on. NGOs are very often at the center of political and social movements, working in coalition with one another often across borders and sometimes across continents. They are networked through, for example, Choike, The Third World Network, Jubilee South, Global South, African Debt and Development Network, and the Philippine-based Freedom from Debt Coalition.

The forums

Thousands gathered in Butan in September 2006 for the International Peoples Forum (IPF), which is held annually and concurrently with the meetings of the WB and the IMF. In 2006 the IPF demanded that the IMF and WB introduce reforms to make them more accountable and transparent, and that the debts of Third World countries be rescinded. The World Social Forum (WSF), along with its regional and national forums and polycentrics, is much larger than the IPF, and given its dispersion, its overall participation is difficult to estimate. A conservative estimate is that at least a million people are involved with the WSF forum in any given year. The WSF's motto is 'A Better World is Possible,' and this principle encompasses participatory democracy, participatory economy, equitable cooperation, and social justice, as well as people's economic rights, indigenous rights, and cultural pluralism (World Social Forum, 2001; International Forum on Globalization 2002; Fisher and Ponniah 2003; Hahnel 2005). Nineteen intellectuals penned the Porto Alegre Manifesto at the WSF in 2005 (Group of 19 2005). They chiefly demanded the end of militarism and runaway capitalism, the advance of universal economic and social protections, and the universal creation of democratic spaces.

One should especially note the differences between 'progress,' as considered as part of the modernity project and the opportunities paradigm, and the utopian impulse inherent in the WSF. Note too that it was not long ago that Derrida (1994) expressed utter despair in his now classic *Specters of Marx*. Something quite amazing is happening. The puzzle is to understand it.

One clue comes from people's movements. Here we could cite many examples: the Burmese Student Movement, Attac in Japan and France, the Oaxaca teachers' mobilization in 2006, the Brazilian Landless Movement, Bayan (the Philippines), Student Activists for Global Equity, and so on. There is no better illustration than Malawi, one of the poorest countries in the world, where a campaign against foreign investors and international organizations has been launched that has united peasants and laborers, rural areas and cities. Called the Shaming Campaign, Malawians are protesting against the IMF and the WTO, demonstrating at foreign banks, the offices of their government that co-operate with foreign investors, and the offices of multinationals (Sahle 2007). Empowered social actors – 'subjects' in Touraine's (1995) terms – have moved to center stage in the shaping of ideas and practices.

The ethical turn

If 1972–3 is the marker for the beginning of globalization – the monolithic economic integration of the globe – it could be said that the beginning of globalism – the awareness of a shared global humanity – was earlier. We put this marker as 20 July 1969, when Neil Armstrong, from the moon's surface, announced to a worldwide television and radio audience, 'A giant leap for mankind.' The event was remarkable; in a moment in time people knew they shared the earth and were themselves connected by that fact (Blau and Moncada 2005: 67). The full significance of this moment was clear by the end of the century. As the philosopher Peter Singer (2002) noted, we live in *one world* and we need to make the best of it. Being newly aware that we all share the same planet must elicit good global citizenship and the recognition that co-operative strategies are the only ones that will work.

The *ethical turn* made its debut in philosophy around the end of the last century (Garber, *et al.* 2000; also see Singer 2002; Bonner 2004). This implies, for the social sciences, a new appreciation of cosmopolitanism and mutuality. We find considerable evidence that sociologists have abandoned the mandates of liberal science and are willing to adopt a new point of view, as we earlier noted. There are other indications of the ethical turn within sociology, such as the emergence of public sociology, public anthropology, experiential learning, service learning, and community economics. Differences between the opportunities paradigm and what we we might call the 'ethical paradigm' are useful to point out. Opportunities, as understood by sociologists, were generated by macro-structures and macro-processes having to do with economic growth, which 'presented themselves' to persons. Now there is no engine of growth, no rosy future, no inevitability, but instead humans are themselves agents, empowered subjects who control their own destinies. Humans, some sociologists write, must be respectful and make ethical decisions (see Sennett 2003). They must be public-minded (Burawoy 2005) and be good cosmopolitan, global citizens (Appadurai 2000). We will make a case that the ethical turn is comprehensive, and may have more far-reaching consequences than are now imagined.

Intellectuals' orientations, as we know, do not evolve in a vacuum. Throughout the world there are growing international contacts and exchanges. These, along with the Internet and news accounts, bring home to Westerners the horrendous and growing gap between poor countries and rich ones. Westerners are also becoming aware that global capitalism was invented by their own Western banks, investors, multinationals, speculators, and inter-governmental agencies, such as the IMF. There is also a new realization that the many decades of Western industrial growth are wrecking havoc on the planet and its fragile ecosystems. On the basis of analyses written by more then 1,300 scientists over the course of four years, the Millennium Ecosystem Assessment Board of Directors (2005) concluded that 'human activity is putting such strain on the natural functions of Earth that the ability of the planet's ecosystems to sustain future generations can no longer be taken for granted' (see also Worldwatch Institute 2006: 1).

Thus, the Global North bears the responsibility for declines in the growth of developing countries and for imperiling ecosystems over the last two centuries, with industrialization and extraction of natural resources. Yet we must explore this a bit more since the US, the world's most powerful and richest country, has been opposed to any redistribution of wealth; steps to curb carbon emissions; curbing commercial exploitation of the rain forests; and regulating multinationals. Some corporations, however, are taking steps themselves towards reform in response to public demands for fair trade over free trade, for the end of child labor, for corporations to be environmentally responsible, and so forth.[5]

It is the US's unqualified support of free-trade policies and financial deregulation that poses the major obstacle to even modest reforms. Such reforms are viewed by US political elites as being economically objectionable. To briefly illustrate, the US favors agricultural aid to Sub-Saharan African countries over direct aid, because that helps American agribusiness (AllAfrica 2007). US firms are the largest exporters of small arms, the very weapons that mostly kill civilians (Small Arms Survey, 2006), and the US sets such ideologically-driven barriers on qualifications for AIDS funds that many countries are ineligible. If, as we will argue, there is a human rights revolution afoot, and the US is not a part of it, we need to understand not only current American foreign and economic policies but the background as well, namely the geopolitical divisions during the Cold War. These divisions affect contemporary policies, and also allow us to assess the extent to which Americans remain unfamiliar with basic human rights.

Human rights, the Cold War, and post-Cold War

The extraordinary 1948 Universal Declaration of Human Rights (UDHR) is a set of principles that now every country in the world has acceded to. It is not a treaty. The goal from the beginning was to create from it a single treaty, but the US waged an intense campaign to prevent this from happening. The argument made by the US at the time was that the UDHR was 'socialist.'

Because the US would not ratify a treaty version of the UDHR, the solution was to divide the UDHR into two treaties: the International Covenant for Civil and Political Rights (ICCPR) and the International Covenant for Economic, Social and Cultural Rights (ICESR). The US ostensibly supported the ICCPR by ratifying it, but added as a reservation that it was 'not self-executing,' in other words, did not apply to the US without enabling legislation that it had no intention of enacting. The US did not ratify the ICESR. In fact, the US has ratified few human rights treaties and only two of the eight International Labour Conventions, but in every single instance of ratification, the US adds the qualification that the human rights instrument is 'not self-executing.' One of the consequences of the US's obstreperousness is that the American public is unfamiliar with human rights thinking and laws. Another, of course, is that the US has become the main obstacle to the advance of human rights in the UN.

Although economic, social and cultural rights have been excluded from American political and social discourse, they are now entering through grassroots movements and the work of NGOs, often drawing from the more focused language of civil rights. Thus, there are campaigns in the US for the rights of migrant workers, the rights of indigenous Americans, workers' rights to sick-leave, a living wage, health-care rights, housing rights, the rights of gays and lesbians, and so forth. Americans do not draw from a comprehensive human rights framework as others do, but they do share with people from all over the world a language of social and economic justice. Besides, the global economy has created economic uncertainty in all countries, including the US, and Americans are concerned about job security (and many with health insurance and housing).

We propose that US sociologists are moving in the direction of adopting a rights-based perspective, as they take heed of human rights campaigns in America. Undoing the assumptions from the Cold War, it is possible for American sociologists to assert that certain rights are inalienable – the right to food security, the right to a job, the right to health care, the right to education, and the right of the elderly to live their remaining years in security.[6] Challenging the assumptions of the tradition of American liberalism, it is also possible for American sociologists to accept cultural and group rights, and, indeed, multicultural perspectives flourish on American college campuses.

An inkling of the human rights revolution

When authors describe the human rights revolution (Orend 2002) they refer to the newly energized civil society organizations and movements or to the new international human rights discourse (Woodiwiss 2005). Although human rights made their first formal appearance in 1948, they only have recently become the predominant theme of people's movements, the focus of NGO activities, and organically incorporated into the ambitious undertakings of the WSF.

Human rights challenge the sovereign authority of the nation-state, and are rooted in an ethic of care, recognition, and respect (Turner 2006a). The American liberal tradition, with its stark emphasis on meritocracy, individualism, and competition, is antithetical to the idea that all humans are entitled to social protections and economic security. The Cold War hardened this perspective even further since the official US position was, and continues to be, that competitive capitalism alone provides people with incentives to work, be industrious, invest, and consume.

The human rights revolution, we argue, is underway and, furthermore, we contend it will be far more significant, far more comprehensive, and far more transformative than those who in 1948 celebrated the adoption of the UDHR could possibly have dreamed. There are three reasons why human rights have literally burst on the global scene only recently: first, because human rights uniquely address the uncertainties of global capitalism, which all people share; second, because human rights are linked with new democracy movements shared by many in Third World countries (Blau and Moncada 2007); and third, because human rights are directly relevant for confronting environmental calamities, which are themselves only recent, at least on such a broad scale (Buttel and Gould 2005). The human rights revolution is on the ground and globally networked, and has penetrated all countries. The centrality of human rights at the WSF (Frezzo 2008) ensures that human rights will be the forefront of global mobilization and international networking of NGOs.

Still, this is not enough evidence to conclude that this revolution will have any staying power. Evidence that this is the case comes from official charters of regional bodies and constitutions. Very recently regional bodies have enacted charters with extensive human rights provisions, including socio-economic rights, cultural and group rights, and the rights of women, minorities, and indigenous populations. These include: the Asian Human Rights Charter, the African Charter on Human and Peoples' Rights, the Arab Charter on Human Rights, the European Charter of Fundamental Human Rights, and the Charter of the Organization of American States (see Heyns, Padilla and Zwaak 2006).

Additionally, countries have revised their constitutions within the last two decades to include human rights provisions. Of the 170 constitutions available online in 2004, 117 included socio-economic rights; 56 have additional provisions for health-care rights; 101 had special provisions for minority, indigenous, or cultural rights; and 129 have provisions guaranteeing the equal the rights of women (Blau and Moncada 2006). Of course, few states have fully implemented all their constitutional provisions. No state really can, given the great dependency of all countries on globalized capitalism. States' own companies and industries compete with companies and industries from all the world, which depresses wages and puts constraints on the taxes states can collect. The global economy, in other words, is a major obstacle to the implementation of human rights, while the same global economy chiefly contributes to the need for human rights protections.

Nevertheless, human rights are advancing everywhere, at the grassroots level and at national and international levels. This is a universal language and a comprehensive set of practices that apply locally, nationally, and internationally. It is finally important to stress that having rights and exercising rights are incompatible with top-down governance structures, and that they require that citizens are informed and empowered (see Gould 2004; Green 1999).

Conclusions

Indeed, it can be said that the human rights revolution is spawning new movements at all our doorsteps. Whether these new movements will converge or not remains to be seen. Capitalism and private ownership pose the chief practical obstacles, and their reformability remains the central question. We take the side of dialecticians, and dialecticians of all stripes – Hegel, Marx, Kracauer – and conclude that capitalism poses now too many human contradictions – moral, material, social, and cultural – for the world to stay the same course.

The human rights revolution affirms humanism as a world view, a humanism that accords dignity to each human person, affirms the realities of their unique personalities, and celebrates the authentic realities of each person's life. It is striking that this revolution veers always in the direction of solidarities, inclusiveness, and harmonization. In part this is due to the inspired model of the WSF, whose organizers have insisted on, quoting from its Charter of Principles, 'respect for Human Rights, the practices of real democracy, participatory democracy, peaceful relations, in equality and solidarity, among people, ethnicities, genders and peoples', while condemning 'all forms of domination and all subjection of one person by another' (World Social Forum 2001). In part too, neoliberalism has brought the world's peoples together, but we cannot underestimate how very recently the world's peoples realized that they shared the same planet.

Notes

1 A crude estimate of the growing popularity of ethnography is the numbers of journal articles in the social sciences that use ethnography as a method. In 1980 there were 261, in 1990, 358, in 2000, 953, and just five yeas later, in 2005, there were 1,560 listed in *Social Science Abstracts*.
2 See Responsible Wealth (http://www.responsiblewealth.org/); Choike (http://www.choike.org/); Wal-Mart Watch (http://walmartwatch.com/); Oxfam Australia (http://www.oxfam.org.au/campaigns/labour/).

3 The Shrink It or Sink It campaign, started by the US Institute for Policy Studies, has had broad coverage; see Focus on the Global South (http://www.focusweb.org/content/view/985/27/).
4 NGOs exhibit varying degrees of formality depending on their resources. The *Encyclopedia of Associations: International Organizations* (2005) lists around 29,000, but these exclude small and relatively informal ones, even those that are registered in the US as 501.C.3s.
5 The aim of the United Nations Global Compact is to promote corporate responsibility.
6 Franklin Delano Roosevelt advocated in his second State of the Union Address in January 1944 a 'Second Bill of Rights,' a comprehensive proposal that encompassed socio-economic rights. He gave the proposal to a congressional committee and after his death in 1945 the committee failed to develop it and did not bring it before Congress for discussion.

Bibliography

Alderson, A. S., Beckfield, J. and Nielsen, F. (2005) 'Exactly How Has Income Inequality Changed? Patterns of Distributional Change in Core Societies,' *International Journal of Comparative Sociology* 46(5/6): 405–23.
AllAfrica (2007) 'Africa: Care to Quite U.S. Food Aid Program.' Available online at http://allafrica.com/stories/200708201175.html (accessed 20 August 2008).
Appadurai, A. (2000) *Modernity at Large*, Minneapolis: University of Minnesota Press.
Bello, Walden (2004) *Deglobalization: Ideas for a New World Economy*, London: Zed Books.
Blalock, H. M. (1991) *Modeling Allocation Processes*, Newbury Park, CA: Sage.
Blau, J. R. (1984) *Architects and Firms*, Cambridge: MIT Press.
Blau, J. and Moncada, A. (2005) *Human Rights: Beyond the Liberal Vision*, Lanham, MD: Rowman & Littlefield.
—— (2006) *Justice in the United States: Human Rights and the U.S. Constitution*, Lanham, MD: Rowman & Littlefield.
—— (2007) *Freedoms and Solidarities: The Pursuit of Human Rights*, Lanham, MD: Rowman & Littlefield.
Blau, P. M. and Duncan, O. D. (1967) *The American Occupational Structure*, New York: Wiley & Sons.
Blumstein, A. and Wallman, J. (eds) (2000) *The Crime Drop in America*, New York: Cambridge University Press.
Bonilla-Silva, E. (2001) *White Supremacy and Racism in the Post Civil-Rights Era*, Boulder, Colo.: Lynne Rienner.
Bonner, S. E. (2004) *Reclaiming the Enlightenment: Toward a Politics of Radical Engagement*, New York: Columbia University Press.
Bourdieu, P. (1984) *La distinction: Critique Sociale du Jugement*, trans. Richard Nice, *Distinction: A Social Critique of the Judgment of Taste*, Cambridge, Mass: Harvard University Press.
Brady, D. (2005) 'The Welfare State and Relative Poverty in Rich Western Democracies, 1967–97,' *Social Forces* 83(June): 1329–64.
Braverman, H. (1975) *Labor and Monopoly Capital: The Degradation of Work in the Twentieth Century*, New York, Monthly Review Press.
Brysk, A. (2005) *Human Rights and Human Wrongs: Constructing Global Civil Society*, New York: Routledge.

Burawoy, M. (2005) 'For Public Sociology,' 2004 Presidential Address, American Sociological Association, *American Sociological Review* 70: 4–28.

Buttel, F. H. and Gould, K. (2005) 'Global Social Movements at the Crossroads: An Investigation of Relations Between the Anti-Corporate Globalization and Environmental Movements,' in Podobnik and Reifer (eds) *Transforming Globalization: Challenges and Opportunities in the Post 9/11 Era*, Leiden: Brill Academic Press.

Derrida, J. (1994) *Specters of Marx, The State of the Debt, The Work of Mourning, and The New International*, trans. Peggy Kamuf, London: Routledge.

Donnelly, J. (1989) *Universal Human Rights in Theory and Practice*, Ithaca: Cornell University Press.

Duneier, M. (1999) *Sidewalk*, New York: Farrar, Straus and Giroux.

Epstein, C. F. (2007) 'Great Divides: The Cultural, Cognitive and Social Bases of the Global Subordination of Women,' 2006 Presidential Address, American Sociological Association, *American Sociological Review* 72(1): 1–22.

Falk, R. A. (2000) *Human Rights Horizons: The Pursuit of Justice in a Globalizing World*, New York: Routledge.

Featherman, D. L. and Hauser, R. M. (1978) *Opportunity and Change*, New York: Academic Press.

Fisher, W. F. and Ponniah, T. (eds) (2003) *Another World is Possible: Popular Alternatives to Globalization at the World Social Forum*, London: Zed Books.

Frezzo, M. (2008) 'Sociology, Human Rights, and the World Social Forum,' *Societies without Borders* 3(1): 35–47.

Gale Research (2005) *Encyclopedia of Associations: International Organizations* (2005) Detroit, MI: Gale Research.

Gans, H. J. (1968) *More Equality*, New York: Pantheon.

—— (1995) *The War Against the Poor*, New York: Basic Books.

Garber, M., Hanssen, B. and Walowitz, R. L. (eds) (2000) *The Ethical Turn*, New York: Routledge.

Goldstein, J. R. (1999) 'The Leveling of Divorce in the United States,' *Demography* 36(3): 409–14.

Goldthorpe, J. H. (1974) 'Social Inequality and Social Integration in Modern Britain,' in Wedderburn (ed.) *Poverty, Inequality and the Class Structure*, Cambridge: Cambridge University Press.

Gordon, D. M., Edwards, R. and Reich, M. (1982) *Segmented Work, Divided Workers: The Historical Transformation of Labor in the United States*, Cambridge: Cambridge University Press.

Gould, C. C. (2004) *Globalizing Democracy and Human Rights*, Cambridge: Cambridge University Press.

Green, J. M. (1999) *Deep Democracy: Community, Diversity and Transformation*, Lanham, MD: Rowman & Littlefield.

Group of 19 (2005) 'Porto Alegre Manifesto'. Available online at http://www.zmag.org/sustainers/content/2005–02/20group_of_nineteen.cfm

Hahnel, R. (1999) *Panic Rules: Everything You Need to Know about the Global Economy*, Boston, MA: South End Press.

—— (2005) *Economic Justice and Democracy*, New York: Routledge.

Harding, S. (2003) 'How Standpoint Methodology Informs Philosophy of Social Science,' in Turner and Roth (eds) *The Blackwell Guide to the Philosophy of the Social Science*, Oxford: Blackwell.

Harvey, D. (2005) *A Brief History of Neoliberalism*, Oxford: Oxford University Press.

Heyns, C., Padilla D. and Zwaak, (2004) 'A Schematic Comparison of Regional Rights Systems,' *Sur: International Journal on Human Rights* 4: 163–71.

International Forum on Globalization (2002) *Alternatives to Economic Globalization: A Better World is Possible*, San Francisco: Berrett-Koehler Publishers.

International Labour Organization (2004) *A Fair Globalization: Creating Opportunities for All*, World Commission Report on the Social Dimension of Globalization, Geneva: International Labour Organization.

International Peoples Forum (no date). Available online at http://www.ipf.homeip.net/

Jackson, T. (2004) *Chasing Progress: Beyond Measuring Economic Growth*, London: New Economics Foundation.

Jameson, F. (1991) *Postmodernism, or, The Cultural Logic of Late Capitalism*, Durham, NC: Duke University Press.

Jencks, C. (1973) *Modern Movement in Architecture*, Garden City, NY: Anchor.

Kuhn, T. S. (1962) *The Structure of Scientific Revolutions*, Chicago: University of Chicago Press.

Kuznets, S. (1966) *Modern Economic Growth: Rate, Structure, and Spread*, New Haven: Yale University Press.

Lamont, M. and Fournier, M. (eds) (1992) *Cultivating Differences: Symbolic Boundaries and the Making of Inequality*, Chicago: University of Chicago Press.

Lin, N. (1999) 'Social Networks and Status Attainment,' *Annual Review of Sociology* 25: 467–87.

Lyotard, J-F. (1992) *The Postmodern Explained*, Minneapolis: University of Minnesota Press.

Mann, M. (1986) *The Sources of Social Power*, Cambridge: Cambridge University Press.

Massey, D. and Denton, N. A. (1993) *American Apartheid: Segregation and the Making of the Underclass*, Cambridge, Mass.: Harvard University Press.

Millennium Ecosystem Assessment (2005) 'Living Beyond Our Means: Natural Assets and Human Well-Being.' Available online at htttp://www.millenniumassessment.org/en/Products.BoardStatement.aspx

Moncada, A. and Olivas, J. (2003) *Hispanos 2000*, Madrid: Ediciones Libertarias.

Morris, A. (2000) 'Building Blocks of Social Inequality,' *Comparative Studies in Society and History* 42(2): 482–6.

Oliver, M. L. and Grant, D. M. (2001) 'The Persistence of Poverty in a Changing World,' in Blau (ed.) *The Blackwell Companion to Sociology*, Malden, Mass.: Blackwell.

Orend, B. (2002) *Human Rights: Concept and Context*, Peterborough, Ontario: Broadview Press.

Paul, J. A. (2000) 'NGOs and Global Policy-Making,' Global Policy Forum. Available online at http://www.globalpolicy.org/ngos/analysis/anal00.htm

Robinson, W. I. (2004) *A Theory of Global Capitalism*, Baltimore: Johns Hopkins University Press.

Sahle, E. (2007) 'Globalization and Politics of Transformation in Africa,' *Societies without Borders* 2(2): 198–221.

Sennett, R. (2003) *Respect in a World of Inequality*, New York: W. W. Norton.

Singer, P. (2002) *One World: The Ethics of Globalization*, New Haven: Yale University Press.

Small Arms Survey (2006) *Small Arms Survey: Unfinished Business*, Oxford: Oxford University Press.

Smith, K. I. (2007) *The State and Indigenous Movements*, New York: Routledge.

Stiglitz, J. E. (2003) *Globalization and Its Discontents*, New York: W. W. Norton.

Strickner, A. (2006) 'Draft WTO Texts Show Broad Differences Among WTO Members,' The Institute for Agriculture and Trade Policy, June 22. Available online at http://www.tradeobservatory.org

Tilly, C. (1998) *Durable Inequality*, Berkeley: University of California Press.

Touraine, A. (1995) *Critique of Modernity*, Cambridge: Blackwell.

Turner, B. S. (1993) 'Outline of a General Theory of Human Rights,' *Sociology* 27(3): 489–512.

—— (2006a) *Vulnerability and Human Rights*, University Park, PA: Penn State University Press.

—— (2006b) 'Global Sociology and the Nature of Rights,' *Societies without Borders* 1: 41–52.

United Nations (2006) *World Economic and Social Survey 2006: Diverging Growth and Development*, New York: United Nations.

Wilson, W. J. (1987) *The Truly Disadvantaged: The Inner City, the Underclass, and Public Policy*, Chicago: University of Chicago Press.

Woodiwiss, A. (2005) *Human Rights*, Abingdon: Routledge.

Woodward, D. and Simms, A. (2006) *Growth Isn't Working*, London: New Economics Foundation.

World Social Forum (2001) Charter of Principles. Available online at http://www.portoalegre2002.org/homepage.asp (accessed 28 August 2008).

Worldwatch Institute (2006) *Vital Signs 2006–07*, London: W. W. Norton.

Wright, E. O. (1979) *Class Structure and Income Distribution*, New York: Academic Press.

9 Corporations and human rights

Gideon Sjoberg

Can human rights standards be employed so as to hold corporations morally accountable? This query calls upon us to examine the theoretical premises undergirding human rights. It also requires us to critically examine the theoretical foundations of how organizations – or, more narrowly, corporations – actually function sociologically. Without an adequate understanding of the sociological nature of corporate entities we are unable to craft an effective course of action that will bring corporations under the human rights umbrella.

In recent years a number of legal theorists have directed attention to the applicability of human rights moral standards to corporations, not just to states. Steven R. Ratner (2001), in his extended essay 'Corporations and Human Rights: A Theory of Legal Responsibility', stands at the forefront of directing attention to these particular non-state actors. He acknowledges that corporations have been held morally accountable to certain human rights standards under state law (in particular, tort law in the US – see e.g. Dale 2007). However, many states are without such a legal framework, and Ratner's objective is to incorporate human rights standards into the international legal system.

Ratner is not alone in this endeavor (cf. Kinley and Tadaki 2004). Philip Alston (2005), a major figure in the field of law and human rights, has edited a book called *Non-State Actors and Human Rights* wherein a number of scholars address the matter of corporations and human rights. While we are in fundamental agreement with the general thrust of these authors' contributions, we are also persuaded that a critical sociological perspective regarding the nature of corporate entities would do much to clarify the issues they are addressing. In a nutshell, our thesis is that the lack of understanding of how corporations function in practice – particularly the relationship between human agents and these organizational structures – is a major shortcoming of current legal theorizing regarding human rights and corporations.

Within the confines of this adumbrated essay, we can only outline the main contours of our argument. We begin with a brief analysis of our orientation towards human rights. After that we discuss the centrality of corporations in the modern world and suggest why human rights standards are so essential if moral accountability for such entities is to be achieved. Within this context we also examine the legal status of corporations that have emerged as creations of the state. With that argument in place we turn to a sociological analysis of the nature of formal organizations, or bureaucracies, that encompass the corporate form. We devote particular attention to the relationship between human agency and the organizational structure. Given this background we can then highlight in a more studied manner our central argument: some fundamental reconfiguration in the legal conception of corporations seems essential if we are to adequately address the issue of how to hold corporations accountable to human rights standards.

The nature of human rights principles

Sociology has been divided, even in its early formation, with respect to the legitimacy of studying what is moral. A major strand of sociology rules out investigation of the moral order. Yet, if the moral order is not god-given or biopsychological (as the utilitarians, for instance, argue) then it is sociocultural in origin. If the moral order is sociocultural in nature, it is a proper subject of sociological analysis.

When we examine the human rights literature, we find, not unexpectedly, various definitions of what are human rights. For us human rights can be most effectively conceptualized as claims of human agents against organized power arrangements so as to advance the dignity of (or equal concern and respect for) human agents (Sjoberg, *et al.* 2001). An emphasis upon the claims of human beings against organized power can be justified by examining how rights, later reconfigured as human rights, came to the fore historically. As we emphasize below, sociologists have typically taken the conceptual frame of duties to a social order as their starting point, and have viewed rights (such as citizen rights) as deriving from a commitment to duties. Such a moral order differs rather markedly from one in which rights are of more fundamental import.

Ironically, a number of scholars (in particular certain positivists) who reject moral theorizing as a sociological way of knowing have unquestioningly accepted the morality of a utilitarian framework. Yet their adherence to some form of the 'pleasure-pain' principle has in practice led them to support a moral order founded on duties. Even sociologists who, following in the footsteps of Durkheim, conceive of morality as a legitimate realm of sociological investigation, have shunned a human rights perspective. In effect they more readily adhere to a duty-based 'system morality' than to one that acknowledges the reality that if the dignity of human beings is to be sustained, human agents must be assured of basic claims against organized power arrangements.

That classical sociologists pushed the rights framework aside is understandable on historical grounds. Although stirrings in behalf of rights have a substantial history (in, for instance, John Locke's theorizing) the 'rights of man' doctrine came into its own in a far more concrete manner during the French Revolution. While the rights doctrine also finds expression in the Bill of Rights of the American Constitution, it is the French revolutionaries who have commanded most attention from scholars. Tellingly, the conservative Edmund Burke voiced opposition to the rights of man doctrine, as did the liberal Jeremy Bentham, who spoke of rights as 'nonsense on stilts'(Waldron, 1987). In turn, the radical Karl Marx derided the French revolutionaries as advancing a far too individualistic conception of man.

Inasmuch as the intellectual traditions out of which sociology emerged raised objections to the rights perspective, the founders of sociology also shied away from a moral order founded on rights. So too, the classical sociological figures regarded duties as far more congenial than rights in their analyses of order.

Still, we find difficulty in imagining that issues such as liberty, equality and fraternity (the rallying cry of the French revolutionaries) could have gained traction without the underlying premise that human beings possess claims on the power arrangements of a social order. The revolutionaries implicitly understood that if appeals to the divine and to tradition are shattered as justifications for power arrangements and if human beings are to achieve some semblance of liberty and equality, then some social space must be carved out for human beings to question and to participate in the decision-making process. Such can be accomplished only if the use of arbitrary power is constrained or limited through a commitment to rights. The broad outlines of our argument find, we believe, support in recent historical scholarship; of considerable import is Lynn Hunt's (2007) *Inventing Human Rights*, a study of the French Revolution.

As we look back on broad historical processes of the past several centuries, we can discern a questioning of centralized authority and power as an ever wider range of persons come to acquire the social and technical knowledge that somehow needs to be tapped into and acted upon if modern social orders are to be sustained. The exclusivity of knowledge within the confines of a small elite cannot sustain modernity. Some version of Jurgen Habermas's (1987) 'lifeworld' appears to be an essential feature of the development of industrialization and urbanization.

Approaching the question of morals from this angle, we can discern how human agents have had to grapple with the construction of a moral order that protects human beings against the arbitrary use of power. Although the rights perspective recognizes that duties are a staple in any kind of social order, members of such a social order must acknowledge that basic rights are essential if limits on arbitrary power are to be affirmed. Furthermore, a. commitment to rights seems essential if minority groups and minority belief systems are to be protected. A moral system founded simply on duties to some larger social order seems incapable of attaining that objective.

The concept of rights emerged within a nation-state framework. During the twentieth century the rights framework was reframed as human rights that are universally applicable. Human rights principles, emerging as they did out of the societal rights tradition, came into their own after World War II, as human agents were confronted with the question of how to create a global moral order that could constrain the arbitrary employment of state power (cf. Kennedy 2006). The Nazi destruction of European Jews and other minorities brought human rights to center stage. The effort to institutionalize a moral order founded on human rights moved forward on several fronts in the years immediately following World War II. The two most salient developments were the adoption in 1948 of the Universal Declaration of Human Rights by members of the United Nations (UN) and the construction of the legal principles underlying the Nuremberg trials, which held state and other officials responsible for the systematic killings of Jews and other minorities. The trials at Nuremberg, while controversial and flawed, lent credence to the concept of 'crimes against humanity,' which privileges human status against power groups who would act to undermine it (see 'Essays on the Laws of War and War Crimes Tribunals in Honor of Telford Taylor' 1999).

Since the creation of the Universal Declaration of Human Rights a number of covenants have been adopted by most member states of the UN, thereby, in theory, anchoring the principles enunciated in the Universal Declaration within the international legal structure. Within a narrower legal framework, the formation of the European Court of Human Rights is a major innovation; its jurisdiction has been framed by the Council of Europe and reaches beyond the confines of the European Union (e.g. Goldhaber 2007). More recently we have witnessed the establishment of an International Criminal Court.

Still, the institutionalization of universal human rights principles remains problematic. The destruction or repression of humans on a worldwide scale persists. The policies of the Bush II administration, in the early years of the twenty-first century, can be read as a sustained effort to undermine strategic features of the human rights doctrine that emerged after World War II, as strategic members of this administration have sought to reassert nation-state prerogatives. The steps taken to by-pass or undermine human rights principles have moved forward on a variety of fronts, including an acceptance of torture, through the use of, for instance, the 'rendition' of prisoners, which is in turn justified by the assertion of the paramount importance of executive power. Nonetheless, elements within the Bush administration have resisted efforts to dismantle the international legal system, and a counterattack by various elements in the broader societal community – one that tacitly, even overtly, accepts human rights principles – seems well underway. These efforts suggest that the international human rights doctrine has become somewhat more entrenched than one might have anticipated.

Thus, one can readily underestimate the emergence of a human rights orientation; conversely, one can overstate its practical saliency in the modern global order. Although human rights theory and practice have come far since World War II, the institutionalization of such a moral orientation is far from complete, particularly with regard to practice. The human rights doctrine remains a work in progress, one that could culminate in failure.

Legal scholars and political theorists, rather than philosophers, have been at the forefront of human rights theory and practice. While we readily acknowledge the contributions of legal/political activists and scholars, we are persuaded that human rights theorizing and practice can profit greatly from an infusion of sociological reasoning. As various elements in the world community attempt to construct a new moral order predicated on human rights principles and seek to convert these into practice, sociological analysis can serve not only to clarify existing debates but also to highlight problem areas worthy of attention. At least two realms can profit from a sociological way of knowing: one is the relationship between human rights principles and nation-state power; the other is the question of extending human rights principles to corporations.

Corporations in the modern world

Why should corporations be held accountable to human rights principles? In addressing this query we consider, first, the social and moral impact of corporations globally and, second, the legal definition of corporations (social entities that have historically been constructed by the state). The latter section provides much-needed background for our core contention regarding the problems confronting scholars and practitioners who argue that corporations should be held accountable to human rights standards.

The impact of corporations

It seems evident that modern globalization processes have been driven by corporations. Nor is the role of corporate entities a recent phenomenon. One much-neglected sub-theme in Adam Smith's (1937) *An Inquiry into the Nature and Causes of the Wealth of Nations* is the master's concern with the East India Company. We judge Smith to be less than enthusiastic about the role that this corporate body played in the expansion of the British Empire.

It was during the late 1800s that corporations as we now know them came into their own. They have, however, been the central organizational structure in the expansion of capitalism. Surprisingly, they have been neglected by such major scholars as Immanuel Wallerstein, who has detailed the expansion of the capitalist world system. We side with John Kenneth Galbraith in his argument for the centrality of the corporate sector: that is, corporations have made possible the expansion of modern capitalism while also generating some of modernity's deepest problems.

Corporations have been deeply implicated in a number of situations involving gross violations of human rights during the twentieth century. They played a crucial role in the genocide practiced by the Nazis. A case in point is the use of forced labor by corporations under the Nazi regime. Furthermore, the killing tools such as gasses employed at Auschwitz, for instance, were manufactured by industrial giants in the Nazi state (e.g. Hayes 1989). The recent struggle over reparations resulting from the Nazis's confiscation of gold and other valuables held by German Jews and the depositing of these items in Swiss banks has thrust into public view the complicity of corporations in the destruction of European Jewry.

We can also single out the apartheid regime in South Africa and what we learned after its overthrow by the African Congress Party. Instead of trying the leaders of the apartheid regime in national or international courts, the Nelson Mandela-led government established the Truth and Reconciliation Commission (1999), whose objective was to further reconciliation through the excavation and exposure of the workings of the apartheid regime. It is difficult to imagine how apartheid could have been sustained without the explicit or implicit cooperation of the large corporations operating in South Africa. Corporate enterprises played a notable role in mining during the apartheid era, and one wing of the corporate sector was deeply involved in the practices of the security industry (and the resulting oppression of blacks) sponsored by the state.

While corporations have been a creation of the state, they are nowadays often multinational or transnational in scope and operate with a notable autonomy from the state. (Admittedly, in some societies corporate entities such as energy companies are state-owned – a complicating factor that we cannot elaborate upon within the confines of this chapter.) Although corporate entities played a strategic role in the international economy of Smith's time, the economic and social impact of multinational corporations (MNCs) today seems vastly more pervasive. John H. Jackson (2006: 28), a noted legal scholar, speaks about the immense power of some of these MNCs and observes that 'the total annual revenue or business status of many MNCs is greater that the gross domestic product (GDP) of all but a dozen or so national economies in the world.'

Managers of corporations may at times shape the manner in which the leaderships of states construct the rules within which corporate activities take place. This is documented in Susan Sell's (2003) compelling account of how the rules regarding intellectual property rights, especially patents, came to be constructed in the Agreement on Trade-Related Aspects of Intellectual Property Rights (TRIPS). As an instance, lobbying led by 12 executives of powerful MNCs based in the US shaped the regulations devised by diplomats in the Uruguay round. Sell (2003: 96) boldly asserts: 'twelve corporations made public law for the world'. Furthermore, corporate-constructed rules regarding patents have permitted a small group of companies to attain near-oligarchic domination in selected economic arenas.

Contestations regarding the activities of large MNCs are rather widespread (Sell 2003). The monopoly over patents has given rise to life-defining debates globally. Should, for instance, the patent rights of corporations take priority over efforts by companies without patent rights to produce inexpensive drugs in the battle against HIV/AIDS? Insofar as the basic health of human agents comes to be defined as a human right, the activities of, for instance, the dominant pharmaceutical companies seem likely to be questioned more intensively. Still, as noted above, a number of large MNCs command greater power and resources than do many states, lending support to the thesis that corporations, like states, should be held accountable to more universal (international) human rights principles.

We should also consider the possibility that a number of modern corporations have become so powerful and strategic that they are 'too big to fail'. Although this concept has typically been applied to banking enterprises, its usage can profitably be extended to other economic spheres as well. Consequently, a state or a coalition of states or an international body may encounter grave risks if they seek to punish large MNCs too severely. After all, the economy on which the well-being of the citizenry rests could be jeopardized, with consequent loss of productive capacity and jobs for wide swaths of the population.

The rise of the corporate control industry has even starker ramifications for human rights than the patterns mentioned above. There is a growing body of literature on corporate control firms. The writings of Peter W. Singer (2003; 2007) are especially instructive (cf. Avant 2005). As the concept implies, these corporations engage in strategic forms of social control or coercion. In some instances violence by corporations has become commodified (Maogoto 2006). Scholars have for some time recognized that in late capitalism the state has outsourced a number of police functions to private industries. But now, corporate control industries have become major players on the world stage. One particularly visible sub-sector of the corporate control industry in the US is the prison-industrial complex.

The war in Iraq has demonstrated the growing power of the corporate control sector and the resultant lack of moral accountability (Sjoberg 2005). Although the private sector has long played a role in wars, the activities of the corporate control industry have reached a new order of magnitude. The use of violence, it would appear, is no longer the sole province of the state. These multinationals in Iraq do not operate merely in a supportive role to the military. Paul Bremer, the viceroy in charge of the Coalition Provisional Authority, was protected not by US army personnel but by guards employed by private corporations. And the employees of these multinational firms have been patrolling the oil pipelines. Some corporate personnel were involved in the Abu Ghraib prison scandal. The reality is that MNCs have been deeply implicated in the Iraq war (e.g. Miller 2006; Scahill 2007).

Reflect for a moment on the social implications of this arrangement. If one accepts the logic of the market, we find that the greater the destruction of the social order in Iraq, the greater the demand for corporate services. Indeed, corporate firms profit from chaos in Iraq; after all, funding for their activities is provided primarily by the US taxpayer. The victims of violence are unlikely to financially underwrite the activities of these corporations.

Additionally, the market emphasizes short-term objectives. Corporate enterprises, with their emphasis on immediate profits, are ill-suited to the construction of new organizations and institutions, a process that requires some collective mobilization of activities in order to achieve long-term objectives. Furthermore, corporations and their personnel typically lie outside the compass of moral accountability as laid down by the Geneva Conventions, whose focus has been on the state apparatus.

The matter of corporate accountability with respect to human rights standards or principles is further complicated by sustained efforts by proponents of 'market forces' to seal off economic activities in general, and corporate activities in particular, within the sphere of 'private law.' For side by side with the human rights endeavor we can discern sustained efforts by powerful private actors to carve out a sphere of private law that lies not only outside the influence of the state but also beyond the reach of the human rights regimen on the international level (cf. Dubinsky 2005). This private legal sphere stresses accountability to the 'laws of the market,' not to human rights standards.

The legal structure of corporations

We have, thus far, taken the nature of business corporations for granted. Inasmuch as, historically, corporations were creations of the state, we should look more closely at how the legal order has come to define corporate entities. In so doing we draw upon the writings of highly regarded legal scholars such as Henry Hansmann and Reinier Kraakman. Their analysis (with others) appears in *The Anatomy of Corporate Law* (Kraakman, *et al.* 2004). Their conclusions are predicated on an analysis of legal systems in the US, the UK, Germany, France and Japan.

These legal scholars identify five core features of the business corporation: '(1) legal personality, (2) limited liability, (3) transferable shares, (4) centralized management under a board structure, and (5) shared ownership by contributors of capital' (Kraakman, *et al.* 2004:5). The notion of legal personality suggests that corporations are treated as if they were 'natural persons'. Thus, inasmuch as corporations or firms posses a 'legal personality' they are capable of signing contracts, and they come to be bound by these contracts. The idea of limited liability means that shareholders or members of corporate boards are in effect shielded from personal liability in the event of a corporation's major financial losses or possible bankruptcy. Somewhat paradoxically, 'shared ownership' suggests a form of 'common property' (a form of property that exists in a social order wherein private property is supposedly the ideal). Hansmann and Kraakman (2001), in an earlier essay, contend that the basic features of this corporate model were in place by the beginning of the twentieth century, and that contemporary corporate law has reached 'the End of History'.

Hansmann and Kraakman (2001: 441) have also elaborated on the broader implications of the legal conception of corporations:

> There is today a broad normative consensus that shareholders alone are the parties to whom corporate managers should be accountable, resulting from widespread disenchantment with a privileged role of managers, employees, or the state in corporate affairs. This is not to say that there is agreement that corporations should be run in the interests of shareholders alone – much less that the law should sanction that result. All thoughtful people believe that corporate enterprise should be organized and operated to serve the interests of society as a whole, and that the interests of shareholders deserve no greater weight in that social calculus than do the interests of any other members of society. The point is simply that now, as a consequence of both logic and experience, there is convergence on a consensus that the best means to this end (that is, the pursuit of aggregate social welfare) is to make corporate managers strongly accountable to shareholder interests and, at least in direct terms, only to those interests.

Corporate law privileges the shareholders to such an extent that Hansmann and Kraakman (2001: 442) observe that 'nonshareholder constituencies … lie outside of corporate law.' Workers can draw on the law of labor contracting, pension law, health and safety law and the like. Consumers in turn can rely on product liability law, antitrust law and so on. Nonetheless, the bottom line is that corporate law serves to insulate managers and shareholders of a corporation from direct legal challenge by other interests in the social order.

The corporation's legal autonomy becomes more pronounced as the economic system (of which the corporation is a key segment) seeks to define itself as possessing an autonomy from the societal system or the broader global system. The international economic order tends toward being encased within the sphere of 'private law.' The market, above all, is perceived as adhering to its own set of laws, namely those of the market. Thus we can delineate two dimensions to the efforts by the economic system to seal itself off from larger social or moral responsibility: first, corporate law protects the corporation from direct intervention by nonshareholders, and, second, the conception of the economic system as possessing an autonomy from larger societal arrangements further insulates corporations from moral accountability, particularly from adherence to human rights principles.

The nature of formal organizations: a clarification of issues

Our central thesis is that if we are to hold corporations morally accountable we must realign the legal underpinnings of corporations with the sociological reality of formal organizations. But what is the sociological nature of the corporate enterprise? We shall outline, in general analytic terms, the structure of such enterprises, grounding our analysis in how complex organizations (or bureaucracies) actually work in everyday life. A number of patterns have become painfully evident as a result of the financial scandals that have plagued corporations, especially in the US, in the twenty-first century. Like Durkheim, we find that deviant activities serve to clarify the nature of the corporation's rules or normative order.

Despite the attention given to Max Weber (1978) and the study of bureaucracy (or formal organizations), this topic occupies an awkward position in contemporary sociological theorizing. Talcott Parsons (1971: 116–17), for one, shied away from investigating powerful complex organizations as he emphasized the centrality of professional and voluntary associations (not of bureaucracy) in modern society. James Coleman (1990), who is identified as a rational choice theorist, incorporated, much to his credit, the notion of the corporate actor (both state and private) into one facet of his theoretical framework, and he stressed the asymmetry of social power between individuals and corporate forms. But Coleman's conception of corporate actors, which is founded on his commitment to methodological individualism, leaves no room for comprehending the internal dynamics of large-scale bureaucratic organizations, be these business firms or state entities. The manner in which human agents interpret, shape, and manipulate organizational rules is of enormous import in addressing the accountability of large organizations.

We should also take note of Anthony Giddens and Pierre Bourdieu, two sociological theorists whose widely influential writings differ significantly in their theoretical thrust. Both, however, can be faulted for their failure to theorize about large-scale multinational enterprises in the modern world, the impact of these behemoths being immense. And although Habermas (1987) takes Weber's iron cage seriously as he challenges Weber's pessimism by contending that modernity has fostered the development of not only political and economic systems but also the lifeworld with its 'communicative rationality'. It is through this lifeworld that human agents are able to overcome the disenchantment that Weber attributed to the growth of bureaucratic structures (and the rationalization process). Still, Habermas's direct theoretical engagement with large-scale corporate systems (public and private) seems severely limited.

While leading social theorists have typically slighted the study of formal or bureaucratic organizations, much research and theory in sub-disciplines in sociology have modified and elaborated upon Weber's conceptualizations. Yet, certain realms remain underinvestigated, particularly the role of human agency in these bureaucratic organizations. True, sociologists have taken tacit account of human agency (in their study of, say, informal arrangements), but we proceed further and seek to integrate a strong version of human agency into our analysis of formal organizations. Our objective serves to link the concept of human agency as advanced by such pragmatists as George Herbert Mead (1934) and John Dewey (1981) with that of the Weberian orientation so as to come to terms with core features of formal bureaucratic organizations (see Vaughan and Sjoberg 1984; Sjoberg, *et al.* 2003; and Tan and Sjoberg 2005). We should remember that although Weber is often read as emphasizing the subjective orientation of the actor, he effectively dropped human agents out of his analysis of bureaucracy.

At this point we digress momentarily in order to consider George Herbert Mead's and John Dewey's conception of human agency. Unlike utilitarians or phenomenologists, for instance, Mead and Dewey conceptualized 'the other' as essential for comprehending the nature of human nature. It is through interaction with others that the 'social self' and the 'social mind' emerge, and inasmuch as humans think and reflect, they are able take the roles of others. We have throughout our analysis assumed that the social self and the social mind are products of interaction with others, and thus individualism, which typifies the modern world, emerges within some larger group experience (the individualism of classical liberalism that undergirds traditional human rights theorizing being severely flawed). Furthermore, the social mind – how one thinks and what one thinks about – is a social process that is grounded in an agent's social interaction with others. Admittedly, there are different layers at which the mind functions, from reflective consciousness (thinking about thinking) to the reliance on habit that Dewey elaborated upon. Dewey's analysis of habit is congruent with Pierre Bourdieu's habitus, as the latter has acknowledged (Bourdieu and Wacquant 1992: 122). Inasmuch as we adopt the Mead and Dewey framework, we are highly skeptical of the rather widespread view that thought processes of the 'social mind' can be reduced to some neurological reality. Although biological conditions are of utmost import, how a person reasons is ultimately a social and cultural process.

These insights directly bear upon the interrelationships between human agency and organizational structures. If we have learned one salient fact from the gigantic cases of fraud perpetrated by managers of some of the largest (and respected) business organizations in the world in the twenty-first century, we have learned that the wide discretion of managers has permitted them, for instance, to manipulate accounting rules or procedures, and to create, as in the case of Enron, new organizational forms that have played a strategic role in the construction of ghost profits, ultimately leading to the restructuring (or even collapse) of certain large-scale corporate structures whose activities have been global in scope. These managerial activities underscore the role of human agency in interpreting rules or norms, oftentimes in diverse ways but nonetheless bounded by structural constraints. The system of hierarchical authority and the division of labor sets limits on how rules may be interpreted or bent. We shall now sketch out the characteristics of formal organizational or bureaucratic structures in the modern world.

We cannot herein analyze the pattern whereby nowadays state entities are frequently labeled bureaucratic, and such an organizational form is said to be nonexistent in the private sector. The premise that large-scale MNCs are not bureaucratic in nature is grossly misleading and empirically incorrect (though we readily acknowledge that some important differences between business corporations and state entities exist).

The structural dimensions of formal organizations – notably hierarchy, the division of labor, and standardization or routinization – loom large. Hierarchy of authority is a hallmark of present-day complex organizations. One pattern is much in evidence: the rules and regulations (internal and external) governing managerial or elite activities are fewer and less constraining than the rules and regulations governing the activities of occupants of lower-ranking positions. Although persons in the lower ranks can attain a degree of autonomy through acquiring even limited expert knowledge, they are nonetheless severely constrained by complex regulations, particularly in dealings with outsiders. One telling consequence of this arrangement is that the bottom layers of the organizational hierarchy, those most constrained by the rules, are expected to interact with, and cope with, the bottom layers of the social order: persons who possess the least knowledge about how formal organizations carry out their activities. This situation reinforces social stratification in the more general social or global order.

Undoubtedly, modern formal organizations, whether public or private, serve to mobilize a vast array of specialists into a more or less co-ordinated whole. This requires rather detailed record keeping and formalized accounting procedures. And the standardization of these activities (note the current efforts to harmonize accounting procedures for business corporations worldwide) enhances the efficiency of formal organizations, particularly within the corporate realm. There is a great deal of discussion nowadays about the ebb and flow of markets, including the massive amounts of capital and information that flow globally. So too, bureaucratic personnel in large-scale corporations come to innovate and at times reshape organizational rules in ways a number of scholars tend to overlook. Nonetheless, the organizational framework within which these activities take place should not be ignored. Modern urban life in advanced industrial societies is highly dependent upon complex organizational structures such as those that deliver electricity and water services and dispose of garbage and sewage.

What is deceptive about these activities is that the complex organizational (or bureaucratic) arrangements that enable, for instance, the distribution of electricity and water are largely invisible to the urban public (including many social scientists) until something goes awry. These organizational structures are typically characterized by a managerial elite, a board of directors and a highly trained cadre of engineers, lawyers and accountants supported by a work force with its own set of specialists; all of these are subject to complex rules and regulations. There are, to be sure, complex processes of outsourcing that distinguish the present from the past, but such more flexible arrangements should not mislead us. The flows of capital and information are typically made possible and shaped by large and complex structural arrangements.

A somewhat closer look at stock exchanges in the functioning of global capitalism is instructive. The New York Stock Exchange, for example, is a formal bureaucratic structure. It is now a public corporation with a CEO and a board of directors, and it encompasses traders (apparently, agents licensed by major shareholders who once owned seats on the exchange), lawyers, accountants and specialized personnel such as those who construct and maintain the computer systems. Additionally, complex formal rules govern a wide range of activities: the nature of companies that can be listed on the exchange, how payments for stocks are to be made, and so on. Some of these rules emanate from within the organization; others are responses to demands imposed by state entities or even international bodies. Thus the data strongly support the view that the massive flow of capital globally is dependent upon large-scale organizational structures – not only stock exchanges but banks and other large financial organizations. Yet, rarely do social scientists or journalists acknowledge the role of bureaucratic organizations in facilitating and, more importantly, shaping the massive capital flows across national borders.

Understanding the formal rules is merely the first step in comprehending the everyday activities of modern complex organizations. For some decades sociologists and other students of organizations have been documenting the saliency of informal rules that supplement formal organizational structures. For instance, when human agents seek to apply the formal rules in a variety of concrete situations, they typically find themselves creating informal arrangements that supplement or modify the formal system. Knowledge of the formal rules is insufficient in and of itself as a guide to understanding a variety of concrete actions. At the same time, the informal activities mirror in a general sense the hierarchical nature of organizations and the division of labor within them.

In addition to the formal and informal rules or norms, secrecy systems emerge within large-scale organizations (both public and private). These secrecy arrangements are both formal and informal. We should not underestimate the power of secrecy arrangements; they are often the basis of corporate fraud or governmental malfeasance (yes, even the violation of human rights). They arise for various reasons. Managers of business corporations, for instance, are often proactive in hiding strategic aspects of their knowledge and activities from underlings and from outsiders. In turn, persons occupying lower positions of power and authority often resort to a secrecy system of sorts in order to protect themselves from the arbitrary use of power by their superiors.

Complicating the lives of personnel within formal bureaucratic organizations is the way in which their activities are anchored within a larger organizational field. Within this often highly contested realm – whether local, national or international – managers depend not only on their own abilities and knowledge but also on the resources of the corporations they command. These large-scale corporate resources both restrain and enable managers as they seek to address a wide variety of economic and political realities.

In addition, certain social processes cut across the hierarchical arrangements. In theory, managers delegate responsibility, but in practice they delegate blameability under the guise of responsibility. Consequently, managers often blame those below for organizational failures or for their own shortcomings. Conversely, situations arise where managers discourage persons below from informing them about questionable activities so as to legitimate their reliance on plausible deniability. Additionally, we should pay heed to the manner in which loyalty systems emerge, particularly between managers and their immediate underlings. These loyalty arrangements bind together strategic elements of the bureaucracy. Perhaps most important of all, organizational personnel, at all levels, take considerable care in crafting and sustaining intricate systems of deference which glue together, on a daily basis, the hierarchical arrangements as well as the division of labor founded on specialized knowledge.

Highlighting the role of human agency in shaping corporate activities are those managers who carry out their tasks through complex forms of reasoning; they do not merely rely upon the means-end logic that Weber emphasized. Rather they employ a number of loosely structured logics, or modes of reasoning, that are yet to be explicated. One pattern can, however, be readily documented. Organizational leaders reason and act in terms of some version of parts-whole logic, where the whole is judged to be more than the sum of the parts. Military commanders have for centuries sacrificed divisions so that the army could be sustained (the actions of the Russian army at Stalingrad in World War II are illustrative of this). So too, managers of corporations justify, say, closing plants (often without consulting the affected constituency) and moving them elsewhere so that the organization will be financially 'healthier' or more efficient. Managers employ a range of other logics as well: classification schemes, analogy, and even versions of the dialectic (for instance, in coping with contradictions within organizations). These modes of reasoning become tool kits for carrying out complex activities and justifying them to members of the organization and other relevant constituents. Effective managing is typically defined by the bottom line, but corporate profits are also dependent on managerial knowledge and decision-making skills, which in turn are enabled and restrained by the corporation's economic and political position in the organizational field. We should not underestimate the manifold interrelationships between human agency and organizational structure.

When we contrast the sociological reality of how corporations function with the legal definition of a corporation, a number of patterns can be discerned. The major scandals that have engulfed large corporations in recent decades underscore the thesis that managers exercise far greater power and authority than is delineated by corporate law wherein shareholders are defined as strategic agents. From the scandal associated with the Bank of Credit and Commerce International (Beaty and Gwynne 1993) in the early 1990s to the demise of Enron, which at the beginning of the twenty-first century was regarded as one of the most successful companies in the US, we have learned that appearances are not necessarily congruent with social reality. In recent years we have had a host of corporations reissue corrected earnings reports because of creative but legally questionable accounting practices.

Nor is it often easy to distinguish between sound business decisions and fraudulent practices associated with the manipulation of accounting rules, for a number of them are subject (within limits) to differing interpretations.

More generally, it should be evident that without basic knowledge of how managers employ secrecy arrangements in covering up abuses of power, we can never come to grips with the matter of the accountability of managers and corporations with respect to human rights standards. The functional fiction on which corporations rest – namely that corporations are analogous to 'natural persons' – must be critically reexamined, even reconceptualized, if accountability to human rights principles is to be advanced. While the empirical features of large-scale organizations, of which corporations are a strategic element, could be more fully elaborated upon, our general sketch of the corporate form should serve to emphasize that corporations in actual practice diverge markedly from the legal construct of what constitutes a corporation.

Where do we go from here?

We share the view that human rights principles should be extended so as to encompass the activities of not only states but also corporations. Yet, if human rights are to be meaningful in shaping corporate activities, the legal underpinnings of corporations will need to be reshaped. Below we articulate several interrelated implications that appear to be congruent with our analysis.

First, the human rights doctrine as defined in practice appears to embody a contradiction of sorts. Acknowledging human rights as claims against powerful organizations, whether state or corporate, brings to center stage the difficulties of challenging powerful organizations. It is not mere happenstance that human rights ideals came to be emphasized in the wake of the Nazi defeat and a public airing of the genocidal process. It then became feasible to try the leaders of the Nazi order at Nuremberg, and this made possible the trial of the heads of collaborating corporations like IG Farben.

Our analysis need not be limited to court proceedings in order to document the difficulties of challenging organized power relationships. The Truth and Reconciliation Commission in South Africa was able to probe deeply into the repression and suffering that were products of the apartheid regime only after a major shift in power had occurred in South Africa. Even so, the leaderships of multinationals chose not to cooperate with the Commission and in the process justify their activities during the apartheid era. By hiding the internal workings of their organizations during the apartheid era from public scrutiny the corporate leadership apparently sought to protect their own legitimacy as well as that of their corporate structures.

We can also single out a variety of cases worldwide where the leadership during the years of repression has apparently escaped formal (particularly, legal) scrutiny, whereas individuals brought to justice have been those occupying positions of much less power (note, for instance, Guatemala). The difficulties of bringing even a fallen repressive leader to justice are reflected in the failed efforts to try General

Augusto Pinochet of Chile. Alternatively, one can point to the Cambodian case and the wanton destruction of human lives during the Khmer Rouge era (1976–9). Now, after some decades, a trial by a UN-backed tribunal is underway (the results of which had not been finalized at the time of writing).

The track record with respect to subjecting leaders of powerful states or executives of major corporations to a formal hearing should give us pause, but we must not assume that human rights standards are doomed to failure. For example, evidence suggests that the European Court of Human Rights (e.g. Ress 2005) has been successful in righting wrongs of state action in limited domains, and its successes provide guidance for one possible course of action that can be pursued in implementing additional human rights standards. And though it is difficult to document this, human rights principles as such might serve to remind leaders of large-scale business corporations how to behave. Thus, public opinion on the international level is not without some role in shaping social activities.

A second implication congruent with our analysis and one step towards holding corporations accountable to human rights standards would be for the world community to designate certain realms of profit-making by business corporations as illegitimate. Prohibiting direct profiteering from coercion or violence (as in the war in Iraq), and thus oppression of human beings, seems a modest first step in advancing the cause of human rights as a standard for holding corporations morally accountable. States (or international governmental entities) are not paragons of virtue, but currently the possibility of holding them and their leadership accountable seems theoretically more feasible than doing the same for large-scale corporations. To permit such firms, financed by taxpayers (as has been the case in Iraq), to profit at the expense of destroying others (particularly civilians) – and to justify this by the claim of market efficiency – is a practice that needs to be considerably modified if the cause of human rights is to be advanced.

If we had more space we might recast the roles of corporations, violence and human rights within a much broader framework and then ask ourselves: How can we rid the planet of war, particularly now that nuclear weaponry is rapidly proliferating (even the theoretical possibility of large corporations possessing such weaponry could become a reality)? In today's world it is utopian in the extreme to entertain the proposition that we might rid the world of war. Yet, sociologists such as Ulrich Beck (2004: 198–99) invoke Kant's ideal of 'perpetual peace.' He has reminded us that the reconstitution of Europe into what is now the European Union has significantly reduced the potentiality of armed conflict among states that once waged long and brutal wars with each other. Ultimately, if we are to examine corporations and nation-states from a moral perspective we must confront the issue of war itself.

A third implication is that the legal structure on which corporations have been founded will in all likelihood require extensive revision. This would seem more likely if we approach corporations from the perspective of international law. Although the notion of international law is sharply challenged in differing quarters of the world community, this form of legal order will likely expand as a result of globalization. And while the concept of corporation has historically been defined by the state, multinational business enterprises are having such a wide-ranging impact globally that the potential for redefinition seems somewhat more likely within the international, rather than in the national, legal order.

One pillar of corporate law – the notion that corporations possess a legal personality – will require considerable reformulation. Treating corporations as if they are 'natural persons' insulates them from moral accountability to human rights standards. In practice the narrow legal conception of corporation comes to be modified indirectly. This occurred at Nuremberg, where political and corporate leaders rather than followers, were put on trial, and it has occurred in a number of proceedings relating to corporate fraud. If we take corporate fraud as a crude analog for the problem we are addressing, we discover that in order to put top managers on trial, prosecutors in the US often reason in bureaucratic terms and thus begin with lower-level officials, who are then likely to expose the activities of their superiors in order to receive lighter sentences for themselves. There are a number of instances in the legal arena where we can point to a tacit recognition that corporations are not considered to be like 'natural persons.' That corporations function as if they were natural persons is a legal fiction far removed from empirical reality; such seems likely to impede any substantial effort to introduce human rights standards as a basis for evaluating corporate activities as morally acceptable.

Defining corporations as encompassing only shareholders and managers also stands in need of fundamental redefinition. It seems possible that human agents could create a legal structure that permits workers employed by corporations (as well as other directly affected parties) to challenge corporations from within, and not have to rely upon legal instruments external to corporate law. Yet other more pressing test cases with respect to corporate law loom on the horizon. To address the potential crises resulting from global warming or climate change or that oil and gas reserves may be finite – when the market for oil and gas is expanding exponentially – we must recognize that the principles underlying corporate law, one that privileges shareholders and managers, are far too restrictive. If indeed environmental degradation falls under the rubric of human rights (an assumption that is gaining increased acceptance), then the actions and profits of shareholders and managers can hardly be considered the be-all and end-all of corporate law. We shall need to confront much larger concerns (cf. Manual on Human Rights and the Environment 2006). Recall that the foundations of corporate law emerged at a time when 'exploitation' of the environment appeared to be acceptable; the social and economic costs of waste products were often conveniently defined as an externality. Although we cannot foretell the specific ways in which corporate law will be redefined, we appear to be on firm ground in contending that major changes in the corporate legal structure are in the offing, if modern industrial-urban social orders are to be sustained reasonably intact in the face of enormous environmental challenges that extend well beyond the boundaries of even major states. The control of carbon emissions into the atmosphere (resulting in major climate change) is worldwide in scope – so too are the issues relating to supply and usage of fresh water. Though markets will occupy a role in coping with the coming crises (which no longer present a far-distant danger), the hidden hand of corporate markets (as presently constituted) will not advance the general welfare or public good with respect to large-scale environmental issues – Hansmann and Kraakman (2001) to the contrary.

A fourth implication congruent with our analysis, and one that is closely related to the third, is the question of how to restrain or punish corporations that transgress human rights standards. It is apparent that we can impose fines upon or reconstitute corporations, but we cannot send them to jail (unlike the pattern with respect to natural persons). After the military defeat of Nazi Germany the victors were able to institute massive revisions in the repressive social arrangements that prevailed. Nowadays corporations or corporate officials who violate the rules and regulations are typically fined (though in some instances corporate leaders may be tried on criminal charges). Yet, simply fining corporations or their managers or shareholders for gross violations of human rights will not resolve the issues inherent in the structural arrangements that gave rise to the violations in the first instance. We need to think through how to reconstitute corporations so that violations of human rights standards will not be constantly repeated. This holds especially for corporate forms that are 'too big to fail.'

On the one hand, it may be possible to restructure corporations by decentralizing some of their strategic activities. On the other hand, certain large-scale organizational arrangements seem to be essential for mobilizing resources and persons so as to effectively confront global economic problems. One potential solution to major social, political and economic issues seems to be the construction of alternative forms of organizational structure that can mobilize a considerable range of activities, all the while inflicting less harm on human beings and their environment. After all, corporations have been creations of the state. Under such circumstances, why is it not in the realm of the possible for states or some international body to reconstitute them?

Conclusions

Among supporters of the thesis that the world community should bring corporations under the human umbrella are certain distinguished legal scholars.[1] Their efforts, with which we agree, are in keeping with our own conception of human rights: notably that human rights are founded on claims against organized power in order to advance human dignity. Inasmuch as a number of MNCs control more resources than do many small states, the efforts to expand the notion of human rights so as to cover corporate activities, in addition to actions by states, seems eminently reasonable.

When we speak of holding corporations accountable, the question arises: What are corporations? These entities emerged as constructs of the state. Nowadays they are defined by a number of characteristics, among these being a legal personality, the limited liability of shareholders and shared ownership by contributors of capital. A central theme of this adumbrated essay is our contention that the legal conception of corporations will require considerable redefinition if substantial progress is to be made in holding corporations, particularly multinationals, accountable to human rights principles. One significant step forward would entail realigning the legal definition of corporations with the sociological reality of formal organizations (or bureaucracies), corporations being a significant organizational form. Issues regarding corporations have been magnified as certain large firms have made enormous profits through being directly involved in the coercion or even the destruction of other human beings (as in Iraq). Rewarding self-interest in this manner is out of keeping with the general welfare of human beings everywhere. The current legal conception of corporations contravenes the sociological reality of how corporate systems actually work. The refashioning of corporations is an especially urgent task as these organizational forms are increasingly called upon to address issues that deeply affect all of humankind.

Note

1   In the future we shall need to look closely at extending the moral framework founded on human rights to cover not only corporations and state structures but also large associations such as non-governmental organizations (NGOs) (which are in effect large formal organizations). Some of these organizations have grown enormously in size, influence and power. John Jackson (2006: 27–8) observes that 'NGOs are remarkably wealthy in some cases. For example, the annual budget of OXFAM (generally viewed as a highly constructive and responsible NGO) is over $300 million – about three times the budget of the entire WTO. Such wealth gives power in the form of the ability to travel, provide research and documentary resources, entertain, and so on. .... NGOs can be remarkably non-transparent, hiding the sources of their funding and thereby deceiving the particular institutions, diplomats and governments about what goals they really seek to achieve' (cf. Jeffrey Jackson 2005). John Jackson's concerns are real: although some of the NGOs have been in the forefront of advancing democracy and the human rights agenda, they have largely shied away from applying the standards they advocate to themselves. Yet, the moral accountability of NGOs and their leadership is heightened as they increasingly wield organizational power in the global setting.

Acknowledgments

I appreciate the comments of two reviewers of this manuscript. Also I am grateful for Boyd Littrell's comments on an earlier version of the manuscript. Additionally, I am deeply indebted to Andree F. Sjoberg for her creative editorial efforts that clarified my own reasoning.

Sources

Alston, P. (ed.) (2005) *Non-State Actors and Human Rights*, New York: Oxford University Press.

Avant, D. (2005) *The Market for Force: The Consequences of Privatizing Security*, New York: Cambridge University Press.

Beaty, J. and Gwynne, S. C. (1993) *The Outlaw Bank*, New York: Random House.

Beck, U. and Willms, J. (2004) *Conversations with Ulrich Beck*, Cambridge: Polity Press.

Bourdieu, P. and Wacquant, L. (1992) *An Invitation to Reflexive Sociology*, Chicago: University of Chicago Press.

Coleman, J. S. (1990) *Foundations of Social Theory*, Cambridge, MA: Harvard University Press.

Dale, J. G. (2007) 'Transnational Legal Conflict Between Peasants and Corporations in Burma: Human Rights and Discursive Ambivalence under the U.S. Alien Torts Claims Act', in Goodale and Merry (eds) *The Practice of Human Rights: Tracking Law Between the Global and the Local*, Cambridge: Cambridge University Press.

Dewey, John (1981) *The Later Works 1925–1953*. 17 vols. Edited by Jo Ann Boydston. Carbondale, IL. South Illinois University Press.

Dubinsky, P. R. (2005) 'Human Rights Law Meets Private Law Harmonization: The Coming Conflict', *Yale International Law Journal* 30: 211–317.

'Essays on the Laws of War and War Crimes Tribunals in Honor of Telford Taylor' (1999), *Columbia Journal of Transnational Law* 37: 649–1047 (special issue).

Goldhaber, M. D. (2007) *People's History of the European Court of Human Rights*, New Brunswick, NJ: Rutgers University Press.

Habermas, J. (1987) *The Theory of Communicative Rationality: Lifeworld and System: A Critique of Functionalist Theory*, Vol. 2, Boston: Beacon Press.

Hansmann, H. and Kraakman, R. (2001) 'The End of History for Corporate Law', *Georgetown Law Journal* 89(1): 439–68.

Hayes, P. (1989) *Industry and Ideology: IG Farben in the Nazi Era*, New York: Cambridge University Press.

Hunt, L. (2007) *Inventing Human Rights*, New York: W.W. Norton.

Jackson, J. H. (2006) *Sovereignty, the WTO, and Changing Fundamentals of International Law*, Cambridge: Cambridge University Press.

Jackson, J. T. (2005) *The Globalizers: Development Works in Action*, Baltimore: The Johns Hopkins University Press.

Kennedy, P. (2006) *The Parliament of Man: The Past, Present, and Future of the United Nations*, New York: Random House.

Kinley, D. and Tadaki, J. (2004) 'From Talk to Walk: The Emergence of Human Rights Responsibilities for Corporations at International Law', *Virginia Journal of International Law* 44(Summer): 931–1023.

Kraakman, R. R., Davis, P., Hansmann, H., Hentig, G., Hopt, K. J., Kanda, H. and Rock, E. R. (2004) *The Anatomy of Corporate Law: A Comparative and Functional Approach*, New York: Oxford University Press.

Manual on Human Rights and the Environment (2006) *Manual on Human Rights and the Environment: Principles Emerging from the Case-Law of the European Court of Human Rights*, Strasbourg: Council of Europe Publishing.

Maogoto, J. N. (2006) 'The Private Military Firm – Subcontracting Sovereignty: Commodification of Violence and Fragmentation of the State's Authority', *Brown Journal of World Affairs* 13(Fall-Winter): 147–60.

Mead, George Herbert (1934) *Mind, Self and Society*. Chicago: University of Chicago Press.

Miller, T. C. (2006) *Blood Money*, New York: Little, Brown.

Parsons, T. (1971) *The System of Modern Societies*, Englewood Cliffs, N.J.: Prentice-Hall.

Ratner, S. R. (2001) 'Corporations and Human Rights: A Theory of Legal Responsibility', *Yale Law Journal* 111(Dec.): 443–546.

Ress, G. (2005) 'The Effect of Decisions and Judgments of the European Court of Human Rights in the Domestic Legal Order', *Texas International Law Journal* 40(Spring): 359–82.

176   *G. Sjoberg*

Scahill, J. (2007) *Blackwater: The Rise of the World's Most Powerful Mercenary Army*, New York: Nation Books.

Sell, S. K. (2003) *Private Power, Public Law: The Globalization of Intellectual Property Rights*, New York: Cambridge University Press.

Singer, P. W. (2003) *Corporate Warriors: The Rise of the Privatized Military Industry*, Ithaca: Cornell University Press.

—— (2006) 'Private Actors, Humanitarian Agents: Implications of the Private Military Industry for the Humanitarian Community', *Brown Journal of World Affairs* 13(Fall-Winter): 105–21.

—— (2007) 'Can't Win with 'Em, Can't Go to War without 'Em: Private Military Contractors and Counterinsurgency', Washington, DC, Brookings Institution, Policy Paper No. 4: 1–21.

Sjoberg, G. (2005) 'The Corporate Control Industry and Human Rights: The Case of Iraq', *Journal of Human Rights* 4: 95–101.

Sjoberg, G., Gill, E. A. and Tan, J. E. (2003) in L. Reynolds and N. Herman-Kinney (eds) *Handbook of Symbolic Interaction*, Walnut Creek, CA: AltaMira Press.

Sjoberg, G., Gill, E. A. and Williams, N. (2001) 'A Sociology of Human Rights', *Social Problems* 48: 11–47.

Smith, A. (1937) *An Inquiry into the Nature and Causes of The Wealth of Nations*, New York: The Modern Library.

Tan, J. E. and Sjoberg, G. (2005) 'Development and the Lifeworld: Individuals, Interstitial Relationships and Social Organizations', *International Journal of Sociology and Social Policy* 25: 145–70.

Truth and Reconciliation Commission of South Africa (1999) *Truth and Reconciliation Commission Report*, London: Macmillan Reference Limited.

Vaughan, T. R. and Sjoberg, G. (1984) 'The Individual and Bureaucracy: An Alternative Meadian Interpretation', *Journal of Applied Behavioral Science* 20: 47–69.

Waldron, Jeremy (ed) (1987) *'Nonsense upon Stilts': Bentham, Burke and Marx on the Rights of Man*. London: Methuen.

Weber, Max (1978) *Economy and Society*, 2 vols. Guenther Roth and Claus Wittich (eds.) Berkeley: University of California Press.

10 A sociology of citizenship and human rights

Does social theory still exist?

Bryan S. Turner

Introduction: cold war political theory

In 1962 Isaiah Berlin, who was then the Chichele Professor of Political and Social Theory at the University of Oxford, published an article with the title 'Does Political Theory Still Exist?' in the famous second series of *Philosophy Politics and Society* (Laslett and Runciman 1962). This article, which had originally appeared in the *Revue Francaise de Science Politique* in 1961, did much to reverse the declining fortunes of political philosophy in Britain, set out a programme of what political theory was about, and distinguished political philosophy from political science. The article outlined his objections to determinism and historical inevitability in the social sciences, which included both American political science and more importantly Marxist historical materialism. Berlin's argument was not something that had occurred to him in the 1960s. In the first edition of his biography of Karl Marx (Berlin 1939), he had explored conflicting interpretations of Marx's political theory between the Hegelian dialectic and an almost Darwinian view of causality. According to Berlin, crass materialism produced a deterministic picture of human history in which political rights played little part in social change. Berlin, who clashed with socialist and Marxist historians such as E. H. Carr, complained that Marxist historians in emphasising social and economic conditions left no space for the role of ideas, beliefs and intentions. The search for what he called 'amoral objectivity' failed to grasp the force of the moral evaluation (Ignatieff 1998: 236). However, the broader intellectual background to Berlin's essay was the impact of linguistic philosophy on the idea of 'political principles' which had led Peter Laslett in the first series of *Philosophy Politics and Society* to declare that 'For the moment, anyway, political philosophy is dead' (1956: vii). The perception that political theory was in decline was the spur behind Berlin's defence of the need for political analysis.

The social and political background to Berlin's liberalism was the Cold War and the struggle to defend liberalism and individual rights. Berlin's covert aim was to defend the idea of philosophical inspection of the causes and nature of politics, and hence the need for political philosophy in the first place. Berlin as a result regarded sociology with some degree of suspicion; it sounded like 'socialism', appeared to embrace deterministic arguments, and claimed to be a science.

Berlin probably also equated sociology with the trend towards positivism in philosophy, which he had criticised in *Concepts and Categories* (Berlin 1978). As a Jewish refugee from Russian communism, he matured intellectually in the context of European fascism. Berlin's commitment to liberal political theory and his antagonism to sociology (or any discipline committed to an assumption about 'historical inevitability') are hardly surprising. He gave public expression to these anxieties in a series of BBC lectures in 1952 which were published as *Freedom and its Betrayal. Six Enemies of Human Liberty* (2002). The six enemies included Saint-Simon (1760–1825) who was arguably the founding father of sociology and an early protagonist for socialism. Saint-Simon's social theories inspired Émile Durkheim to publish a volume on *Le Socialisme* (1928) in his unfinished study of the history of socialism in which he regarded Saint-Simon and not Auguste Comte as the founder of sociology. Berlin's conviction that socialism and sociology shared a common inheritance was not wide of the mark.

It is perhaps also interesting to compare Berlin's liberalism with the social philosophy of another intellectual refugee from Poland, namely Leszek Kolakowski. In 1968, Kolakowski had been forced out of Poland and became eventually a fellow of All Souls College Oxford, where of course Berlin was a Fellow until his death in 1997. As a Catholic philosopher, Kolakowski was critical of Marxism, but recognised in his monumental *Main Currents of Marxism* (1978) the appeal and achievements of Marxism in developing a comprehensive doctrine in which the social inequality and injustices produced by capitalism were both explained and exposed. However, like Berlin, Kolakowski was highly critical of the bureaucratic, authoritarian and elitist consequences of Party domination over civil society and the loss of civil liberties. Kolakowski was criticised by the Left for leaving Marxism and thereby apparently selling out to bourgeois capitalism. Famously in 1973, in an open letter to *The Socialist Register* E. P. Thompson attacked Kolakowski for abandoning the Marxism of his youth and for allowing his experiences of actually existing socialism in Poland to cloud his understanding of socialist ideals. Kolakowski replied in 'My Correct Views on Everything' (1974) to say that one cannot save socialism from the historical failures of Marxism or save Marxism from the failures of communism in the name of an ideal that is allegedly grounded in material reality. This conflict between Thompson and Kolakowski was symptomatic of a deep division between Western intellectuals who had no direct experience of communism and intellectuals from the Soviet Union and Eastern Europe who had suffered under its crushing cultural monotony and political authoritarianism.

While Kolakowski was primarily critical of Eastern Europe, in *Main Currents of Marxism* he was also deeply critical of China where he argued that the commitment to egalitarianism in fact masked a profound political inequality as illustrated by the absence of any public access to information. Kolakowski (1978: 519) claimed that in this respect 'the Chinese population is more deprived than that of the Soviet Union. In China everything is secret'. Like Berlin, Kolakowski was therefore shocked by the naivety of Western intellectuals who, while condemning the militarism of the US, ignored the militarization of Chinese society or the enforcement of punitive labour discipline, or the suppression of freedom of religion. *Main Currents* concluded with the observation that 'Marxism has been the greatest fantasy of our century'. In our own time, these prejudices of Western intellectuals appear to continue since, while being critical of American military interventions in Iraq and Afghanistan, they remain silent about Chinese adventures in Tibet or Beijing's plan to create an administrative region for the Paracel and Spratly islands or Chinese harassment of Falungong.

One problem facing the creation of a sociology of human rights is the analytical tensions between civil liberties (or individual rights) and social rights. This tension was present in the philosophical debates associated with the French revolution, it emerged again in the works of Marx, and it is manifest in the conventions of the Declaration on Human rights. This conflict between social and economic rights (to health, education and welfare) and individual rights (of freedom of religion, conscience, assembly and so forth) was exaggerated by the Cold War in which writers like Berlin and Kolakowski sought to demonstrate that individual freedoms cannot be lightly ignored and that the aspiration to achieve social equality in the Soviet Union and communist China often disguised political authoritarianism. My proposal is that the sociology of rights will be centrally concerned with the nature, history and consequences of this tension. In this chapter, I also have to assume that, while all rights are in a sense social rights, there is historically and intellectually a difference between a liberal view of rights from John Locke onwards and a social view of rights that has been associated with various strands of socialism. The latter critique of liberal rights is *prima facie* compatible with sociology insofar as the sociological tradition from Saint-Simon to Pierre Bourdieu (1999) has been critical of the notion of the individual as self-contained and autonomous and critical of the association of individualism and capitalism. This debate about the social nature of rights is the subject of this chapter.

Reviving sociology

Why should contemporary sociologists take Berlin and Kolakowski seriously? Berlin in particular challenged sociological explanations because deterministic accounts of human behaviour prevented sociology from engaging in moral argument and criticism, and its apparent commitment to 'historical inevitability' ruled out the possibility of human agency in social change. Sociology appeared to deny human autonomy – a necessary condition for regarding humans as morally accountable for their actions. By in fact reducing 'the political' to 'the social', sociology had failed to understand how intentional political action can change the course of history. As a result of his liberalism, Berlin like Kolakowski became the target of much radical criticism, but he remained profoundly influential in British university life, becoming the founding master of Wolfson College Oxford (1966–75). Berlin was socially and politically influential for his Cold War politics and his liberalism, both of which were compatible with the views of the British establishment and the political class. This attempt to use Berlin as a pretext for redefining social theory in relation to human rights is a deliberate challenge to sociologists to produce an article of similar status and to answer the challenge of Kolakowski against the legacy of Marxist theory. To Kolakowski, we could of course add the names of Agnes Heller, Zygmunt Bauman, and Ernest Gellner.

In the 1950s then there was a sense of malaise in (British) political philosophy. It is also clear that there was by the end of the twentieth century a similar malaise in (British) social philosophy or social theory in which the ravages of posthumanism, poststructuralism and postmodernism had brought many to the conclusion that with the 'cultural turn' there is little to distinguish literary theory from social theory, and social theory, if it survives at all, is increasingly subsumed under cultural studies or cultural theory. I propose immodestly that to revive sociology we need an argument that will answer the question 'Does social theory still exist?' with the decisiveness that Berlin answered Laslett's challenging observation that political thought was moribund. In this chapter, I make no serious distinction between sociological and social theory. The former can be regarded as a subset of the latter. In this sense, social theory is an umbrella term that embraces, not only sociological theory, but social philosophy, psychoanalytical theory, critical theory, and so forth. Sociological theory underpins an academic discipline; social theory does not. The distinction is important, but not for my immediate purposes. In addition, to develop this argument more fully, one would need to make careful distinctions between types of social theory, but here again I am more interested in a range of generic problems, paying thereby less attention to the variety of traditions in social theory. Having said that, the contention of this paper is that social theory is primarily concerned with the nature of 'the social' and that the social can only defined by reference to a set of contrasts between the social world and the not-social world. From Aristotle onwards, the principal contrast has been between the social and nature, a domain in which the idea of agency has no place (Brogan 2005).

The Cold War is over, communism has been largely dismantled, and political philosophy flourishes at both Oxford and Cambridge and globally through such journals as *Political Theory*, but 'does social theory still exist' and how can we make sociology relevant to the times in which we live? In this chapter, I want to respond in particular to Berlin's article which I shall use a pretext for considering the possibility of developing the sociology of rights. In developing a theory of rights, it may be that context is everything. Berlin argued that political philosophy exists only in societies in which ends collide. By implication, the Soviet Union could not have political theory because the Party controlled civil society, and he criticised both Comte and Saint-Simon for regarding the study of ends (goals and values) as merely empirical and technical. We may define mainstream sociology as simply the study of the social and by the latter I mean, following Durkheim, the study of institutions. In my own sociology, I have attended primarily to three institutions: religion, medicine and law. These three institutions can be said to define the social by producing individuals who are socialised or disciplined to follow rules, but rule-following can never be merely mechanical and, while institutions are by definition supra-individual, social life cannot expunge individual choice. Individuals are involved in evaluating, interpreting and managing institutions. In a voluntaristic theory of social action, individuals are always selecting means to achieve ends by reference to norms and values in contexts where values and ends often conflict (Rex 1961: 92). In this sense, sociology is a science of institutions, social interactions and social actions. The social is institutionalised but it cannot remove individual action. This schematic comment on the sociology of social action is a basic assumption of all sociological theory (Rex 1961: 92). In addition, classical sociology (Durkheim, Max Weber and Talcott Parsons) rejected the idea that free will simply meant random, haphazard or irrational actions. It is only in a context of norms that we can act rationally, otherwise free will can only be exercised by people who are eccentric, that is literally falling outside socially normal behaviour. In any case, for both Rickert and Weber, while the natural sciences are interested in mapping reality in terms of a series of abstractions that reduce complexity, the cultural sciences are *Wirklichkeitswissenschaften*, that is sciences of concrete reality that are interested in the individual and qualitative properties of reality (Oakes 1988). The discourse of natural laws and the discourse of rights are epistemologically very different.

It is clear that this conventional conundrum of institution and action is yet another way of describing the debate about agency and structure, or 'structuration theory' in the language of Anthony Giddens in *The Constitution of Society* (Giddens 1984). However, in retrospect it seems to me that the real point of the debate about agency was lost in theories that became too abstract to be useful in understanding the real world. Sociology in becoming too absorbed with the personal – for example in Giddens's *The Transformation of Intimacy* (1992) – also became too remote from the analysis of institutional politics to be relevant to the study of macro-social change. If you over-emphasise structure, you have a deterministic theory of action. If you over-emphasise individual agency, then you have an individualistic, not a sociological, theory of the social. But what, apart from a debate in epistemology, is the real point of this contrast between the agency of individuals and the constraining (and alternatively empowering) role of structures or institutions? My argument is that if modern sociology wants to be relevant to modern society, especially in a period of globalisation, it has to develop the sociology of rights, an understanding of how the rule of law functions, the centrality of concepts of legality and legiti-macy to authority, and it has to have an objective theory of justice. To do this, it needs, among other things, to go beyond its current implicit acceptance of 'cultural relativism'. As sociologists we need to accept that people can only have rights if they have moral autonomy, that is if they are moral agents. This moral autonomy cannot work if we assert a mechanistic theory of causality that expunges any role for action, decision or judgement. We need to distinguish clearly between general moralising about topics with little regard to the facts and moral clarification and evaluation that is disciplined by evidence and research. In defending the idea of the 'public intellectual' in sociology, we need to distinguish between opinion and judgement.

In many respects, this is the classical liberal Berlin-type argument, and it is correct. It is however not that far removed from the discussion of value freedom and value neutrality in Weber's *The Methodology of the Social Sciences* (1949), in which he struggled to distinguish 'causal adequacy' at the level of meaning, rational action, causal mechanisms, the role of interests, and the nature of the 'cultural sciences'. Of course, this sensitive account of methodology has to be balanced against Weber's criticism of natural law and his view of law as command. I shall return to the ambiguities of Weber's legacy shortly. He was clear that social action, as opposed to behaviour, involved action directed by reference to norms. In modern parlance, action is rule-following conduct. Now, if people have rights, in the strong sense, then they have duties. Where does a sense of duty come from? Moral duties are typically inscribed in what we as sociologists call 'culture' – an umbrella term that includes morality, values and religion. In a largely implicit way, sociology is the study of the duties (mores, morals, norms, and values) that are important in creating the social. This study of mores, or norms, was the topic of Parsons's sociology and it was essentially a Durkheimian project. The study of rights has been largely the concern of jurisprudence and political philosophy; the study of duties – or normative institutions – can be seen as a traditional task of sociology, but in the strong programme of rights you cannot have a right without a duty and vice versa.

The fit between rights and duties is never entirely perfect. Most legal typologies of rights and duties start with a model developed originally by the American jurist Wesley Newcomb Hohfeld (1919). He divided legal relationships between rights bearers and rights addressees into four fundamental dyadic relations. This produced the following list of legal relationships: (1) y has a duty to do something and x has a claim to receive this contribution (such as parental support): (2) y has a privilege or liberty to do something over which x has no rights (I can lie in bed on a Sunday morning); (3) y has immunity from a claim for which x has a disability (I am too old to serve in the army, therefore you will have to take my place); (4) y has a power to bring something about and hence x has a liability to do something (I may ask you to write an essay; you have a liability to produce one). Individuals may be right-holders with respect to: claims, liberties, immunities or powers. This model is useful, and describes four fundamental legal relationships: right/duty; privilege/no-right; immunity/disability; power/liability (Freeden 1991: 44–8). The core of this classification is the notion that only some rights (for example claims) typically exercise constraint on others. This legal classification can be interpreted as a sociological typology of social interaction. We may notice however that some persons such as unborn babies have rights (claims on their parents) without duties. Disabled people or the mentally retarded who cannot work may also have claims on society. One obvious role for sociology is to explore the empirical relationships between rights and duties, and to criticise the rationalist-cognitive assumptions of jurisprudence which appears to assume that rights-bearers are mature, rational, able people.

One further conclusion to this introduction is that one cannot have political philosophy without sociology, but conversely sociology has been especially impoverished by its separation from political theory for at least one obvious reason. Political theory has been especially concerned with questions of rights and justice, whereas sociology rarely considers justice; its major concern has been inequality – the sociology of stratification – not injustice. When sociology comes to study justice, it is often simply concerned with the subjective apprehension of justice. The examples are few and far between: Barrington Moore's *Injustice* (1978), Morris Ginsberg's *On Justice in Society* (1965) and Garry Runciman's *Relative Deprivation and Social Justice* (1963). In American sociology, the problem of racial inequality has also produced many major works on racial injustice such as Kenneth Clark's *Dark Ghetto* (1965), but generally speaking justice is not overtly a sociological topic. Relativism means that sociologists cannot as sociologists criticise modern day societies, only describe and account for their ideologies. In short, sociologists have been mainly concerned with the subjective sense of relative injustice, for example in subjective opinions about fairness in income distribution.

Cultural relativism appears automatically to entail moral relativism, and both imply that sociology does not make judgements, for example as to whether a regime is progressive or reactionary or authoritarian. Sociologists take an anti-Platonic view of social reality in which sociological theories describe social reality from within the cave. The point of this argument was brilliantly put by Alasdair MacIntyre (1971: 278) in 'Is a science of comparative politics possible?', where he observed that 'to insist that political science be value-free is to insist that we never use in our explanations such clauses as "because it was unjust" or "because it was illegitimate" when we explain the collapse of a policy or a regime'.

The most important aspect of modern globalisation is the growth of human rights institutions. Legal globalisation is a product of yet another aspect of the global, namely the modernisation and globalisation of technological warfare. To be relevant to the modern world, sociology will, among many other possible lines of inquiry, need to develop a robust analytical programme for the study of rights, duties and justice. This is a formidable task, but a necessary one if we are to give a positive answer to the perennial question 'Does social theory still exist?'.

For social theory to exist in some sense as a vibrant and important part of sociology as a discipline, it has to throw light on problems of major contemporary concern. A relevant social theory should not be a theory about theorising or simply a history of ideas; it must be something more than a meta-theory. In my estimation the major contemporary problems are the changing nature of warfare, the impact of biotechnology on human expectations, the destruction of the natural environment through industrialisation and pollution, neoliberal globalisation and the growing incivility of the public sphere. In these crisis situations, the assertion of, and claims for, rights are major pre-conditions for social reform. There are many forms of rights, but in this chapter I am primarily concerned to distinguish between two systems of rights: human (or individual) rights and social (or collective) rights.

These two rights systems are very different. Human rights are enjoyed by human *qua* humans; there are no specific human duties; and human rights are claimed to be universal. Social rights are basically the rights of citizens in return for the duties they perform in society. These two systems tend to overlap. The Universal Declaration of Human Rights was adopted in 1948 by the United Nations (UN), but it was not converted into legally-binding treaties until 1966 with the promulgation of the International Covenant on Economic, Social and Cultural Rights (ICESCR) and the International Covenant on Civil and Political Rights (ICCPR). These covenants came into force in 1976. The ICESCR includes rights that are also common to the social rights of citizens in nation states. The ICCPR are the classic rights of liberalism. This distinction is also an important division between politics and sociology.

As we have already observed, there is an important distinction between sociology and politics in that political philosophy has been primarily concerned with the question of justice, and hence the analysis of rights arises necessarily from a concern with the justice and legitimacy of political regimes. By contrast, sociology often portrays itself as 'value neutral', and hence it does not raise normative questions about justice or rights. Sociology approaches these normative issues indirectly, for example through the study of inequality. The paradoxical consequence of this concentration on empirical studies of such issues as income inequality is that sociology typically does not study equality directly. Equality is merely the absence of inequality, and not as it were an independent phenomenon. Normative debates about equality and justice get buried under empirical and descriptive analyses of inequality and injustice. Because anthropologists and sociologists have typically been either positivists or relativists, they have not developed an analysis of justice and rights, and therefore they have failed to engage with one of the most significant institutional revolutions of the twentieth century – the growth of universal human rights. Because sociology has withdrawn from the issues covered by international relations as a subject area, it does not have much to say about contemporary political issues: regime change, international intervention, international wars, famine relief, authoritarianism, the global drift towards totalitarianism, global poverty, the persistence of slavery and so forth.

While many rights activists find the philosophical problems relating to relativism to be an irrelevance, the issue of cultural relativism has major practical implications and consequences. If there is a right to intervene in the internal politics of other societies, then there is a problem relating to the legitimacy of human rights interventions. The right to intervene to prevent or to remove human rights abuses cannot be justified without some legitimate notion of universalism. The point of this chapter is to challenge this legacy of positivism and relativism, and to promote a sociological approach that starts with the idea of embodiment and human vulnerability. Human rights can be defined as universal principles, because human beings share a common ontology that is grounded in a shared vulnerability. Sociology is also well positioned to study the failure of institutions that exist to protect human vulnerability. In developing this perspective, the aim is to construct a normative sociology (Turner 2006).

In summary, sociologists have felt comfortable with research on citizenship but not on human rights. They have understood perfectly the issue of the absence of effective social rights in relation to social inequality, but have been analytically blind to human rights. When sociologists do contribute to human rights debates, it is typically to enforce the notion that equality of social conditions, for example in terms of international labour law, is a necessary foundation for the effective enjoyment of rights (Woodiwiss 1998). My argument is that as sociologists we cannot simply ignore the issues that are covered by ICCPR, because the justice or otherwise of a social system will depend critically on how those are recognised and enforced. A revival of social theory will hinge on reconciling the tensions between social and human rights which, I argue, are institutional or jurisprudential expressions of the traditional problem of 'agency and structure' in sociological theory.

Social and human rights

Social citizenship is constructed historically from a set of contributory rights and duties that are related to work, public service (for example in the military) and parenthood or family formation. It defines membership of a society through the entitlements associated with service, and is perhaps most clearly evident in a national system of taxation. This model of social rights has been closely associated with the legacy of the English sociologist Thomas H. Marshall (1950). Marshallian citizenship has been subject to extensive criticism over the last two decades and the social model of citizenship has been somewhat overshadowed by theories to emphasise the flexibility of social membership, the limitations of citizenship as a set of exclusive rights, and by perspectives that emphasise identity and identity politics. Concern to defend human rights has often outmatched the defence of citizenship as entitlement, status and social membership.

Although the origins of the Western institution of citizenship can be sought in the political cultures of ancient Greece and Rome, citizenship rights became significant as an aspect of modern politics only when certain key revolutionary events had appropriated the political norms of ancient Greece and Rome as their own: the English Civil War, the American War of Independence, and the French Revolution. These radical political changes had much in common; for example, the evolution of citizenship, involving a set of exclusionary rights that established claims to collective resources, and contributing to the formation of the state and then the nation. There was a common emphasis on the contributions of the 'common man' in services to the state through taxation and military service. Each revolution, however, appropriated and interpreted citizenship quite differently. The republican French tradition assumed the suppression of differences between citizens, who were to share a common loyalty to the republic in which religious identities were excluded from the public domain. French notions about citizenship were the results of the rational Enlightenment and were expressed radically in the writings of aristocrats like the Marquis de Condorcet who among other things championed the rights of women as citizens in his essay of 1790 'On giving women the right of citizenship' (McLean and Hewitt 1994). In the US, citizenship emerged with the characteristics that were described classically by Alexis de Tocqueville (2003) in his two volumes on *Democracy in America* in 1835 and 1840. The citizen was seen to participate in the state through civil society, which was composed of a multitude of voluntary associations such as chapels and denominations. Citizens shared a radical doctrine of egalitarianism, and there was a profound suspicion of central institutions of government. In the British case, citizenship was constituted within the framework of the common law, which safeguarded the privileges of property owners, and was a barrier against the power of the state over the individual. Parliament and the rule of law established a system of checks against the rise of an absolutist state. The rights of the citizen were essentially negative freedoms from interference rather than positive rights to enjoy certain privileges. These forms of citizenship were very different from social citizenship in Bismarck's Germany where rights to social security were more important than civil liberties.

While investigating citizenship had been an important concern of political thought for centuries, it is in the early modern era, at the onset of the three revolutions mentioned earlier, that we see the separation of subjects from citizens. While Thomas Hobbes was at pains to recognise the citizen, Baruch Spinoza declared that 'I call men citizens in so far as they enjoy all the advantages of the commonwealth by civil right; and subjects in so far as they are bound to obey the ordinances or laws of the commonwealth' (Spinoza 1958: 285). Early modern political thought had, therefore, already concentrated on the rights and obligations of citizens in relation to the state. By contrast, modern social thought initially concentrated on the social structures that have distorted and limited the formal rights of citizens, and these structures are typically social class, gender and race. The debate about citizenship in the US has focused heavily on the issues of slavery, race and immigration, whereas the debate in British sociology has been conducted in terms of the tensions between citizenship, capitalism and class structure. Marshall developed the principal theory of citizenship within the context of postwar welfare institutions.

In this discussion I have been primarily concerned with the origin of rights in Western societies, but one central unresolved problem for rights research is the entitlement of aboriginal peoples to recognition. Tocqueville had recognised clearly the plight of native Americans whom he thought were bound to extinction and the black Americans who were bound to personal servitude in his discussion of 'the three races in the United States' in volume one of *Democracy in America*. We might note that Western citizenship as a status position within the nation-state emerged during the 'the great land rush' of 1650 to 1900 (Weaver 2003) and hence the acquisition of social rights in the West occurred alongside the suppression or extinction of aboriginal communities. Colonial land rights were often based upon a political myth, as in Australia, of *terra nullius*. The struggle to legitimise the assertion of sovereignty over these 'virgin lands' preoccupied jurisprudence for centuries from at least, for example, the work of Hugo Grotius with the rise of Dutch power in the East Indies (Van Ittersum 2006). The residue of this expansion is the unresolved issue of legal pluralism, state sovereignty and native title to land.

Citizenship versus human rights

It is often claimed that modern politics is a politics of identity in which claims over resources depend less on social class membership and more on ethnic, religious or cultural identities. These identity struggles that are now associated with recognition and citizenship rights for minorities are actually an aspect of a still more complex issue which is the relationship between the human rights of people *qua* humans and the rights of citizens as members of a nation or the state. Human rights and citizenship, and state sovereignty and rights are often contradictory couplets. The declaration of the National Assembly of France in 1789 claimed that 'the natural and imprescriptible rights of man' were 'liberty, property, security and resistance of oppression'. It went on, however, to assert that 'the nation is essentially the source of all sovereignty' and that no 'individual or body of men' could be entitled to 'any authority, which is not expressly derived from it'. While human rights are regarded as innate and inalienable, the rights of citizens are created by states. These two contrasted ideas – the imprescriptible rights of human beings and the exclusive rights of citizens – have remained an important dilemma in any justification of rights.

Social rights are entitlements enjoyed by citizens and are upheld by courts within the framework of a sovereign state. These can be called 'contributory rights', because effective claims against a society are made possible by the contributions that citizens have made to society typically through work, war, or parenting (Turner 2001). By contrast, human rights are rights enjoyed by individuals by virtue of being human, and as a consequence of their shared vulnerability. John Rawls (1999: 79) in his *The Law of Peoples* has asserted that 'Human rights are distinct from constitutional rights, or from the rights of liberal democratic citizenship', and he calls human rights 'a special class of urgent rights' that protect people from slavery, mass murder and genocide. They are deployed in states of emergency where states have failed to protect their people or indeed have been instrumental in genocide as appears to be the case in the Darfur region of the Sudan.

Hannah Arendt (1951) developed the most devastating criticism of 'the rights of Man'. She complained that these inalienable rights are said to exist independently of any government, but once the rights of citizenship have been removed, there is no authority left to protect people as human beings. Human rights that cannot be enforced by a sovereign power are mere abstractions. They are almost impossible to define and it is difficult to show how they add anything to the specific rights of citizens of nation states. The 'right to have rights' only makes sense for people who already enjoy membership of a political community. Arendt concluded ironically that these arguments against abstract human rights were originally put forward by conservatives like Edmund Burke who argued that the rights of an Englishman were more secure and definite than any number of abstract rights of man. Recent attempts, for example by Peg Birmingham (2006: 45–6) to distinguish Arendt's criticism of human rights from the work of Burke on the grounds that, in defending the rights of Englishmen, Burke was in fact a racist are hardly convincing. While Burke was certainly a conservative, his principal concern appears to have been to defend liberty against oppressive and bad government. Hence he defended American independence as a genuine demand for freedom and while his attitudes towards India were often incoherent he came eventually to criticise the East India Company because he recognised the suffering of the people of India just as he had recognised the suffering of Catholics in Ireland (O'Brien 1997). These attitudes do not appear to be those of a racist.

Romantics have often claimed that the state, through taxation, imposes a burden on aboriginal or native communities who have been torn from a 'state of nature' by colonisation or modernisation. While it is true that state formation typically involves an alienation of indigenous rights, especially where a number of distinctive ethnic communities are coerced into an emerging state, it is also the case that a viable state is important as a guarantee of rights. Human rights abuses are characteristically a consequence of state tyranny, dictatorship, and state failure resulting in civil war and anarchy. There is some validity to the argument by Burke: the liberties of citizens are better protected by their own state institutions than by external legal or political intervention. Nation-states are the principal political instruments through which human rights legislation is enforced. Perhaps even more strongly, there is no international law of human rights and 'the purpose of international concern with human rights is to make national rights effective under national laws and through national institutions' (Henkin 1998: 512). In addition, the chaotic outcome of 'human rights wars' in East Timor, Kosovo, Afghanistan, and Iraq should cause us to look with some scepticism on those governments that claim a right to intervene in the name of protecting citizens from their own states (Chandler 2002). In any case, human rights wars tend to occur selectively when powerful states have a direct interest in the conflict. The US and other Western governments have shown little interest in intervening militarily on Darfur, but they have committed billions of dollars to intervene in Afghanistan and Iraq in their 'war against terrorism'. International interest in Sudan's oil reserves means that without Chinese co-operation the UN is unlikely to intervene. The security provided by an authoritarian government might be preferred to fragile democracy which requires foreign armies to sustain it. From a Hobbesian point of view, a strong state will be required to enforce agreements between conflicting social groups. Another way of expressing this idea is to argue that we need to maintain a distinction between the social rights of citizens that are enforced by states, and the human rights of persons that are protected, but frequently and inadequately enforced, by both states and international institutions.

Karl Marx on human rights

Marx also recognised a distinction between citizenship and human rights. He was a trenchant critic of the doctrine of individual rights which he defined as 'bourgeois rights', that is the claims of a capitalist class to be free from interference. In European languages, there is an important connection between the idea of 'civil rights', 'civil society' and the bourgeoisie. The citizen was closely connected historically and etymologically with the rise of the European city, with the virtues of civility, and the spread of civilisation. The term 'citizen'is derived from the Anglo-French *citeseyn*, *citezein* or *sithezein*. A citizen was originally a member of a city and as a result he enjoyed certain privileges and was burdened with obligations and duties. Service in the city militia was a typical duty of the citizen. A citizen was originally a denizen of a city as a legal entity. A citizen was a burgess or freeman of a city, and citizenship has been associated with bourgeois culture. The citizen was characterised by civility. The countryside was pagan and uncivilized. Pagans were lacking in urbanity, whereas citizens were part of the *civitas* – the urban culture of the city and church. While we can trace these components of citizenship from the Greek polis and the early church, citizenship is most appropriately regarded as a modern concept that first emerged with the creation of autonomous cities in medieval Europe, but came to fruition with the revolutions that created the modern world, namely the American and French Revolutions. In European culture, 'citizen' is made possible by the rise of 'civil society' (*die burgerliche Gesellschaft*), and they are both dependent on the emergence of a bourgeois civilisation. The citizen is a member of civil society who is the carrier of bourgeois civility. The liberal notion of citizenship (*Staatsburgerschaft*) has this ambiguity, because it is a conduit of individual rights, but it is also a reflection of the growth of state power over civil society.

Marx's equation between the bourgeoisie and the doctrine of rights was perfectly intelligible. What Marx added to this debate was a vision of human rights and the related doctrine of individualism as a form of alienation. Marx followed Hegel in taking the isolated individual as the guiding thread of theories of the individual and natural rights, but he rejected the view that all that was needed was the restoration of a moral community to provide an ethical life. For Marx, the lack of ethics was a function of poverty and exploitation in capitalist society. In 'On the Jewish Question' (Waldron 1987), Marx argued that the political emancipation of the Jews was irrelevant unless there was a corresponding social and economic revolution to convert them into citizens. Apart from his criticism of Jewish emancipation as a consequence of the French Revolution, this argument is important because it subordinates in theoretical terms 'the political' to social and economic determination. In turn, the implication is that political rights are subordinate to a set of prior social and economic transformations of society. Crudely speaking, this argument lent force to subsequent developments in 'actually existing communist societies' that the assertion of civil liberties of individuals was counter-revolutionary.

Whether Marx (and hence Marxist-Leninism) was hostile to human rights has been an important issue with major implications for modern politics. First, Marx appears in his criticisms of the French revolutionary declaration of rights to suggest that the rights of citizens must always have priority over the rights of 'Man' (that is of 'egoistic man'). Second, he appears to argue that political rights can only be exercised when an egalitarian political community has emerged that expresses the nature of humans as communal beings. Third, rights can only be enjoyed when real religious freedom is available and where the limitations of inequality have been eliminated, thereby making possible a genuine community. Finally, only with these economic changes will the imaginary single isolate of bourgeois theory become a full sovereign being.

In defence of Marx, it is often argued that his apparent hostility to rights talk is based on the misleading interpretation of Marxism as simple materialism. In this crude interpretation, human rights do not really matter because the legal superstructure of society will always be determined by the mode of production, and so scientific attention should be directed to these laws of historical motion. Against such a view there is the humanistic interpretation of Marx in which there is a far more subtle interpretation of legal ideas (Lefebvre 1968).

The Marxist theory of history is controversial because it was also applied to Russia by writers such as Karl Wittfogel (1957) in *Oriental Despotism* to argue that the great bureaucratic systems of pre-modern times, which were often associated with state control of water management and supply, produced despotic regimes and were not conducive to the growth of bourgeois democracy. The Soviet system had reproduced the authoritarian and bureaucratic systems of the past. There was no security of property in the Soviet system and the collectives had not improved agricultural production. The Soviet Revolution had merely replaced one autarky with the cult of Stalin and the central power of the Party. A similar conclusion had been reached by Weber (1995) in his essays on the Russian Revolutions. Russia suffered from late industrialisation, the political immaturity of the bourgeoisie, and the inability of the Tsar to find a compromise with bourgeois politicians. The Russian Revolution blocked off the possibility of liberal bourgeois capitalism. From a Marxist perspective, Russia was also not ripe for a proletarian revolution since its material conditions and the political development of its small working class were inadequate social circumstances in terms of producing an advanced socialist system based on a mature, urban proletariat. Russia's premature revolution raised the question of Russia's isolation from the European working class. Was the Bolshevik Revolution to remain merely a peculiarity of the Russian nation?

Although one can defend Marx, Marxist-Leninism was therefore, in practice, as Berlin argued, hostile to political rights. The historical problem was that the triumph of Bolshevism in Russia meant that a minority party had gained power by force and hence it was profoundly undemocratic. Elections would almost certainly have given power to a conservative peasantry. The solution was developed by Leon Trotsky. The political doctrine of 'socialism in one country' was formulated towards the end of 1924 by Josef Stalin in reply to Trotsky's theory of the 'permanent revolution'. The leaders of the October uprising were convinced that the Revolution would quickly spread to other European societies and that the Russian Revolution itself could only succeed through expansion. The 1905 bourgeois revolution would pass quickly into the socialist revolution involving a series of subsequent revolutions in the more advanced economies of Europe. Lenin retained the orthodox view that by the laws of history the revolution would eventually embrace the Western world, if not the entire globe. Trotsky followed Lenin in arguing that the choice was between either international socialist revolution or sliding back into capitalism. There was therefore no place for socialism in one society. Communism required the creation of a world economy under the dominance of the various proletarian movements and in the interests of the workers (Trotsky 1967).

However as the prospects of a general revolutionary conflict receded, the communists resolved to guide the socialist transformation of Russian society in international isolation. Stalin's attack on Trotskyism was an attempt to counteract the negative psychological impact of the failure of world communism on the morale of party workers (Kolakowski 1978:190). Throughout his *History of the Russian Revolution*, Trotsky had maintained the view that a proletarian revolution in Russia was dependent on the support of the Western proletariat, and that 'socialism in one country' was a dangerous error. By 1926 Trotsky recognised that

Trotskyism – essentially the thesis of permanent revolution – had been officially branded as incompatible with Bolshevism (Trotsky 1967, 3: 352).

A similar problem has existed in China where a centralised revolutionary party was confronted by a large conservative population of peasants, a hostile set of international forces and internal opposition from nationalists and others. Contemporary official resistance to human rights and human-rights movements is associated with the fact that the Chinese Communist Party regards human-rights norms as simply an aspect of Western globalisation and as an unwarranted intrusion into its internal political affairs. While the Party's view of Western antagonism may be paranoid, the Party has been conscious of the role of rights talk in the fall of the Soviet system in 1991–2, especially the role of Solidarity in the transformation of Eastern Europe. Human-rights criticism of Chinese politics was particularly important as a consequence of the backlash after the Tiananmen Square massacre in 1989. The so-called June 4 movement played an important role in shaping official fear of political opposition. The international erosion of communism in the wider world has often reinforced the conservative determination of the CCP to remain loyal to Marxist-Leninism. Contemporary Western pressure on the Party to liberalise its policies is often seen within the framework of Chinese history as simply further evidence of foreign meddling in Chinese society. The perception that the West manipulates opposition movements in China, such as 'heretical sects' to cause embarrassment to the Party also explains official attitudes towards Roman Catholicism, but suspicion about the disruptive potential of sects and cults has a long history in Chinese politics, thereby explaining the current hostility to Falungong.

China has found it easier to support social and economic rights which are seen to be more consistent with its own emphasis on development. The ICESCR came into force in China on 27 June 2001, but by 2005 the ICCPR had not been ratified. If we take the view that economic development is a necessary precondition for the enjoyment of rights, then China has made great progress towards establishing a human rights regime. Whereas somewhere around 22 million people had died of starvation during Mao's Great Leap Forward, China has managed to feed its own population which represents 22 per cent of the world's population on only 7 per cent of the world's arable land. This economic growth is compatible with the notion of a right development that was accepted by the Vienna Declaration in 1996.

However, the Chinese view of rights departs significantly from the Western legal view. In Chinese jurisprudence, rights are not natural and inalienable, but given by the state and defined by the law. Constitutional rights are not regarded as limitations on the law and human rights affairs are domestic, not international, issues. Because the Chinese government regards states, not individuals, as the subjects of international law, human rights cannot be used as a justification to interfere in state sovereignty.

The future of citizenship and human rights in China will depend in part on the nature of American foreign relations with respect to China, Taiwan and North Korea, and pressure from the UN and human rights agencies for *de facto* compliance. Secondly, it will depend heavily on sustaining economic growth, redistributing wealth, creating an effective taxation system and eliminating corruption. Thirdly, it will depend on how the CCP responds to both external and internal political pressures such as the growth of political parties, the Internet and the continuation of Hong Kong's special status. Finally, it will depend on how well the modernisation of its legal system can successfully institutionalise the rule of law and how effective those juridical institutions are in sustaining the improvement in criminal proceedings.

At present the prospects for human rights in China are not promising. In reviewing China's achievements, it is useful to conclude with a comparison of the recent history of Russia. With the collapse of the Soviet empire in 1992, there was of course considerable optimism about the prospects of human rights improvements. In November 1994 President Yeltsin decided to attack the Chechen capital Grozny to crush the separatist movement of Jokhar Dudayev. Human-rights critics of the war, such as Sergei Kovalev, having been denounced as enemies of Russia, predicted that the war would result in intolerance, revenge and civil violence (Gilligan 2005). These criticisms came horribly true at the school massacre in Beslan. While Kovalev was highly critical of the Chechen leadership, he argued that the second war in Chechnya allowed Vladimir Putin to consolidate his power. Putin, who has done much to curtail human rights, undermine foreign non-governmental organisations (NGOs), silence opposition and restore centralised power, has enforced the ideology of the Great Power and the doctrine of *derzhavnost* – the view that the state is a superior mystical being that every citizen must serve without question. The good citizen is a *derzhavnik* who is indifferent to the fate of other citizens and accepts state crimes as necessary and justified. In China, the rule of virtue may also ultimately entail the subordination of the citizen to the state as a morally superior being.

Max Weber on natural law

So far I have attempted to spell out some of the complexity between the social rights of citizens and the individual human rights of persons. Sociologists have been critical of the notion of 'human rights' because they have inherited a legacy of social criticism from Marx of 'bourgeois rights' but they have also from Weber inherited a criticism of 'natural rights'. Addressing this dual legacy is an import precursor to a restoration of social theory.

Although sociology has, as we have noticed, made major contributions to citizenship studies and thereby indirectly to social rights research and analysis, it lacks a genuine approach to human rights for reasons which are related to the relativism of classical sociology. Weber's attack on natural law in which he rejected any possibility of establishing, among other things, a hierarchy of values, remains a definitive sociological critique. Leo Strauss's response (1950) is well known outside sociology among theorists of natural law, but it has had little lasting influence in recent years on the sociology of law. The consequence of this Weberian legacy is that sociology does not have a basis for contributing to the discussion of the legality of law, an issue which has been central to Jurgen Habermas's attempt to develop a communicative action approach to law and politics (Habermas 1996).

In *Natural Right and History* Strauss showed how Weber's philosophy of social science was incompatible with any scientific defence of values. For Weber, science cannot provide rational guidance as to what is justice; in this scheme, science is primarily about the selection of means to ends, rather than the determination or selection of goals. Natural law, which is fundamentally concerned with justice, cannot be sustained by such rational inquiry. Sociology can tell us about facts and causes, but it cannot adjudicate between conflicting value systems, such as between Buddhism and Christianity. Science can provide no reliable knowledge about what we ought to do; it can clarify values in order to make our decisions more reasonable, but it cannot guide us in the face of competing values. Strauss argued that while Weber's sociology resulted in nihilism, it was 'noble nihilism', because his ethical imperative was, following Nietzsche, 'Become who you are', that is choose your own fate. Without an ethical commitment to realistically following one's vocation, a human being cannot achieve 'personality'. In Weber's ethical system, having personality meant having devotion to a cause or acting passionately in terms of a career or course of action that one has rationally chosen. But Strauss points out that, given Weber's value neutrality, it is difficult to see how one could rationally justify such an attitude. Hence relativism is self-defeating.

Strauss attacked Weber's relativistic nihilism by showing its inconsistency. For instance, Weber constantly makes value judgements in his sociology of religion where he praises the high moral calling of the prophets, rejecting magic and sorcery as base forms of religiosity. Weber's approach to religion was basically Kantian in regarding religion as subservient to morality. Both Weber and Kant followed German Lutheranism in elevating moral self-determination as the highest goal – as an expression of the Enlightenment freedom from tutelage.

This observation provides Strauss with a general criticism of Weberian sociology. We should try to imagine a sociological description of a concentration camp, including a factual account of the motivation of the guards. Furthermore we should imagine that this sociological account of concentration camps had nothing to say about cruelty (Strauss 1950: 52). Strauss also argues that in his sociology of religion Weber did (and must be able to) make distinctions between false or pretended and real or authentic charismatic authority. Again this raises the general problem of whether interpretative sociology can provide understanding without judgements between and about values.

Strauss's attack on Weber ultimately comes down to a criticism of Nietzsche. Weber takes struggle and conflict as necessary and inevitable conditions of politics. As a result Weber tends to regard peace and the quest for peace as wishful thinking. Strauss (1950: 65) observes that:

> If peace is incompatible with human life or with a truly human life, the moral problem would seem to allow of a clear solution: the nature of things requires a warrior ethics as the basis of a "power politics" that is guided exclusively by considerations of the national interest.
>
> (Strauss 1950: 65)

Because Weber takes for granted the importance and inevitability of the struggle for space ('elbow room'), he cannot take the quest for universal brotherhood or universal peace seriously. There is no place in Weber's sociology for an analysis of human rights, but interestingly he does provide an early theory of citizenship in his account of the universalistic implications of the occidental city (Weber 1958, 1981). Christianity played an important role in destroying the tribal basis of the urban community. Religious faith became the basis for urban collectivities. In this respect, the rise of the nation-state as the framework for citizenship undermined much of the universalistic thrust of natural law with its conception of a foundational groundwork for human rights as part of the legacy of world religions, particularly in Pauline Christianity and Quranic Islam. The Universal Church and the Islamic *ummah* created global communities within which, in principle, ethnic or regional divisions were irrelevant to the notion of a person's worth *qua* human being. It was precisely the collapse of the natural law theory of rights which led Weber in his sociology of law to promote a relativistic view of authority. Citizenship rights do not extend beyond the legal boundaries of the nation-state; in this sense, they are particularistic and local rights.

In this clear division between ethics and politics (in the famous dichotomy between the ethics of responsibility and ultimate ends), Weber accepted Wilhelm Dilthey's vision of the 'anarchy of values', but rejected his notion of *Erlebnis* (unmediated or lived experience) as an underlying psychology by which cultural difference could be reconciled in the aesthetics of emotion. For Dilthey and his followers, the cultural relativism of *Historismus* was to be overcome by translating the Pietist notion of religious feeling into the foundation of a common humanity via a radical hermeneutics. Weber not only reformulated the idea of *Verstehen* as sociological understanding, but argued that sociology had nothing to do with ethics. In his Freiburg Address of 1895, Weber argued that it is not the task of political economy to formulate 'recipes for making the world happy'. Population pressure ruled out 'eudaemonism' and any earthly happiness could only be won by the struggle for 'elbow room' (Weber 1989: 196–7). In the case of German power politics, this struggle meant the conquest of Eastern Europe and Russia.

To some extent, Weber's view of rights is a reflection of the fact that in German legal theory rights were not of the people but of the state. While in Hobbes's world brutish individuals struggled for survival, Samuel Pufendorf and Gottfried Leibniz recognised that individuals had a right and an obligation to perfect themselves through education and that the state was to function as a moral guide to the individual. In his *On the Duty of Man and Citizen According to Natural Law*, Pufendorf, emphasising the moral component of right as a social bond, warned the citizen 'not to give his mind to revolution' but to conduct his or her life with dignity and scrupulousness (Turner and Hamilton 1994: 316–17). These themes of perfectability were taken up by Kant who rejected the possibility of the legality of popular opposition to the state. Weber's political sociology with its assumptions about the limitations of mass democracy in capitalism in the notions of 'leadership democracy' and 'plebiscitary democracy' perpetuated the assumptions of passive citizenship in both Lutheranism and German jurisprudence. For Weber, any legal norm is justified if it is issued by a recognised authority and the rationalisation of law, from the point of view of sociology, had nothing to do with its normative validity. Moreover, for Weber, law is command, and recognition of the existence of a coercive apparatus is essential for any sociological definition of law. An argument against Weber is that whether or not a law is normatively justified is in fact a condition for its social acceptance and thus normative considerations (what is the legality of law?) can play a causal role in sociological explanations (of political behaviour).

Because Weber's philosophy of social science involved the formal separation of facts and values, it required a careful division between moral analysis and sociological inquiry. This position (that the task of sociology is not to make people happy) was explicitly embraced, as we have noted, by Weber in his Freiburg Inaugural Address where he framed German foreign policy in terms of the struggle for space in Eastern Europe. Weber's 'perspectivism' was based therefore on the assumption that rights are merely outcomes of power politics. The paradox is of course that the (factual) separation of facts and values is itself a value position. Despite Weber's commitment to value neutrality and to the fact-value distinction, a religious tension was necessary if values are to have any vitality. Strauss clearly recognised this important feature of Weber's outlook:

> He had to combine the anguish bred by atheism (the absence of redemption, of any solace) with the anguish bred by revealed religion (the oppressive sense of guilt). Without that combination, life would cease to be tragic and thus lose its depth.
>
> (Strauss 1950: 66)

There is much that can be said about Weber's theory of value neutrality and his analysis of the vocations of politics and science (Lassman and Velody 1989). One issue with his legacy is outlined implicitly in Berlin's essay on political philosophy. In the 'real world' of politics, political leadership involves taking decisions between competing courses of action – choosing in Weber's terms between a politics of responsibility and a politics of ultimate ends. Berlin (1962: 17) says that there will always be politics wherever human beings conflict over ultimate and incommensurate values. As a result political theory cannot 'avoid evaluation; it is thoroughly committed not only to the analysis of, but to conclusions about the validity of, ideas of the good and the bad, the permitted and the forbidden'. He concludes by saying the notion of 'a completely *Wertfrei* theory (or model) of human action (as contrasted say, with animal behaviour) rests on a naïve misconception of what objectivity or neutrality in the social sciences must be'. In the real world, human actors are forced to make evaluations and decisions about conflicting values, and it is precisely at this point that a value-neutral sociology declares that it must remain silent – apart from providing evidence about the likely consequences of different choices. Because human rights interventions require such value-laden choices, sociology has been largely absent.

Conclusion: agency and structure

This chapter has concentrated on the distinction between the social rights of citizenship and the rights of human beings. This contrast was basic to Kant's recognition that universal rights would require a universal government and a world of perpetual peace. The problematic relationship between the two systems was also a basic issue in Marx's discussion of 'the Jewish question'. The same dilemma has been recognised by Habermas in his contrast between the two dominant ideas of modern law: individual rights and popular sovereignty. This chapter has primarily therefore explored two issues: (1) sociology has been principally concerned with citizenship and popular sovereignty, but a comprehensive sociology of rights would also have to address the issue of individual rights, and (2) the sociology of individual rights is a feature of the agency and structure debate, in which a sociology of rights would have to address the issue of human autonomy. Both issues require sociology to take a more positive view of liberal philosophy, for example taking Berlin seriously. We might add to these two issues the fact that sociology cannot ignore human rights if it wants to take the process of globalisation seriously.

Mainstream sociology in following Marx and Weber has been implicitly, and occasionally explicitly, critical of John Locke's version of liberalism, partly because they have followed C. B. MacPherson in condemning the Lockean notion of 'possessive individualism' (1962), even where there are good grounds for rejecting this critical interpretation of Locke (Dunn 1979: 39). This sociological orthodoxy – social rights trump individual rights – is difficult to sustain given the history of twentieth-century communism in the Soviet Union, China, Vietnam and the Eastern European autarkies such as Romania. These examples of 'actually existing communism' suggest that property rights, along with the right of political opposition and disobedience are in fact crucial ingredients of personal freedom (from intolerance, arbitrary rule and compulsion).

These arguments might as it were be regarded as substantive claims about a rights tradition. But what are the theoretical underpinnings? An intellectually exciting sociology can never be merely the study of a random collection of contemporary problems such as housing, poverty or ageing. It has to make a more substantial contribution to the development of sociological theory. What examples do we have from British sociology that might illustrate this claim, given my focus on Isaiah Berlin and British liberalism? In the case of John Rex, his *Key Problems in Sociological Theory* (1961) was a key text of postwar sociology. There is an important relationship between his empirical research on social class and race and his interpretation of Weber's sociology as a theory of social action. A major but neglected figure in British sociological theory was Alan Dawe. His article 'The Two Sociologies' (1970) played a significant role in shaping the sociological imagination in the mid-1960s. Dawe stressed the connection between certain forms of sociological theory, social action, political responsibility and sociological theories of action. This influence of Dawe can for example be seen in Anthony Woodiwiss's contribution to the study of human rights (Woodiwiss 2003).

In short, the debate about agency and structure is as old as sociology itself, but the implications of this distinction have not been adequately expressed. It is necessary to retain a vision of human autonomy and agency (against behaviour) if we are to regard social actors as moral agents capable of choice. The sociology of Parsons retained this distinction in the theory of voluntary action in *The Structure of Social Action* (1937) – a theory that is distinctively Kantian. Sociological theory needs to maintain a clear notion of the voluntary character of social action and hence the possibility that humans can be held accountable for their actions. The role of 'social structure' is to draw attention to the limitations and constraints on social action. In retaining a notion of 'structuration', it does not follow that social theory supports a theological notion of free will, but it also means that it does not accept a positivist version of determinism. Social theory can have a positive role in modern society and I want to follow Arendt (2003) in *Responsibility and Judgment* in order to argue that things can always be otherwise. Sociologists, for example Erving Goffman, have often been concerned to understanding the roles we play and the masks we acquire to perform socially. Arendt said that these are necessary if society is to function, but she reminded us of the Roman legal distinction between *persona* (somebody who possesses civil rights) and *homo* (somebody who is nothing but a member of the species). It is in the public sphere of action that human beings achieve their moral standing as beings above nature. In order for social theory to continue to exist, it needs to retain this legacy of a critical theory the purpose of which is to uncover the constraints that prevent the moral action (of people with rights) as opposed to the conditioned behaviour of members of *Homo sapiens*.

What are the conditions necessary for a revival of social theory? The implications of my argument are that social and political theory should not be divorced. Social theory may however be the handmaiden of politics in the sense that its role may be negative. It is to explore those conditions of social life – in fact, the conditions of civil society – that make the achievement of moral autonomy and responsibility impossible. As a critical theory the role of sociology is to consider those circumstances that artificially constrain the voluntary character of choice. By taking this moral issue seriously, of course sociology must continue to assert that the isolated existence of the autonomous individual is a fiction. In a more positive note, social theory does not have to choose between social rights of citizens living in a moral community and the civil liberties of asocial liberalism. Finally, I have argued that the conventional relativism and perspectivism of traditional sociology may prove an impoverished basis for contemporary sociology that needs to go beyond Marx's rhetorical pamphlets and Weber's pessimistic vision of the night of polar darkness.

Bibliography

Arendt, Hannah (1951) *The Origins of Totalitarianism*, New York: Harcourt Brace.
Arendt, H. (2003) *Responsibility and Judgment*, New York: Schocken Books.
Berlin, I. (1939) *Karl Marx*, London: Home University Library.

—— (1962) 'Does Political Theory Still Exist?', in Laslett and Runciman (eds) *Philosophy Politics and Society* (Second Series), Oxford: Basil Blackwell.

—— (1978) *Concepts & Categories. Philosophical Essays*, London: Hogarth Press.

—— (2002) *Freedom and Betrayal. Six Enemies of Human Liberty*, Princeton and Oxford: Princeton University Press.

Birmingham, P. (2006) *Hannah Arendt and Human Rights: The Predicament of Common Responsibility*, Bloomington and Indianapolis: Indiana University Press.

Bourdieu, P. (1999) *The Weight of the World. Social Suffering in Contemporary Society*, Cambridge: Polity Press.

Brogan, W. A. (2005) *Heidegger and Aristotle: The Twofoldness of Being*, New York: State University of New York Press.

Clark, K. B. (1965) *Dark Ghetto*. New York: Harper Row.

Chandler, D. (2002) *From Kosovo to Kabul: Human Rights and International Intervention*. London: Pluto.

Dawe, A. (1970) 'The Two Sociologies', *British Journal of Sociology* 21(2): 207–18.

Desai, P. (2006) *Conversations on Russia: Reform from Yeltsin to Putin*, Oxford: Oxford University Press.

Durkheim, É. (1928; reprint 1991) *Le Socialisme*, Paris: Alcan.

Dunn, J (1979) *Rethinking Modern Poltical Theory*, Cambridge: Cambridge University Press.

Freeden, M. (1991) *Rights*, Milton Keynes: Open University Press.

Giddens, A. (1984) *The Constitution of Society. Outline of a Theory of Structuration*, Cambridge: Polity Press.

—— (1992) *The Transformation of Intimacy: Sexuality, Love and Eroticism*, Cambridge: Polity Press.

Gilligan, E. (2005) *Defending Human Rights in Russia: Sergei Kovalyov, Dissident and Human Rights Commissioner 1969–2003*, London: Routledge Curzon.

Ginsberg, M. (1965) *On Justice in Society*, London: Penguin Books.

Habermas, J. (1996) *Between Facts and Norms*, Cambridge: Polity Press.

Hohfeld, W. N. (1919) *Fundamental Legal Conceptions*, New Haven: Yale University Press.

Henkin, L. (1998) 'The Universal Declaration and the US Constitution' *Political Science* 31(3): 512–15.

Ignatieff, M. (1998) *A Life of Isaiah Berlin*, London: Chatto & Windus.

Ittersum, M. J. v. (2006) *Profit and Principle: Hugo Grotius, Natural Rights Theories and the Rise of Dutch Power in the East Indies (1595–1615)*, Leiden: Brill.

Kaldor, M. (2003) *New & Old Wars. Organized Violence in a Global Era*, 2nd ed, Cambridge: Polity.

Kolakowski, L. (1974) 'My Correct Views on Everything: a Rejoinder to E. P. Thompson', in *The Social Register*, reprinted in (2005) *My Correct Views on Everything*, Chicago: St. Augustine's.

—— (1978) *Main Currents of Marxism. The Breakdown*, Oxford: Clarendon Press.

Laslett, P (1956) 'Introduction' in Laslett (ed.) *Philosophy Politics and Society*, Oxford: Basil Blackwell.

Lassman, P. and Velody, I. (eds) (1988) *Max Weber's 'Science as a Vocation'*, London: Unwin Hyman.

Lefebvre, H. (1968) *The Sociology of Marx*, Harmondsworth; Penguin Books.

MacIntyre, A. (1971) *Against the Self Images of the Age: Essays on Ideology and Philosophy*, London: Duckworth.

McLean, I. and Hewitt, F. (eds) (1994) *Condorcet: Foundations of Social Choice and Political Theory*, Aldershot: Edward Elgar Publishing.

Macpherson, C. B. (1962) *The Political Theory of Possesive Individualism*, Oxford: Oxford University Press.

Marshall, T. H. (1950) *Citizenship and Social Class and Other Essays*, Cambridge: Cambridge University Press.

Moore, B. (1878) *Injustice. The Social Bases of Obedience and Revolt*, London: Macmillan.

Oakes, G. (1988) *Weber and Rickert: Concept Formation in the Cultural Sciences*, Cambridge, Massachusetts: MIT Press.

O'Brien, C. C. (1997) *Edmund Burke*, London: Sinclair-Stevenson.

Parsons, T. (1937) *The Structure of Social Action*. New York: McGraw Hill.

Pufendorf, S. (1994) 'On the Duty of Man and Citizen According to Natural Law', in Turner and Hamilton (eds) *Citizenship: Critical Concepts*, London: Routledge.

Rawls, J. (1999) *The Law of Peoples*, Cambridge, Mass.: Harvard University Press.

Rex, J. (1961) *Key Problems of Sociological Theory*, London: Routledge & Kegan Paul.

Runciman, G. W. (1963) *Relative Deprivation and Social Justice*, London: Routledge & Kegan Paul.

Spinoza, B. d. (1958) *The Political Works*, Oxford: Clarendon Press.

Strauss, L. (1950) *Natural Right and History*, Chicago: University of Chicago Press.

Tocqueville, A. d. (2003) *Democracy in America*, London: Penguin Books.

Trotsky, L. (1967) *History of the Russian Revolution*, London: Sphere, three volumes.

Turner, B. S. (2001) 'The Erosion of Citizenship', *British Journal of Sociology* 52(2): 189–209.

—— (2006) *Vulnerability and Human Rights*, University Park, Pennsylvania: Pennsylvania State University Press.

Turner, Bryan S. and Peter Hamilton (eds) (1994) *Citizenship: Critical Concepts*, London, Routledge.

Waldron, J. (ed.) (1987) *Nonsense upon Stilts: Bentham, Burke and Marx on the Rights of Man*, London: Methuen.

Weaver, J. C. (2003) *The Great Land Rush and the Making of the Modern World 1650–1900*, Monreal: McGill-Queens University Press.

Weber, M. (1949) *The Methodology of the Social Sciences*, New York: Free Press.

—— (1958) *The City*, Glencoe, Illinois: Free Press.

—— (1989) 'The National State and Economic Policy', in Tribe (ed.) *Reading Weber*, London and New York: Routledge.

—— (1995) *The Russian Revolutions*, Cambridge: Polity Press.

Wittfogel, K. (1957) *Oriental Despotism: A Comparative Study of Total Power*, New Haven: Yale University Press.

—— (1998) *Globalisation, Human Rights and Labour Law in Pacific Asia*, Cambridge: Cambridge University Press.

—— (2003) *Making Human Rights Work Globally*, London: Glasshouse Press.

Index

Entries in **bold** denote references to graphics.

torture: definition of 93; and democracy 9; and ECHR 92; game theory analysis of 28; and health 45; in Pinochet case 95–6; scale of 32; and war on terror 37, 98, 160
Torture Victim Prevention Act (TVPA) 97
trade unions 109–10, 145
Trotsky, Leon 190–1

United Kingdom (UK): and anti-terrorism law 88–9, 98–9; human rights teaching in 7; and indigenous rights 83; and Pinochet trial 95–7
United States (US): debate about citizenship 186; and international human rights 92, 95–9, 125, 160; labour law in 113–15; social inequality in 141–2; support for neoliberalism 149–50; and war on terror 99, 125, 188

Universal Declaration of Human Rights (UDHR): analyses of 123–4; anthropologist opposition to 3; and Cold War 150; and health 48, 59; and human rights norms 29, 159–60; intentions behind 87; and international law 95; lack of absolute rules 93; tensions between liberties and rights 159, 179, 183–4
universalism 69, 75, 82, 90, 111, 184
utilitarianism 50–1

war atrocities 28
warfare, new forms of 16, 35, 183
Weber, Max 24, 110–11, 165–6, 169, 181–2, 190, 192–7
World Social Forum (WSF) 144, 147–8, 151–2

Yugoslavia 2, 92